Critical Essays on

BEN JONSON

CRITICAL ESSAYS
ON
BRITISH LITERATURE

Zack Bowen, General Editor
University of Miami

Critical Essays on
BEN JONSON

edited by

ROBERT N. WATSON

G. K. Hall & Co.
An Imprint of Simon & Schuster Macmillan
New York

Prentice Hall International
London Mexico City New Delhi Singapore Sydney Toronto

Copyright © 1997 by G. K. Hall

All rights reserved. No part of this book may be reproduced or transmitted in any form or by any means, electronic or mechanical, including photocopying, recording, or by any information storage and retrieval system, without permission in writing from the Publisher.

G. K. Hall & Co.
An Imprint of Simon & Schuster Macmillan
1633 Broadway
New York, NY 10019

Library of Congress Cataloging-in-Publication Data

Critical essays on Ben Jonson / edited by Robert N. Watson.
p. c. — (Critical essays on British literature)
Includes index.
ISBN 0-7838-0043-6
1. Jonson, Ben 1573?–1637—Criticism and interpretation.
I. Watson, Robert N. II. Series.
PR2638.C68 1997
822'.3—dc21 97-28769
CIP

The paper used in this publication meets the minimum requirements of American National Standard for Information Sciences—Permanence of Paper for Printed Library Materials. ANSI Z39.48-1984. ∞™

10 9 8 7 6 5 4 3 2 1

Printed in the United States of America

To Jonathan K. Probber—a true friend, and a true Jonsonian spirit

Contents

General Editor's Note

♦

The Critical Essays on British Literature series provides a variety of approaches to both classical and contemporary writers of Britain and Ireland. The formats of the volumes in the series vary with the thematic designs of individual editors and with the amount and nature of existing reviews and criticism, augmented, where appropriate, by original essays by recognized authorities. It is hoped that each volume will be unique in developing a new overall perspective on its particular subject

Robert Watson has set himself the formidable task of seeking to resurrect a vital Ben Jonson from his entombment in classical Renaissance comedy. Watson's lively, imaginative introduction deftly and briefly presents a vivid picture of a larger-than-life personality writing an angst-ridden satiric comedy out of his own bodily poles.

Watson's selection of essays pairs early critical commentaries with modern interpretive responses that examine Jonson's timeless insights from a contemporary perspective. While Jonson's poetry and masques are addressed by several essays, the major portion of the critical selection is given over to a drama in which the problematics of Jonson the person and his responses to his antagonists in the literary/social wars gain a new modern credence in this engrossing, innovative (re)presentation of one of the most singular, controversial figures in English literature.

ZACK BOWEN
University of Miami

Publisher's Note

♦

Producing a volume that contains both newly commissioned and reprinted material presents the publisher with the challenge of balancing the desire to achieve stylistic consistency with the need to preserve the integrity of works first published elsewhere. In the Critical Essays series, essays commissioned especially for a particular volume are edited to be consistent with G. K. Hall's house style; reprinted essays appear in the style in which they were first published, with only typographical errors corrected. Consequently, shifts in style from one essay to another are the result of our efforts to be faithful to each text as it was originally published.

Abbreviations

Journals frequently cited throughout this text may be identified by the following abbreviations:

E & S	*Essays and Studies*
ELH	*English Literary History*
ELR	*English Literary Renaissance*
MLN	*Modern Language Notes*
MLQ	*Modern Language Quarterly*
RES	*Review of English Studies*
SAQ	*South Atlantic Quarterly*
SEL	*Studies in English Literature*
SP	*Studies in Philology*
SQ	*Shakespeare Quarterly*
SS	*Shakespeare Survey*

Introducing Ben Jonson

ROBERT N. WATSON

The first collection of literary commentary memorializing Ben Jonson was published just a year after his death. Its title—*Jonson Virbius*—sets an example this new volume seeks to follow, despite New Critical and Post-Structuralist doubts about the centrality of the author to the functions of literature. I want to bring the figure of Jonson back from death.

So my unofficial subtitle is *Jonson Virbius II.* Virbius was a minor mythological figure commonly identified by Renaissance mythographers as Hippolytus returned to life after being torn apart. In the 1638 volume, the 33 elegists and their editor, Bryan Duppa, evidently sought to repair the damage Jonson suffered from attacks during his long decline, when he could no longer defend himself as ferociously as in his ambitious youth. My primary task is to rescue Jonson from an opposite danger: not ridicule, but what T. S. Eliot rightly identified as "the praise that quenches all desire to read the book . . . the most perfect conspiracy of approval."[1]

In literary history, then, Jonson's has been a death by asphyxiation rather than dismemberment. His achievements—like his admirers—have been locked into the library, escaping only for occasional riotous nights out at the theater. The proprietary classicism by which Jonson sought to exalt himself has become his half-acre tomb, and the realistic details of urban life and language that invigorated his comedies have been buried, in shards, among the glossary notes. The obsolescence of the masque, the devaluation of classical Greek and Roman culture, and the ascendancy of Romantic criteria for lyric poetry have all made Jonson seem archaic as well. But the essential Jonson is not really contained in those closed books. That students so rarely warm to Jonson is merely frustrating; that they can be brought to like him better only by learning that he was a drunken brawler and cold-blooded killer is at least ironically revealing.

The transformation of Jonson into a literary missing person has happened very much against his will. He was always inserting himself into his work: with bumptious prologues and epilogues, for example, or with interjections of his corpulence into love poems, virtually eclipsing their exquisite erotic pretensions (like a parody of glossy modern fashion magazines). In this, he mimics the Renaissance painters who depict themselves peering out conspiratorially at the viewer from a corner of the greater scene. But Jonson cannot remain in his observational corner. He might not have been satisfied to achieve what Thomas Greene perceptively called a "centered self,"[2] if it were in the background: he demands downstage center.

To the centuries-old practice of comparing Jonson to Shakespeare, I would therefore add that Jonson is a great egoist, just as Shakespeare is a saint of self-effacement; if Shakespeare exemplifies the transparent artist, Jonson often resembles a privileged spectator partly blocking our view. In this sense, the other familiar contrast—Jonson versus Donne as patriarchs of Cavalier and Metaphysical poetry respectively—is no contrast at all: these two men are speaking proof of the narcissistic potential of English culture at the turn of the seventeenth century.

Jonson grew up with a large chip on his shoulder—a chip that eventually worked its way down to his waist. He expressed his hatred for his enemies with scorn and violence, and so loved this world that he felt compelled to condemn and destroy it; his only begotten comedies struggle to punish his very powerful appetite for the infinite variety of worldly entities, the infinite objects of human production, admiration, and language. The Jonson who ate himself fat and then mocked his waistline resembles the Jonson who humiliates his comic gulls for greedily consuming the million modern things of his world, things Jonson could never portray with such delightful anatactic richness unless he understood their appeal only too well. Nor could he have assailed his rivals with such brutal accuracy unless he knew too well how it felt to be mocked and dismissed.

With Jonson, ignoring the body that held the mind that wrote the works is an even graver mistake than usual, because (like Donne) he was almost obsessed with bodies and the limitations they place on literate fantasies and immortal longings. In "My Picture Left in Scotland" and the "Celebration of Charis," he ruefully mocks the inability of his lovely verse to erase his physical unloveliness. In the "Expostulation with Inigo Jones," he expresses similar exasperation with the way the physical media of the masque threaten to eclipse its literary conceits. Even in burying his infant daughter, he speaks the spiritual commonplaces, but ends up focused on the bodily remains; and in burying his son, he relinquishes "Ben Jonson his best piece of poetrie."

In drama Jonson not only respected the physical presence implicit in the dramatic unities, he added another unity, that of the human being, often making his drama out of precisely the inextricability of what Donne's "The Extasie" calls "That subtle knot, which makes us man." Thus, the comedies often reach their limits when a grandiose scheme encounters an inconvenient but incontrovertible physical fact. And it is usually a degrading one, somewhere in the Bakhtinian lower bodily stratum: Epicoene's male genitalia, and perhaps Volpone's; Mistress Overdo's need to urinate; and the *Alchemist* conspirators' need for a little more space and time to keep their schemes from smashing up as Surly's lust and anger, and Dapper's fatigue and hunger, break through the artificial barriers. Jonson could praise his patrons in the exalted, body-denying language of Augustan eulogy, but such eulogy always provoked the Swift within him into a corrective scatological satire on some adjacent target, as in "The Famous Voyage." Behind all this, I believe, lies a heightened Renaissance anxiety about the dependence of the mind on the body, and hence the vulnerability of all perception and knowledge to erasure by physical death. Imagine, too, the bitterness of Jonson's long later years after a stroke had left him trapped in an immobile trunk and hindered the working of his brain. The potentially comic plot of his life, in which he rose from obscurity and took his many pleasures, turned sour in much the way his satiric plots do. So did the creative zeal of Renaissance English Culture.

At first glance, Jonson's comedies most resemble the work of David Mamet, a playwright who loves scams and their jargon. Audiences are taken into another world, but it is a golden one only in its profitability. The verbal capitalism of pun and neologism mirrors economic capitalism in this world, which is circumscribed by animal instinct and bodily function but richly decorated with opaque rather than transparent language.

These comedies, however, also have the intellectual and allusive range of Tom Stoppard, as well as Stoppard's remarkable ability to make the audience think not just in between but actually through its laughter. In Jonson as in Stoppard, and in Shaw as well, what is most funny is often what is most profound, not just a way of cajoling the audience into awaiting the next sententious moment. Jonson's allusions—especially in a masterpiece such as *Volpone*—are so deeply apt as to merit comparison with Milton's similes in *Paradise Lost.*

The tragedies are also oddly realistic, through the same allusive classicism that allows Jonson to describe his feeling for lost children or hated competitors most honestly by near translation of ancient authors. He was much condemned for merely quoting extensive passages from famous classical orations—an allusive yet literal- and historical-minded form of realism—and perhaps the tragedies failed because they inverted the naturalistic mode of the comedies, where the rhetoric seemed to spring from the bodies onstage, and their needs, in an intensely present tense. Also—and I believe this is unusual and costly—the world of Jonson's tragedies accepts a simpler moral calibration than his comedies.

This brief introduction has put a heavy emphasis on those comedies; so will the essays that follow. I agree with the consistent judgment of centuries of critics and audiences: only comedy allowed Jonson's true genius—which is to say, his violently contradictory aspects—full expression. It is worth looking back through those centuries of responses, because a volume of essays on Jonson offers a rare opportunity for historical perspective on criticism itself. Because Jonson succeeded so well in making himself known as an author so early in the history of that profession, this volume can provide evaluations of Jonson from his own time that compare instructively with those produced by the modern academic system. He was so combative a personality that he both wrote aggressive defenses of his own works and provoked aggressive attacks on those works and their creator, leaving us perhaps the best early case study of English literary criticism, the clearest evidence of the purposes and principles by which pre-Enlightenment literature was produced and judged.

It seems both just and illuminating to know the standards by which Jonson himself probably sought to succeed, as well as the prejudices which may have helped or hindered him. Therefore I have tried to pair brief early commentaries on Jonson with modern ones on the same works. I am deeply indebted to D. H. Craig's *Ben Jonson: The Critical Heritage 1599–1798* (London: Routledge, 1990) for bringing many of these responses to my attention, though I have returned to the original texts of nearly all of them, and silently modernized the spelling where I felt it would improve the clarity of reading without decreasing its richness.

Some of these early commentaries may stretch the category of "Critical Essays," but in compensation I have stuck to modern instances that fit the bill fairly closely: not textual studies, not performance histories, not sociopolitical critiques, but interpretive responses to the works as we have inherited them, responses that help us read the plays, poems, and masques with greater thoughtfulness and greater pleasure.

All modern Jonson scholars are indebted to the great editorial work of C. H. Herford, Percy Simpson, and Evelyn Simpson; unless otherwise noted, their edition of the *Works* (Oxford: Oxford University Press, Clarendon Press, 1925–52)—hereafter abbreviated as H&S—provides the basis for all citations of Jonson's own writings within the modern essays.

No one has performed the professed task of this volume—putting Jonson back together—as well as David Riggs, who connects Jonson's psychological needs with the details of court politics and professional competition in the period. Riggs's *Ben Jonson: A Life* is the most illuminating biography I have encountered of any Renaissance literary figure. The rich particularities of its historical and psychoanalytic explanations are impossible to reproduce here, but (at the author's suggestion) I am including the brief, lucid introductory overview of the argument about Jonson's fundamental conflicts, trusting that it will lead students of Jonson and his period to the book itself.

After Riggs's brief contribution I have placed William Drummond's equally brief summation of Jonson, an early version of the tell-all biography, based on remarks the distinguished visitor presumably made while intoxicated by alcohol and perhaps by a seemingly reverential Scottish audience to whom he thought he could safely vent his rivalrous opinions. The other primary document excerpted here, Chapman's knotty and naughty "Invective," shows how nasty these rivalries among the London literati became.

The opening section of Russ McDonald's *Shakespeare and Jonson, Jonson and Shakespeare* offers a superb overview of the history of the relentless comparison, acknowledging both its real bases and its illusory superstructures. McDonald also shows that the binary function of this comparison has obscured the important elements of conversation and even cooperation between the two great playwrights as their careers traced parallel arcs.

Afterward I offer some especially interesting early versions of the comparison (which still controls Jonson's reputation), including Aphra Behn's unorthodox remarks on the learnedness and hilarity of Jonson's drama, as compared to Shakespeare's. Among seventeenth-century commentators, Margaret Cavendish, Thomas Fuller, and Edward Phillips establish the conventional line in making Jonson the laborious version—impressive but pedantic—of the greatness Shakespeare achieved with breathtaking ease. Finally, like a modern literary theorist, Alexander Pope qualifies that neat binary distinction by analyzing the cultural dynamics that produced it.

Jonson's costliest handicap in this competition is his failure as a tragedian, and Anne Barton explains the probable causes, and the partial injustice, of that failure. Barton is probably our greatest cardiologist of the corpus of Renaissance dramatic literature (as Helen Vendler is of modern poetry): she sees what happens at the heart of it with astonishing clarity, and she describes it so plainly that we wonder why we didn't see it for ourselves. Here she contributes a chapter on Jonson's neglected *Catiline,* which she sees as significantly "anti-tragic."

Appended to Barton's essay are Fletcher's prefatory endorsement of the 1611 Quarto of *Catiline* and Jonson's own, no less defensive preface to the 1605 Quarto of Jonson's other classical tragedy, *Sejanus;* also appended are the specific complaints of the acerbic Thomas Rymer—the John Simon of the seventeenth-century theater—that articulate the preference for Jonson the comedian which has remained stubbornly in force from Jonson's time to our own. It would doubtless have been some consolation to Jonson that this attack on his tragedies nonetheless ranks them far above Shakespearean excrescences such as *Othello.*

The volume then turns to comedy—but not lightheartedness. Kristen McDermott's "'He may be our father, perhaps': Paternity, Puppets, Boys, and *Bartholomew Fair,*" building partly on Riggs's work, traces Jonson's paternal anxieties from their obvious literary and biographical instances in the epitaphs on his children, through his deep concerns about child actors, and into the spectral representations of childhood that permeate *Bartholomew Fair.* Interweaving the threats that theatrical careers presented to the children's sexual innocence, personal identity, and very survival, McDermott displays the full complexity of this great egoist's most altruistic side and of this professedly good-natured comedy's most uneasy moments.

The brief afterword to this essay belongs to the great conservative Edmund Burke, whose youthful commentary worships in Jonsonian comedy the ethical as well as aesthetic balance McDermott explicates, the way Jonson stands in implicit and sometimes explicit reproach to the degeneracies of his time.

In Katharine Eisaman Maus's "Impotence and the Satirist's Vocation"—part of a book-length study of the problems of selfhood and evidence in Renaissance drama—the litigation of the Essex-Howard annulment provides illuminating background not only for the peculiar rape-trial scene in *Volpone,* which turns into an impotence trial, but also for the general social ethics of *Epicoene,* in which "Jonson makes the conundrum of Morose's marital fitness a kind of metonymy for far more general problems of sexual identity and theatrical representation in Jacobean London." Maus convincingly describes the play's concern with the ways urban life had disabled "shaming rituals designed to be intensely humiliating in the intimate context of village life," and Jonson's concern, as a practicing satirist, with the impossibility of correcting a shameless society rather than (as in the earlier comedies) with merely humiliating "individually grotesque humors characters." As in several other New Historicist studies of Renaissance drama, the playwright becomes a kind of social engineer, and the critic a skeptical interpreter of the adjacent political and legal history. But Maus complicates the formula by acknowledging the way words and bodies compete as reality in the theater, and as proof in the courtroom. She even connects *Epicoene*'s gender trouble not only to the ambiguously gendered boys who performed it, but also to the grammatical gendering of English and Latin.

Following Maus's essay I have placed John Dryden's extensive commentary on *Epicoene;* Dryden's delight in the play reminds us how thoroughly Jonson anticipated and probably shaped Restoration literary tastes, but the accompanying reservations also remind us that Dryden anticipated and probably shaped modern literary criticism.

Gabriele Bernhard Jackson writes about *Every Man In His Humor* as a "comedy of non-interaction" in which Jonson produces at once a hilarious commentary on the malfunctions of Elizabethan society and an ironic commentary on the premises of Elizabethan theater. Jonson's switch throws the centripetal engine of drama into reverse, making its meaning not from the unnaturally focused struggle between characters in a single action but instead from an arguably more realistic series of failures of the characters to communicate, or even cohabitate.

Though it was not praised as tactical, Jonson's reluctance to portray warm human intimacy was already noted by contemporaries such as William Cartwright. Thomas Shadwell's preface and epilogue to *The Humorists,* and William Congreve's letter to John Dennis, provide Restoration perspectives on Jonson's "humors" drama; and Thomas Davies seems to provide almost a rough draft for Jackson's reading of *Every Man In.*

My own contribution is an essay sketching the "literary imperialism" of Jonson's comedies in general, and describing *The New Inn* as Jonson's negotiated settlement with the forms of social inauthenticity and traditions of romantic drama he had parodied for so long. Ten years ago, in *Ben Jonson's Parodic Strategy* (Cambridge: Harvard University Press, 1987), I described Jonson's comedies as themselves a competitive device, subsuming the works of his literary rivals, in a humiliating form, into his own plots. Thus, Celia and Bonario fail because *Volpone* refuses to respect their standard plot of romantic heroic innocence. In *Every Man In His Humor,* Kitely humiliates himself by frantically combating a cuckolding plot that no one around him would have thought to stage without his deluded prompting. The titular character of *The Devil Is an Ass* finds that his morality-play schemes and special effects are no match for the deviltry of Jonson's street-smart London connivers. In this regard, Jonson kept trumping himself, as the wits of *Every Man Out of His Humor* find themselves at a loss for stories or values once they have finished exposing the hollow theatricality of all the plots and purposes around them; the satiric exposer Surly finds himself exposed as a hackneyed Jonsonian debunker at the end of *The Alchemist;* Volpone and Mosca fatally mistake themselves for that same triumphant cynic; and theatrical wit itself must finally yield to real life at the end of *Bartholomew Fair,* where Jonson surrenders, affectionately, to the old forms. This exploration of *The New Inn* is a sentimental coda to that study, as the play was to Jonson's own career.

The New Inn may now seem an obscure topic, but in Jonson's time it was hugely controversial. Appended to my essay are several installations of the debate. Jonson began it by indignantly attacking the play's initial detractors in his "Ode to Himselfe," drawing a vituperative response in "The Cuntrys Censure" and a more measured one in Thomas Carew's "To Ben Johnson," which damns the play with faint praise; Carew, the most glib of the Cavalier Tribe of Ben, concedes that neither the play nor Jonson's indignation augments his stature, and affirms the familiar charge that Jonson wrote slowly, but insists that *The New Inn* still outclasses the competition. John Suckling's "A Sessions of the Poets" also offers an affectionate if left-handed compliment to the discredited playwright, answering Jonson's angry vanity (concerning his collected works generally and *The New Inn* particularly) by offering him an apt consolation prize in the literary competition. Also here is Charles Fitzgeoffrey's playful praise of Jonson's borrowing, the strategic illusion of plagiarism, which my aforementioned book as a whole attempts to trace. Finally, I append Jonson's prologue to *The Sad Shepherd,* in which he attempts a more genial defense of the sentimental, popularizing tendencies of his last plays.

Stephen Greenblatt's "The False Ending in *Volpone*" demonstrates a genius for making complicated literary observations both lucid and far-reaching—the talent that has made Greenblatt the most cited and influential scholar in his field. Though the article is mostly a superb close structural reading of the play, it shows the unmistakable seed of Greenblatt's subsequent work on "Renaissance self-fashioning," which engendered New Historicism. Exploring why neither Jonson nor his audiences could settle for the triumph they had wished on Volpone, Greenblatt finds a parable of the entire Renaissance, a story in which the abundance of dazzling props and verbal energy are the only stay against the void, and in which the doomed struggle of the "theatrical self" to survive allows us to "feel ourselves present at the very fountainhead of modern consciousness."

Two brief but distinguished early commentaries on *Volpone* follow Greenblatt's, and they too bear on the question of the authenticity of self in this play and beyond. John Dennis expresses reservations about the characterological verisimilitude, comic decorum, and structural unity of the play, and adds another vote against Jonson's ability to represent nobler passions. Richard Steele, on the other hand, insists that the authentic characterizations, and the way they drive the plot, put the works of Jonson's contemporaries—presumably including Dennis—to shame.

Turning to Jonson's verse, an insight similar to Greenblatt's propels Joseph Loewenstein's "The Jonsonian Corpulence, or The Poet as Mouthpiece," which makes Jonson the spokesman for an insatiable complaint about the "failed sovereignties of a modern self." Again, a brilliant close reading—this time of the "Invitation to Supper"—gestures toward literary history and psychobiography, but then opens out into a complex perspective on the functions of desire in a modern world. Loewenstein's justly renowned perspicacity concerning publication practices in the Renaissance produces both specific revelations about Jonson's poem and suggestive metaphors for the multiple strategies for multiplying the self that propelled Jonson's careers as both a producer of art and as a consumer of food. As a brief afterword to Lowenstein's essay, I attach Francis Beaumont's laudatory poem from the 1616 Folio, the book by which Jonson materialized and multiplied his literary self.

John Hollander's "Ben Jonson and the Modality of Verse" provides an excellent introduction to poetry, not merely to Jonson's. Its exegesis of poetic modes allows modern readers to understand Jonson's verse in the terms and on the principles Jonson himself would have applied. In doing so, Hollander blames the modern eclipse of Jonson by Donne on the impressionistic and expressionistic ideas imbued by Romantic poetry, and thereby enables us to bring Jonson back out into the light of reason and tradition. He also shows that old-fashioned literary history provides an indispensable basis for any study of literature's political import. The essay stands in explicit as well as implicit reproach of this volume's emphasis on Jonson's dramatic writing; but if any single essay can help readers appreciate the range of Jonson's poetry, this one can. Following this essay are contrasting comments on Jonson's poetic modes by his contemporaries: the snarlingly dismissive "On Jonson's Epigrams" ("Scribimus indocti doctique epigrammata passim"), and a virtual reply by Edward Howard, which credits Jonson with establishing and purifying English as a poetic language.

Finally, for a look at the Jonsonian masque and at a new direction in Jonson studies, the volume concludes with Kim Hall's "Sexual Politics and Cultural Identity in *The Masque of Blackness,*" which takes that strange literary event out of the category of literary history, where it has been safely stowed for centuries, and restores its context of racial and sexual politics. I say "restored" because this is not an anachronistic imposition or application of current political values in the academy: Hall shows how deeply this performance (and its uneasy reviews) participated in Jacobean discourses of racial stereotype and colonial authority. She also, thereby, shows that Jonson's supposedly arcane work can sometimes be productively adduced in the liveliest arguments of contemporary cultural criticism. I follow Hall's essay with Jonson's own 1606 defense of *Hymenaei,* a masque that would eventually be tainted less by any internal faults than by the sensationally sordid history of the marriage (of Lady Francis Howard) that it celebrated. History has a way of catching up with literary creations and consuming them for its own purposes—as it surely will the morsel called *Critical Essays on Ben Jonson.*

Notes

1. T. S. Eliot, "Ben Jonson" (1992), quoted by David R. Riggs, *Ben Jonson: A Life* (Cambridge: Harvard University Press, 1989), 238.

2. T. Greene, "Ben Jonson and the Centered Self," *SEL* 10 (1970):325–48.

Prologue to *Ben Jonson: A Life*

DAVID RIGGS

Some people regarded Ben Jonson as a scoundrel; others took him for a sage. There was ample basis for both views. A biographer who concentrated on contemporary gossip, satires, court records, and private correspondence could easily conclude that Jonson was a notorious reprobate and public nuisance: a drunken, swaggering, murderous sponge who gained his livelihood by writing libelous plays and flattering poems, and routinely attacked his friends behind their backs. His admirers have sought to discredit such charges on the grounds that Jonson was the innocent victim of his enemies' malice. At the age of forty-seven, however, in the course of extended private conversations with William Drummond, the Laird of Hawthornden, Jonson spoke quite openly about his drinking bouts, petty animosities, killings, womanizing, and criminal record. But the autobiographical passages in Jonson's published work, and tributes and memorabilia written by his friends, tell a very different story; a biographer who took these portrayals at face value could just as easily conclude that Jonson was a discreet and scholarly man who treasured his solitude and the society of a few intimate companions. He portrays himself as a "modest" individual, "known only to that *Few* which are truly able to know him," as his friend John Selden put it; his poetry and criticism mirror the same qualities of plainness, moderation, and sober rationality that inform his everyday existence. He discourages readers from inquiring too closely into his personal life by insinuating that there is not much to know about it. He has "*ever trembled to thinke toward the least prophanenesse*"; his project, both in his writing and his life, is to curb extravagance.[1]

Taken separately, these two protagonists can only perpetuate sterile controversies about the nature of the "real" Jonson; taken in conjunction, they offer a remarkable opportunity to study the interplay of reckless self-assertion and rationalistic self-limitation in a single life. Jonson is like a prudent businessman who periodically feels an irresistible urge to go to the racetrack. Just as one would expect, he loses everything he owns by the end of the day; within a few months, however, Jonson is wealthier, and more prudent, than

From *Ben Jonson: A Life* (Cambridge: Harvard University Press, 1989), 1–5. Reprinted by permission of Harvard University Press.

ever. The oscillations between defiant risk taking and sober retrenchment are less drastic after he reaches his mid-thirties, but the pattern persists until the end of his life.

My objectives are to keep both sides of Jonson's personality in perspective and to reconstruct the individual who negotiated between these extremes. In this biography, therefore, I analyze Jonson's behavior from two complementary points of view. When he is acting like a professional artist making practical choices, I adopt the outlook of a social historian. In these sections of the book, my aims are to reconstruct his social and intellectual milieu; to describe the conditions within which he produced his plays, poems, and masques; and to relate his writing to his personal circumstances at any given moment. When Jonson's behavior resists this kind of explanation, I seek out a psychological one. These parts of my narrative are frankly speculative and treat the ramifications of his childhood experience, the enactment of persistent neurotic impulses, and the therapeutic functions of his writing.

The two strands of my argument converge in the analyses of Jonson's plays. In writing his satirical comedies for the London stage, Jonson simultaneously released his pent-up aggressions and reconstituted himself as a man of letters, a leading figure in the literary avant-garde of Renaissance England. When his enemy Inigo Jones complained to Jonson that "no ill thou couldst so taske dwells not (in thee) / and there the store house of your plotts wee see," he spoke more wisely than he knew (H&S, XI, 385). In the last analysis, I argue, Jonson's writings reveal the malcontent troublemaker, astute careerist, and literary artist to be one and the same person.

The dominant motifs of Jonson's professional life are social and literary ambition. Between his early twenties and his mid-forties the upward trajectory of his career is breathtaking: forsaking his apprenticeship in the Bricklayers' Guild, he was by turns a journeyman actor touring the provinces, an innovative playwright trying to reach both a popular audience and an educated readership, a court poet to the household of King James I, the first English dramatist to bring out his works in folio, and a royal pensioner whose verse manuscripts circulated among a select circle of gentlemen and ladies. By the time of his death two decades later he had become the most celebrated poet of his age, a man who outshone even Shakespeare and Donne in the eyes of his contemporaries. Since his career coincides with the rise of the literary profession in England, his personal success story takes on the characteristics of a cultural phenomenon: in following his rise we are also witnessing the emergence of authorship as a full-time vocation.

Jonson not only prevailed over external obstacles that were built into the fabric of his society; he also overcame psychological disabilities that would have doomed a lesser man either to oblivion or to extinction at an early age. The record of his misadventures rivals the story of his success and is too long to be explained away on the grounds that he was a victim of circumstances, or lived in a more boisterous age than our own. Contemporary sources reveal that he killed two men for no apparent reason, went to prison on three separate occasions, was "almost at the Gallowes" (*Conv*) and wore the brand of a convicted murderer on his thumb, enjoyed sleeping with other men's wives (but not with single women), sired one or more illegitimate children, was paraded through the streets of Paris in a drunken stupor, and narrowly escaped having his ears and nose mutilated after collaborating on a play that lampooned King James I. In his thirty-third year, his own mother was on the verge of bringing his life to an end and acquired a dram of "Lustie strong poison" (*Conv*), for that purpose. This turbulent personal history goes back to the formative stages of Jonson's career and indicates that the course of his development was far more checkered than he cared to admit in public. The facade of a swift and sure ascent to Parnassus concealed a maze of personal and professional crises; the man who encouraged the reading public to view him as a model of even-tempered rationality had a foul mouth, a violent temper, and could be recklessly self-indulgent.

The progress of Jonson's literary career reflects his growing ability to cope with these inner demons and to achieve a degree of the self-mastery that he prized so highly. The key to psychological health, it is now widely believed, lies in the adaptive styles that enable individuals to resolve inner conflicts in a constructive fashion. If Jonson's instinctual drives were unusually fierce, his repertory of defense mechanisms was correspondingly rich and effective. Humor, which Freud regarded as "the highest of these defensive processes" because it "scorns to withdraw the idea bearing the distressing affect from conscious attention,"[2] was the main catalyst in his personal and professional growth. When Jonson's wayward impulses led him to commit overtly antisocial acts, he placed his future in jeopardy; but when the same psychological disorders found expression in his stage comedies, they became a source of strength and launched the professional career that ultimately secured his future.

Although he continued to exhibit the same disabilities throughout his life, the mature artist discovered a wealth of creative uses for them. His greatest comedies, *Volpone* and *The Alchemist,* are replete with adaptive devices that transform the dross of lust and aggression into the gold of artistic creation. That he consciously grasped the analogy between his experience and his art is more than we can say, but his continuing preoccupation with alchemy, sublimation, mock encomia, self-transformation, and the psychopathology of the bodily humors suggests that he was at least intuitively aware of it.

The most rigid of Jonson's defenses was reaction formation, which can be defined as behavior that is "diametrically opposed to an unacceptable instinctual impulse." The autobiographical passages in his critical dialogues, prefatory letters, prose jottings, and poems repeatedly insist on the changeless purity of his inner self, even when the factual record belies such assertions. Although self-transformation is the most compelling aspect of his biography, the actual experience of growth and change left him unsatisfied; his ultimate, and unrealizable, ambition was to transcend his origins, to preserve the product of growth while discarding the process. Karen Horney characterizes the compulsion to triumph over one's own past as "*the drive towards a vindictive triumph.*" This project "may be closely linked to the drive for actual achievement and success," she writes, but "its chief aim is to put others to shame, or defeat them through one's very success." Its "motivating force," she continues, "stems from impulses to take revenge for humiliations suffered during childhood."[3]

A simple, yet revealing, example of Jonson's tendency to efface his origins is the spelling of his last name. The title pages of the first three printed works that bear his name all refer to him as "Johnson." Since he carefully prepared these texts for the printer, and was quite finicky about such matters, we can be reasonably sure that this spelling, which also appears in all the early manuscript copies of his poems, was the one he employed for the first thirty years or so of his life. In his thirty-second year, however, he switched to "Jonson," and when he reprinted the three earlier texts in the 1616 *Works* he expunged his name from their title pages. "Johnson" thus became a nonperson, and the question of why he chose to adopt the anomalous spelling that set him apart from his contemporaries has never even been posed.

Turning to the matter of his ancestry—the usual starting point for a biographical narrative—we find another instance of retrospective self-fashioning. The first three court records that allude to his social status variously describe him as a "player," a "yoman," and a "bricklayer and citizen of London," phrases which indicate that he was not of gentle birth. In his thirty-third year, however, a fourth court record refers to him as "Armiger," a gentleman entitled to bear the heraldic arms of his ancestors. This document does not indicate who the ancestors were, but many years later, during his conversations with Drummond, Jonson remarked that "his grandfather came from Carlisle and he thought from Anandale to it, he served King Henry 8 and was a Gentleman."[4] Although this gentlemanly forbear gave the erstwhile bricklayer a crucial link to an earlier generation of landed gentry, he is a relative latecomer in the chronicle of Jonson's own life. At some point between the third and fourth appearances in court, around the time when he changed the spelling of his name, Jonson persuaded the Herald's Office that he was descended from the Johnstones of Annandale and purchased the right to bear their hereditary coat of arms. Ben Johnson, the journeyman bricklayer, disappeared in the wake of Ben Jonson, the courtier's grandson.

However instrumental these maneuvers may have been in furthering Jonson's career, or fortifying his self-esteem, they provoke precisely the kind of speculation they were meant to discourage. Jonson inadvertently calls attention to the side of himself that he wants to conceal; the adult's eagerness to rearrange his past arouses our curiosity about the child who came before him.

Notes

1. *Underwood,* 14, "An Epistle to Master John Selden," line 86; H&S, XI, 383–384; Dedication of *Volpone,* H&S, V, 18.

2. Freud, *Jokes and Their Relation to the Unconscious,* ed. and trans. James Strachey (London, 1960), p. 233. Where Strachey translates Freud's "Vorstellungsinhalt" as "ideational content," I have substituted the less cumbersome "idea."

3. George E. Vaillant, *Adaptation to Life* (Boston, 1977), p. 385; Horney, *Neurosis and Human Growth,* in *The Collected Works of Karen Horney,* vol. 2 (New York, 1964), pp. 26–27.

4. *Conversations.* For the title pages of the early quartos, see H&S, III, 195, and H & S, IV, 24, 197. For early documents relating to Jonson's social status, see H & S, I, 217–219, and H & S, XI, 572, 579.

From *Conversations* (1619)

William Drummond

He is a great lover and praiser of himself, a contemner and Scorner of others, given rather to lose a friend, than a Jest, jealous of every word and action of those about him (especially after drink, which is one of the Elements in which he liveth); a dissembler of ill parts which reign in him, a bragger of some good that he wanteth, thinketh nothing well but what either he himself, or some of his friends and Countrymen hath said or done. He is passionately kind and angry, careless either to gain or keep, Vindicative, but if he be well answered, at himself. For any religion as being versed in both. Interpreteth best sayings and deeds often to the worst. Oppressed with fantasy, which hath over-mastered his reason, a general disease in many poets. His inventions are smooth and easy, but above all he excelleth in a translation. When his Play of a Silent Woman was first acted, there was found Verses after on the stage against him, concluding that, that play was well named the Silent Woman: there was never one man to say *Plaudite* to it.

These are Drummond's concluding remarks to his summary of a conversation with Jonson in 1619 in Scotland. They were first published in 1711, but best recorded in an early transcription by Robert Sibbald.

An Invective Wrighten . . . Against Mr. Ben Jonson (1623 or later)

GEORGE CHAPMAN

Great-Learned witty-Ben: be pleased to light
the world with that three-forked fire; Nor fright
All of thy sublearned with Luciferous Boast
that thou art most-great-most-learned-witty most
of all the kingdom; nay of all the earth
As being a thing betwixt a human birth
and an infernal; No humanity
Of the divine soul showing Man in the[e]
Being all of pride composed and surquidry
        Thus it might Argue; if thy petulant will
may Flyblow all men with thy great swans Quill
If it Can write no plays; if thy plays fail
All the Earnests of our Kingdom straight must veil
to thy wild fury; that, as if a fiend
had slipped his Circle; showest thy breast is spleened
Frisking so madly that gainst Town and Court
Thou plantest thy battery in most hideous Sort
If thy pied humours suffer least impair
And any vapour vex the virulent Air
The Dunkirks keep not our coal ships in awe
More than thy Moods are thy Admirers Law—

        Thou must be Muzzled Ringed and led In Chains
Lest dames with child abide untimely pains
and Children perish: didst thou not put out
A boy's Right eye that Crossed thy mankind pout
if all this you find pardon Fee and grace

Excerpted and modernized from D. H. Craig, *Ben Jonson: The Critical Heritage 1599–1798* (London: Routledge, 1990), 134–39, which draws on the Bodleian MS Ashmole 38. Chapman is evidently responding to Jonson's "Execration upon Vulcan," which lamented the burning of Jonson's library in 1623.

The happiest outlaw th'art that ever was
Goodness to virtue is a godlike thing
And man with god Joins in a good doing king
But to give vice her Name, and on all his
(As her pure Merits) to Confer all this
who will not argue it redounds, whatever
vice is sustained with all, turns pestilent fever
what nourishes virtue, ever more Converts
To blood and spirits of nothing but deserts

Now to your parts Called good; your sacred desk
(The wooden fountain of the Mighty Muses)
(Alas) is burned; and there all their wealth failed
(That never Can with all time be retailed
Why then as good not name them) yes, O yes
Ten times repeated will all brave things please,
Not with their Titles yet, and poor self praises.
He lives yet (heaven be praised) that Can write
In his ripe years much better, and newborn
In spite of Vulcan, whom all true pens scorn
Yet let me name them in meantime to Cheer
his greedy followers with a pricked-up ear
It does himself ease and why them no good
Come serve it in then give him golden food.
Nobody (he dares say) yet have sound parts
Of profound search and Mastery In the arts
And perfect then his English Grammar too
To teach some what their nurses could not do
The purity of Language, and Among
The rest; his Journey into Scotland song
And twice twelve years stored up humanity
With humble gleanings in Divinity
After the fathers and those wiser guides
That faction had not drawn to steady sides
Canst thou lose these by fire; and live yet able
To write past Joves wrath, fire and Air things stable
yet Curse as thou wert lost for every babble

The sun in challenge for the heat and light
Of both heavens influences which of you two knew
And have most power In them; Great Ben 'tis you
Examine him some truly Judging spirit,
That pride nor fortune hath to blind his merit
He matched with all book fires he ever read

His Desk poor Candle Rents; his own fat head
With all the learned worlds; Alexander's flame
That Caesar's conquest cowed, and stripped his fame,
he shames Not to give reckoning In for with his:
As if the king pardoning his petulencies
Should pay his huge loss to in such a score
As all earth's learned fires he gathered for.

Odious Tandem

RUSS McDONALD

Literary history has separated William Shakespeare and Ben Jonson, created two distinct personae, taught us what to think about each in relation to the other, and established a simplified construction of each dramatic style in relation to its antithesis. Although the division has probably increased in our time, increased even in the past few decades, it is by no means a recent phenomenon. "In the seventeenth century it was fashionable, and profitable, to compare them, as Dryden did, to set them side by side as the two giants of the English theater, to discuss their respective virtues and evaluate their respective merits. By the time the century was over criticism had rendered its verdict: Shakespeare's preeminence would henceforth pass unchallenged. But by this time the luckless Jonson was yoked to Shakespeare in an odious tandem from which two centuries of subsequent comment would scarcely suffice to extricate him."[1] Thus Jonas A. Barish summarizes the process which has dissociated Shakespeare and Jonson from each other or, rather, joined them in a familiar and invariable relation. This book attempts to challenge the segregation of the two playwrights' work.

Personal mythology has helped to shape critical response. Barish goes on to point out that eighteenth-century editors of Shakespeare "discovered early that a convenient and safe way to praise 'their' poet was to abuse Jonson. The well-authenticated tradition of Jonson's conviviality gave way to a fraudulent countermyth: that Jonson, throughout his life, harbored an envenomed dislike of Shakespeare, whom he lost no opportunity of reviling and ridiculing, despite the fact—so ran the tale—that it was Shakespeare to whom he owed his start in the theater."[2] These myths were nourished, one suspects, by the differences in the two dramatists' origins: Shakespeare's Warwickshire boyhood distinguishes him from the urban Jonson, and the warm country heart has been preferred to the sharp urban eye. Such legends of personality might be passed over with a word or two about outdated prejudice did they not still influence our thinking about the men and their achievements. Shakespeare as

Reprinted from *Shakespeare and Jonson/Jonson and Shakespeare* by Russ McDonald, by permission of the University of Nebraska Press. Copyright 1988 by the University of Nebraska Press.

the genial natural who composed romantic comedies, Jonson as the crabbed classicist who spat forth bilious satires—these myths die hard, and even critics who consciously reject them still describe the works in terms that reflect such assumptions.

Neither in critical studies nor in lecture halls are the two most important playwrights of the English Renaissance normally brought together. Robert Ornstein's suggestion that they may be seen "either as the twin pillars of Elizabethan comedy or as its opposite poles" illustrates the space usually assumed to exist between them, and rarely has this critical structure been challenged.[3] Jonson has for many years been a whipping boy for Shakespeare, and most students of the period either whip him or seek to protect him. Many of Shakespeare's partisans are offended by the suggestion that Jonson might have been considered the more significant figure in the seventeenth century and insulted by the idea that the two playwrights should be compared at all.[4] On the other side are those sympathetic critics of Jonson's work who, leery of the power of traditional prejudice, find it advisable to remove their subject from the shadow cast by the colossus of Shakespeare.[5] The boundaries probably became even more rigid during the period of the New Criticism, when the preference for discrete units of art and organic literary careers fostered the treatment of each dramatist's work in isolation. From time to time voices have been raised against these ironclad categories, but only recently have critics in any number begun to reconsider the contemporaneity of the two playwrights and thus tentatively to explore the artistic connections between them and their work.[6] If the post-structuralist subversion of canons and literary authority has loosened the prevailing division somewhat, there is still much to be said.[7]

Jonson himself must bear partial responsibility for his critical estrangement from Shakespeare, for he seems to have wanted it that way. Passages from the inductions, prologues, poems, and reported commentary indicate that Jonson conceived of himself, and offered himself to the public, as one who wore the ancient, honorific mantle of Poet, a persona that required him to elevate his Works above the entertainments of mere playwrights. As he became more successful and well-known, he also became increasingly candid in his attacks on Shakespeare's dramatic predilections. Yet these celebrated pronouncements are only part of the story. The more we study Jonson the more we recognize discrepancies between his dogma and practice,[8] and it strikes me that his dealings with his colleagues—notably John Marston—are among the most revealing of these inconsistencies.[9] The Olympian declarations about his fellows must be considered in the larger context of a professional connection that included personal acquaintance, suspicion, certain common assumptions, theoretical disagreement, professional association, artistic borrowing, and in some cases even collaboration. In short, we should not allow ourselves to be hoodwinked by Jonson's claims to uniqueness, nor should we accept as gospel his shrill insistence upon the great distance between his work and Shakespeare's. It is highly ironic that literary critics have used Jonson's self-proclaimed singularity against him and perpetuated the opinion that he and his rival have nothing in common, but in the sense opposite to that intended. The artistic distinctions that Jonson established have become canonical, but now it is Shakespeare who is beyond compare.

Shakespeare contributed to the traditional separation, perhaps unwittingly, perhaps not, by saying nothing at all, or very little. He refused, so far as we can tell, to participate wholeheartedly in the imbroglio known as the War of the Theaters, and he mostly eschewed prologues, inductions, and theoretical asseverations. By remaining aloof from public controversy, Shakespeare allowed future generations to imagine him as the private, diligent artist, untainted by the personal and literary squabbles of the time. This image may be accurate, but it is almost surely an oversimplification promoted by scant evidence, and it has had far-reaching consequences. Two similar biographical passages, written over two hundred years apart, illustrate the tenacity and power of fable. As late as 1970 Ivor Brown, in an essay tellingly entitled "Not So Big Ben," could write:

> The two men met and matched their wits amid the canakin's clink of the inns, but Will kept sober while nimbly outwitting the heavier and more learned man. He remained a countryman at heart and went home to Warwickshire as a man of property. Jonson, of Scottish origin on his father's side, was essentially a Londoner, with no idea of becoming a landowner. He said that in all his life he made only two hundred pounds in the theatre. The masques were his prop.
> Will was a friendly and agreeable person; there is no sign of his dominating in company. Ben became, from the City to Westminster, increasingly a public figure and a Personage. If Will had died in London would he have been buried in the Abbey? Ben was. One feels that he had to be.[10]

Are the prejudices here much different from those contained in the following forged sentence which Robert Shields added to Drummond of Hawthornden's recollections in 1753?

> [Jonson] was in his personal character the very reverse of Shakespear, as surly, ill-natured, proud, and disagreeable, as Shakespear with ten times his merit was gentle, good-natured, easy, and amiable.[11]

Jonson as public, bellicose, and censorious, Shakespeare as private, affable, and above dispute—these characterizations have proved to be durable. Rarely is it profitable to contest such familiar legends, which are usually fairly harmless, but in the cases of Shakespeare and Jonson, the personae have unjustly limited critical response to their work, particularly their comedies; and our conception of their dramatic styles, in turn, has reinforced the outlines of their portraits. Surmounting the obstacles erected by biographical mythology may afford a fresh and expansive view of territory traditionally separated and may reveal that Shakespeare's and Jonson's artistic concerns and achievements are not as distinct as the supposed personalities of their creators might imply.

No one denies that Shakespeare and Jonson were personally acquainted, but the critical segregation of their work has brought with it a tendency to minimize evidence of professional interchange or even to exaggerate suggestions of rivalry into acrimony and dislike. Jonson's complaints about romantic comedy are often interpreted personally, for example, or his association with the children's companies is sometimes assigned more importance than it warrants, and these distortions have created the impression that Shakespeare and Jonson were leaders of warring camps who attacked each other from across the Thames. In fact there is little proof of enmity and considerable evidence of artistic cooperation. In the first place, the two playwrights often wrote for the same actors.[12] Shakespeare's commitment to the Lord Chamberlain's–King's Men was official and constant, in that he was a shareholder who composed all except perhaps his earliest works for these players; Jonson, on the other hand, was a sometime contributor of scripts. Still, while Shakespeare was actively associated with it the company produced six of Jonson's most significant plays (*Every Man in His Humour, Every Man out of His Humour, Sejanus, Volpone, The Alchemist,* and *Catiline*); Shakespeare participated in the staging of at least two of these. The list of actors in the 1616 Folio version of *Every Man In* places Shakespeare's name at its head, and even disallowing Rowe's claim that Shakespeare sponsored the production,[13] he was still a party to Jonson's first hit on the London stage. Although the newcomer withdrew from the company after the failure of *Every Man Out* in 1599, giving his next two comical satires to the children (and sniping at some of his former colleagues), he returned in 1603 with *Sejanus,* and again Shakespeare took a role, perhaps acting Tiberius. This evidence of professional contact reminds us that Shakespeare was not oblivious to Jonson's work, that he could not have escaped familiarity with the younger playwright's dramatic tastes, prejudices, methods, and accomplishments. He knew at least parts of two of Jonson's plays, a comedy and a tragedy, by heart. Although proof that Jonson was similarly associated with the performance of any of Shakespeare's plays is wanting, it is superfluous in light of Jonson's repeatedly declared objections to them. Recognition of personal and professional fraternity is the first step in judiciously defining the relationship between the two dramatists and properly comparing their theatrical styles.

Jonson's gibes at Shakespeare begin early, in *Every Man Out* (pub. 1600), and continue long after Shakespeare's death, in the "Ode to Himselfe" (1629).[14] Scrutiny of some of these discloses a primary source of modern thinking about the relationship. Occasionally Jonson permits himself a personal jab, as when he mocks Shakespeare's recently acquired coat of arms, with its motto *Non sanz droict:* Puntarvolo recommends that the parvenu

Sogliardo make the motto for his crest *"Not without mustard."* And there is resentment at the public favor that came easily to Shakespeare and often eluded Jonson, as in the contention that the audience that had disliked *The New Inn* would have preferred "no doubt a mouldy tale, / Like *Pericles.*"[15] But the personal allusions matter less than the complaints about Shakespeare's dramaturgic choices, and such criticism is directed chiefly at the means of theatrical mimesis and the moral function of drama.

Shakespeare's liberal approach to verisimilitude offended Jonson's classically derived view of how truth can be most effectively represented on the stage. Thus, most of the familiar reflections on Shakespeare's lapses, the body of proof "That Shaksperr wanted Arte," are devoted to sins against credibility. (It is worth remembering that Jonson abandoned an adaptation of one of Plautus' comedies because he could not cast it with actual twins.) The notorious Prologue to *Every Man In,* possibly written as Jonson was preparing text for the Folio, is a representative statement of the aesthetic objections that Jonson regularly lodged against his most famous rival. The speaker laments that other playwrights—the principal offender, though unnamed, is obvious—are willing

> To make a child, now swadled, to proceede
> Man, and then shoote up, in one beard, and weede,
> Past threescore yeeres: or, with three rustie swords,
> And helpe of some few foot-and-halfe-foote words,
> Fight over *Yorke,* and *Lancasters* long jarres:
> And in the tyring-house bring wounds, to scarres.
> He rather prayes, you will be pleas'd to see
> One such, to day, as other playes should be.
> Where neither *Chorus* wafts you ore the seas;
> Nor creaking throne comes downe, the boyes to please;
> Nor nimble squibbe is seene, to make afear'd
> The gentlewomen; no roul'd bullet heard
> To say, it thunders; nor tempestuous drumme
> Rumbles, to tell you when the storme doth come;
> But deedes, and language, such as men doe use:
> And persons, such as *Comoedie* would chuse,
> When she would shew an Image of the times,
> And sport with humane follies, not with crimes.
> (lines 7–24, Folio text)

Alluding unmistakably to the *Henry* plays and perhaps glancing at *Pericles, The Winter's Tale,* and *The Tempest,*[16] this anatomy of abuses backhandedly commends "realism," local specificity, recognizable persons, and morally significant situations. It is the same antiromantic conviction that gives rise to the tart critique of improbable fictions in the Induction to *Bartholomew Fair:* "If there bee never a *Servant-monster* i' the *Fayre;* who can helpe it? he [the author] sayes; nor a nest of *Antiques?* Hee is loth to make Nature afraid in his *Playes,* like those that beget *Tales, Tempests,* and such like *Drolleries*" (lines 127–30). Shakespeare's imaginative genius is never at issue; it is the use of that gift that disturbs Jonson. He protests especially Shakespeare's neglect of the didactic opportunities provided by the stage. Mitis's desire to see a romantic comedy instead of something "thus neere, and familiarly allied to the time" is met by Cordatus with the pseudo-Ciceronian definition recorded by Donatus: proper comedy is an "*Imitatio vitae, Speculum consuetudinis, Imago veritatis;* a thing throughout pleasant, and ridiculous, and accommodated to the correction of manners" (*EMOH,* III.vi.200–201, 206–9). Virtually all of Jonson's comments, personal and theoretical, must be interpreted in light of such assumptions.[17] Finally, there is the problem of the Folio poem, which I take to be a document of genuine, if reserved, respect. Most of the comments cited are familiar and amusing. Their acerbity should not be dismissed, but the artistic assumptions from which they proceed and the specific contexts in which they appear must be kept in mind.

Knowledge that Shakespeare acted in two of Jonson's plays does not tell us what he thought of his younger colleague's work. There is little to go on except for some oblique remarks on the War of the Theaters. Rosencrantz's gossip about the "eyrie of children, little eyases" who are "now the fashion" (*Hamlet,* II.ii.337, 339) reveals little beyond possible resentment at the faddish popularity of the recently revived children's companies and perhaps some implied censure of Jonson's encouraging such pointless competition.[18] In the Prologue to *Troilus and Cressida,* Shakespeare's armed speaker is apparently an imitation of the identical device in *Poetaster,* which probably preceded *Troilus* by a season. Whereas Jonson's presenter announces that he is prepared for attack in the theatrical wars, Shakespeare's disclaims local associations and explains his costume as appropriate to the dramatic subject ("suited / In like conditions as our argument" [lines 24–25]). This is probably a witty defense of drama against topical commentary—a private joke attacking private misuse of the stage—and thus one of the rare instances in which Shakespeare glances disapprovingly at Jonson's work.

The search for portraits of Jonson in certain Shakespearean characters, a sport that flourished in the nineteenth century, produced some ridiculous conclusions, and modern suggestions of this kind, while more judicious, have won little support. For instance, few critics accept that Jaques himself represents Jonson, although his satiric credo may fairly be called Jonsonian. The most nearly convincing work in this line has been done by William Elton, who makes a forceful case for identifying Ajax in *Troilus* with Jonson.[19] He believes, on the strength of the biographical parallels and the nasty pun on Ajax's name ("A-jakes" or "privy"), that *Troilus* is the "purge" that Shakespeare is said to have administered to Jonson as revenge for the attack on the Chamberlain's Men in *Poetaster.*[20] Such personal comment is inconsistent with almost everything we know about Shakespeare's usual practice,[21] and yet

Troilus itself is similarly anomalous. Whatever the truth may be, to conclude that Shakespeare rarely remarked publicly on Jonson's (or other dramatists') work is not to claim that he was ignorant of or uninterested in it.

Jonson's theoretical prolixity and Shakespeare's reticence make for a basic difference that is consistent with other important distinctions, most of them unexceptionable and familiar. First is the issue of professional orientation. Shakespeare apparently considered himself a commercial playwright who from the beginning to the end of his professional life was concerned chiefly with the attraction and satisfaction of paying customers, whereas Jonson thought of himself as a Poet, a historically distinguished vocation that included the activity of writing for the stage. Shakespeare retired from the theatrical and urban scene while still creative, while Jonson remained until his death a central fixture in the London literary milieu. Shakespeare seems to have shown no interest in publishing his plays, and the fact that his was the usual practice made Jonson's presentation of his *Works* in 1616 all the more egregious. Jonson's exalted view of the poet's role is responsible for his well-known insistence on the moral and social functions of dramatic writing. In dedicating *Volpone* to the two universities, Jonson differentiates between his own and others' views of "dramatick, *or (as they terme it) stage*-poetrie" (lines 36–37), an analysis that Shakespeare probably would not have disputed. Shakespeare evidently conceived of the theater as an end in itself, not as a vehicle for instruction or revelation. This is not to say that he rejected the Horatian dicta of *utile et dulcere,* but doubtless his interpretation of the utility of drama was considerably less specific than his colleague's. Jonson's didactic impulses have sometimes been overstated or misconstrued: the morality of *The Alchemist* is vastly more subtle and sophisticated than that of *Poetaster,* for example. But Jonson and Shakespeare would have certainly disagreed on whether a poem should mean or be.

Jonson's famous left-handed compliment, that Shakespeare ranked with the ancient masters despite inadequate classical learning, points to the celebrated difference in their response to classical literature. Jonson advertises his allegiance to the ancient poets repeatedly, in his extra-dramatic commentary, such as Cordatus's coaching of Mitis; in depicting himself as Horace in *Poetaster;* in his scrupulous citation of Latin sources in the quarto text of *Sejanus;* in the philosophical assumptions that govern the dedicatory letter to *Volpone;* in his frequent dependence on Lucian; in his attraction to the epigram; in his portrait of Cicero in *Catiline;* and in his occasional remarks on Shakespeare's betrayal of classical rule. Jonson's reverence for antiquity constitutes one of his trademarks, and Shakespeare did not share this passion, at least not in the same way. Shakespeare seems generally to have preferred contemporary authors, from whom he took most of his plots. Despite the Plautine sources of *The Comedy of Errors* and the ancient settings of many of the tragedies, Shakespeare's classical plays have a modern stamp upon them: he reached Rome by North. The pen-and-ink sketch (attributed to Peacham) of an early performance of *Titus Andronicus* with the actors in Elizabethan interpretations of Roman costume captures the essential relation between Shakespeare and the ancient masters. The classics were useful to him, but no more than any other kind of literature.

These distinct responses to classical example account for the disagreement over the unities. Jonson subscribed to the ancient doctrine because he believed that it helped to sustain dramatic illusion, to bridge the gap between nature and art, to present "things (like truths) well fain'ed" (Second Prologue to *Epicoene,* line 10). For instance, the unity of time demarcates and comments on the action of *Volpone:* the opening speech is an aubade, the Fox is in the full heat of passion at noon, and his gold is confiscated and his scheme exploded as darkness descends. In *The Alchemist* the unities of time and place contribute an invaluable sense of claustrophobia and potential comic calamity.[22] That his commitment to the unities was not absolute is revealed by the time sequence in *The Case Is Altered* or *Sejanus,* but Jonson claims that the principles are fundamental to his strict conception of dramatic mimesis.[23] Shakespeare's celebrated flouting of the unities reflects not only his relative indifference to classical stipulations but also his more flexible attitude toward dramatic representation in general. At times Shakespeare seems to have been willing, as in the choral admonitions from *Henry V,* to credit the spectator's imagination with greater power than Jonson was. At other times, however, he seems to have doubted the possibility of bridging the gap between life and art, believing with Dr. Johnson that the audience is always conscious that "the stage is only a stage, and that the players are only players."[24] Even when he strives to create an illusionistic fiction, he does so with other means than the unities.

Contrary ideas on the functions of drama led Shakespeare and Jonson to select different kinds of stories to dramatize. The plays that make Shakespearean romantic comedy what it is, those from *Dream* to *Twelfth Night,* derive from narratives of love and courtship, tales that Shakespeare found in fiction (in both poetry and prose) by Ariosto, Lodge, Barnabe Rich, and Spenser. A similar predilection is apparent in virtually all the other comedies, which originate in stories by Montemayor, Giovanni Fiorentino, Painter, Golding's Ovid, Cinthio, and the *Gesta Romanorum.* Shakespeare could invent actions when he wished to but was mostly content to adapt the narratives of his contemporaries and of comparatively modern English and Continental authors. If Jonson read such tales he did not dramatize them; in fact, the search for Jonson's sources is almost pointless because he invented most of his comic actions. With notable exceptions, such as Coleridge's commending the plot of *The Alchemist,* criticism has tended to underrate the contribution of action to Jonsonian comedy, but still it is a fact that story was less important to Jonson than to Shakespeare. He concocted the fable to suit his thematic and heuristic purposes. For tragedy, Jonson went directly to classical sources, at least for the two tragedies by which he wanted to be remembered, *Sejanus* and *Catiline:* from the mine of ancient history he chose two careers offering unmistakable moral patterns.[25] Shakespeare, again, preferred modern sources for tragedy, adapting the stories of Belleforest or Cinthio or plays with proven appeal, and when he did select an ancient subject, he relied upon Elizabethan intermediaries such as North or Chapman. Shakespeare's choice of sources, unlike Jonson's, does not bespeak an informing dramatic theory or predetermined aim.

Jonson's suspicion of narrative for its own sake is accompanied by a commitment to and a gift for satiric portraiture. Nevill Coghill, in an influential discussion of the two dramatists' different styles, remarks upon the primacy of character in Jonsonian comedy:

> Like Chaucer, [Shakespeare] never troubled to invent a plot if he could find one invented by somebody else. A good story was the first necessity in imagining his plays.
>
> Ben Jonson worked differently. Satire was his object and he therefore had to begin with *character* (or a group of characters) fitted to his lash. He then placed them in a certain situation calculated to show them at their worst, and by a prodigious intellectual mastery contrived the complete series of their logical development into successive scenes, working from his data to his Q.E.D. with the stunning ingenuity of a master in algebra. By doing so he almost in some cases achieved a story.[26]

Overlooking the manifest preference in this summary (indeed, it is usually necessary to ignore the evaluative tone of such formulations) we find a clear statement of the orthodox view. Evidence of this difference in emphasis is that it is often difficult to recall the events in Jonson's comedies but easy to remember the persons who perform them. Jonson's corrective bent, especially his interest in manners, prompted him to imagine characters guilty of outlandish moral and social faults. Shakespeare, of course, began with no such agenda, and their difference on this point results in two styles of characterization. "It is a truism that [Shakespeare's] characters are 'round' where Jonson's are 'flat,' that they have changes of mood and motive, that they develop and surprise us. . . . his people seem 'natural' to us, like people that we know, like ourselves. This is never so in Jonson."[27] Coghill's last pejorative phrases reflect the taste, stimulated by influences such as the Victorian novel and the criticism of A. C. Bradley, for "real people." But the central article in the analysis is indisputable: Shakespeare took a greater interest in character for its own sake, as he did in story, than did Jonson. For the most part, Jonson seems to have regarded his characters as means to an end; Shakespeare rarely did so. These technical biases naturally produce two very different kinds of comedy.[28] Shakespeare's geniality toward his persons and their actions is consistent with his fundamental interest in narrative, especially tales of love and courtship; and Jonson's satiric asperities proceed naturally from his primary concern with eccentric figures whose interactions constitute a dramatic action.

These several oppositions of technique and taste signify two distinct attitudes toward experience, two visions that may fairly be described in antithetical terms: tolerant versus critical, optimistic versus pessimistic, positive versus negative, progressive versus conservative. Shakespeare offers a version of life that admits the opportunity for happiness, for improvement, for second chances. Oliver repents his tyranny over Orlando and mends his behavior; Don "John is ta'en in flight, / And brought with armed men back to Messina." Even when the agents of folly and evil are allowed to escape or remain uncorrected, there is the suggestion that they may be entreated to a peace, as Orsino urges for Malvolio. If humans are not perfect, they are at least corrigible, and it is on this possibility that Shakespeare throws the dramatic pressure. His characters are assisted by luck, by good fortune, by chance, by Providence, and such happy coincidence is the manifestation of benevolent natural forces. Shakespeare uses all his dramatic expertise to attract his audience and encourage participation in the theatrical transformation, a strategy altogether appropriate to a vision that urges us to accept people for what they can become. Jonson's depiction of humans in society disturbs us, for he is pessimistic about the penalties of Adam. His characters are rarely better off at the end than at the beginning of his comedies, and those who accidentally profit do so only financially. The Jonsonian world is static and confined, hardly subject even to change, much less amendment. Shakespeare's benevolent Providence, which links effects to causes and ironically converts mischance into fruitful possibility, is here replaced by a universe that is random and perilous. When Fortune does intrude, it is usually in the form of hard luck for everyone concerned. There is a logic to experience, but it is a scheme tied to human will and fallibility. Shakespeare observes and smiles at humanity and its ways; Jonson mocks and fulminates.

It would be pointless to dispute these antitheses, for they are generally valid, their familiarity being a result of their utility. There is some point, however, in attempting to modify them, to state them more precisely, and we may begin by recognizing that the accepted oppositions derive from the juxtaposition of certain typical plays—say *Dream, Much Ado, As You Like It,* and *Twelfth Night* against *Every Man Out, Volpone, The Alchemist,* and *Bartholomew Fair*—and that it is risky to generalize about either comic style on the basis of a few works, however important and representative. Too often each category is stretched to encompass virtually all the comedies of each dramatist, so that Jonson's "satiric realism" is invoked in discussions of plays to which it scarcely pertains, such as the unrevised *Every Man In* or *The New Inn.* Or a play may be wedged into a category, a process that often requires distortion or peculiar emphasis. Occasionally the familiar labels attach themselves even to noncomic texts, so that Shakespeare's romantic idealism is extended even to his tragedies. Most readers of Renaissance drama are capable, when studying the work of either dramatist alone, of making fine discriminations, of noticing the darker shades in *Twelfth Night* or of appreciating the boisterous mirth of

Volpone, for example. Yet once Shakespeare and Jonson are placed next to each other, the well-known differences assert themselves and some of our most sensitive readers are satisfied with clichés. Criticism has been restricted by a monolithic conception of each style, an assumption evident in Ornstein's metaphor of "the twin pillars." If each canon is regarded as homogeneous and fixed, then we can do little more than look upon this picture and on this.

In fact, however, each canon is various and irregular, containing experiments and false starts and atypical plays, and such variations arise from conceptions of experience that are dynamic and complicated. Every text of each dramatist embodies a vision of life marked by tensions and competing impressions: in any of Shakespeare's comedies, for instance, faith in human resiliency and providential aid is subverted by doubts about universal weakness and inevitable limitation. Similarly, in each of Jonson's comic masterpieces, the critique of self-interest and baseness coexists with awareness of and respect for man's extraordinary powers of imaginative invention. When all these particular responses and conclusions are collected into the abstraction that we call Shakespeare's or Jonson's artistic vision, we have a very capacious and sophisticated thing indeed. Even though the two visions are distinct from each other, it is also true that they contain similar subjects, parallel shapes, related colors, and that they blend together at the edges. A similar relationship obtains among the dramatic means employed to mediate these visions. Shakespeare's exploitation of romantic conventions depends upon ironic and even satiric tactics that serve to qualify and, paradoxically, to amplify the effect of romance, while Jonson's assault on human failings is sometimes supported by romantic possibilities that must be denied or displaced. In short, the complexity of the two visions makes them appropriate for comparison: their contents and the strategies that convey them are more closely related than most criticism has been willing to allow.

The traditional polarization of Shakespearean and Jonsonian comedy has tended to obscure the two dramatists' attraction to similar themes. *Twelfth Night* and *Every Man Out,* plays from roughly the same period, are usually (and rightly) held to represent the two types of Elizabethan comedy, romantic and satiric, New and Old. Yet the source of conflict, the focus of attention in both works is the human penchant for affectation and self-absorption. The fantasies and self-delusions that Jonson derides in Puntarvolo, Fastidious Briske, and Sordido also afflict Orsino, Olivia, and particularly Malvolio. This simple instance of likeness within difference attests to a pervasive thematic consistency. Both dramatists were concerned with what Sidney called "the common errors of our life," and even though Jonson's response to the ubiquitous evidence of humanity's fallen state is usually more contemptuous than Shakespeare's, both devote their attention to the irresistible pressures of the flesh, the inevitable defeat of innocence, the familiar desire to take advantage, the lamentable effects of inconstancy. In play after play audiences are invited to contemplate that weakness that comprehends and fosters many others—

human pride. Exploration of its power and influence is not confined to the comedies, however. Numerous characters suffer from self-love and from exaggerated conceptions of themselves, and the actions devised to puncture such inflated ideas may be comic, tragic, or satiric. Both dramatists also seem vitally interested in the natural impulse to transcend natural limitations. The lawyer's clerk in *The Alchemist,* the young nun in *Measure for Measure,* the aging lovers in *Antony and Cleopatra,* the Stoic Germanicans in *Sejanus*—all these very different figures exhibit a will to overcome mortal restrictions of one kind or another, and the vastly different nature of their actions or of the responses they provoke ought not to obscure the similarity of their desires. One token of the significance of this effort at transcendence is the two playwrights' similar fascination with the uses of language. This subject may be of greater obvious importance to Jonson—indeed it is the mainspring of *Poetaster*—but throughout both canons (and in the nondramatic works as well) we find an abiding interest in the power of words.

Words are the medium of the imagination, and virtually all of Shakespeare's and Jonson's dramas address themselves directly to the problem of the imaginative faculty. The human imagination is presented as a gift and a curse, and both dramatists show special concern for its misapplication or perversion. The connection between words and imaginative ability is clearly discernible in any number of their comedies and comical satires, in figures such as Master Ford, Thorello, Giuliano (Downright), Mistress Quickly, Puntarvolo, Beatrice and Benedick, Dogberry, Captain Tucca, Don Armado, and many others. In most of the romantic comedies Shakespeare addresses himself to the creative value of fancy, and in the comical satires Jonson is concerned to show the products of the disciplined imagination in Crites and Horace. But many of their greatest plays, notably Shakespeare's major tragedies and Jonson's middle comedies, are based upon the experience of imaginative idealists who seek to impose subjective visions of experience upon an intractable world. The result of these imaginative efforts is failure. And yet the very works that generate such doubts about the imagination imply that its greatest fulfillment is to be found in the dramatic artifact itself. It is therefore appropriate that late in their careers both playwrights take what we might call a romantic turn: pessimism and failure are supplanted by a new perspective and confidence in the compensatory and even redemptive powers of the imagination.

A Note on Texts

I quote from *Ben Jonson,* ed. C.H. Herford and Percy and Evelyn Simpson, II vols. (Oxford: Clarendon Press, 1925–52). Jonson's spelling of *i/j* and *u/v* has been modernized, and citations from *Every Man in His Humour* refer to the Quarto edition of 1601.

Notes

1. Jonas A. Barish, "Introduction" to *Ben Jonson: A Collection of Critical Essays* (Englewood Cliffs, N.J.: Prentice-Hall, 1963), p. 1.

2. Ibid.

3. Robert Ornstein, "Shakespearian and Jonsonian Comedy," *SS* 22 (1969): 43.

4. A typical example of this approach is found in David L. Frost's *The School of Shakespeare: The Influence of Shakespeare on English Drama, 1600–1642* (Cambridge: Cambridge University Press, 1968). Frost attacks Gerald Eades Bentley's argument, derived from contemporary allusion, that Jonson was the more highly regarded playwright in the seventeenth century. Bentley's work is *Shakespeare and Jonson: Their Reputations in the Seventeenth Century Compared,* 2 vols. (Chicago: University of Chicago Press, 1945). In general, Bentley's thesis has met with vigorous objection; whether it is true or not, the negative response to it indicates the firmness of modern taste.

Frost goes on to dismiss Jonson from his analysis of Shakespearean influence with the remark that "their activities were not parallel" (p. 20). Similarly, Peter G. Phialas insists that Shakespeare and Jonson adopted different methods to "dramatize two different responses to the human situation." See "Comic Truth in Shakespeare and Jonson," *SAQ* 62 (1963): 80. Virtually all such phrases are euphemisms for a manifest preference.

5. For a statement of this point of view, see George Parfitt, who asserts that Jonson is surely Shakespeare's greatest contemporary but "the most consistently unlike Shakespeare in dramatic method." *Ben Jonson: Public Poet and Private Man* (London: J. M. Dent, 1976), p. 132. Similarly, Gabriele Bernhard Jackson's fine book on Jonson contains only two references to Shakespeare, one proclaiming the impropriety of comparison: "Jonson has had much to bear from critics irresistibly tempted to set him against his greatest contemporary. . . . Apart from date, however, there is very little similarity in the intention or achievements of their work to make such comparisons fruitful." *Vision and Judgment in Ben Jonson's Drama,* Yale Studies in English, 166 (New Haven: Yale University Press, 1968), p. 93.

6. An early dissenter from the prevailing wisdom was E. E. Stoll, who recognized that too much attention was being paid to the doctrine of the humours, that the simplicity of Jonson's style of characterization was often exaggerated, and that simultaneous study often produced distortion. See his sensible and careful chapter entitled "Shakespeare and Jonson" in *Shakespeare and Other Masters* (Cambridge: Harvard University Press, 1940), pp. 85–120. This essay has received less notice than it deserves.

A stimulating comparison of themes is offered by S. Musgrove in the second of three lectures, "Tragical Mirth: *King Lear* and *Volpone,*" collected under the title *Shakespeare and Jonson,* Auckland University College Bulletin no. 51, English Series, no. 9 (1957). Musgrove's method in this lecture is, to my way of thinking, sensible: "In comparing these two plays I am not, in the main, looking for literary borrowings of a direct kind, nor for verbal indebtedness: but for larger likenesses of theme and imaginative invention" (p. 21). The volume begins promisingly, with a desire "to see [Jonson and Shakespeare] not as 'classicist' set against 'Elizabethan,' but as two men working within the same dramatic kinds and with similar dramatic intentions" (pp. 3–4); but too often the argument descends into speculation about echoed lines and possible cases of influence. For treatment of parallel themes, see Harry Levin's brilliant essay, "Two Magian Comedies: *The Tempest* and *The Alchemist,*" *SS* 22 (1969): 47–58.

Maurice Charney contributes some extremely sensible remarks on the impropriety of segregating Shakespeare from his contemporaries in "Shakespeare—and the Others," *SQ* 30 (1979): 325–42.

Critics who have attempted to describe the relationship more precisely include Anne Barton and Ian Donaldson. See, in addition to Barton's *Ben Jonson, Dramatist* (Cambridge: Cambridge University Press, 1984), the paper she delivered before the Second Congress of the International Shakespeare Association at Stratford in August of 1981: "Jonson and Shakespeare," in *Shakespeare, Man of the Theater*, ed. Kenneth Muir, Jay L. Halio, and D. J. Palmer (Newark: University of Delaware Press, 1983), pp. 155–72. Donaldson has edited a collection of essays entitled *Jonson and Shakespeare* (Totowa, N.J.: Barnes and Noble, 1983). Few of the papers contained therein are as fresh as one might wish—some concern themselves only with Shakespeare or with Jonson—but the idea of the collection is laudable. See Donaldson's admirable introduction; D. H. Craig's "The Idea of the Play in *A Midsummer Night's Dream* and *Bartholomew Fair*," pp. 89–100; F. H. Mares's "Comic Procedures in Shakespeare and Jonson: *Much Ado About Nothing* and *The Alchemist*," pp. 101–118; Ann Blake's "Sportful Malice: Duping in the Comedies of Jonson and Shakespeare," pp. 119–34; and Anthony Miller's "The Roman State in *Julius Caesar* and *Sejanus*," pp. 179–201.

Two studies that would seem pertinent but which I have not found very helpful are Nicholas Grene's *Shakespeare, Jonson, Molière: The Comic Contract* (Totowa, N.J.: Barnes and Noble, 1980), and Zvi Jagendorf, *The Happy End of Comedy: Jonson, Molière, and Shakespeare* (Newark: University of Delaware Press, 1984).

7. The most important of such studies is probably Jonathan Goldberg's *James I and the Politics of Literature* (Baltimore: Johns Hopkins University Press, 1983), esp. chs. 3 ("The Theater of Conscience") and 4 ("The Roman Actor: *Julius Caesar, Sejanus, Coriolanus, Catiline,* and *The Roman Actor*"). Goldberg's role in developing the new historical criticism means that he is interested less in particular texts and authors than in broad theoretical questions, as the argument of his book indicates: "The underlying thesis of this study is that language and politics—broadly construed—are mutually constitutive, that society shapes and is shaped by the possibilities in its language and discursive practices" (p. xi). Such criticism is certainly not limited by the stereotypes I have deplored—indeed, it breaks down categories with a vengeance—but concentration on the linguistic medium and its relation to political authority makes it less useful than it might be to one interested in literary forms and the treatment of them by individual artists. Much the same may be said of some of the new linguistic studies: for example, see Patricia Parker, "Deferral, Dilation, Diffé*r*ance: Shakespeare, Cervantes, Jonson," in *Literary Theory / Renaissance Texts*, ed. Patricia Parker and David Quint (Baltimore: Johns Hopkins University Press, 1986), pp. 182–209.

8. Alexander Leggatt has identified many of the contradictions between Jonsonian theory and practice: *Ben Jonson: His Vision and His Art* (London: Methuen, 1981). See especially pp. xv–xvi and ch. 6, "The Poet as Character," pp. 199–232.

9. In 1601 Jonson pilloried Marston in *Poetaster*, portraying him as Crispinus, the title character whose barbarous vocabulary attests to his artistic incompetence; yet four years later Jonson collaborated with Marston and Chapman in composing *Eastward Ho!* Likewise, Marston ridiculed Jonson harshly and repeatedly at the turn of the century, and then in 1603 dedicated *The Malcontent* to him. Such curious patterns of censure followed by collaboration should teach us how to interpret Jonson's legendary blasts at Shakespeare.

10. Ivor Brown, "Not So Big Ben," *Drama* 99 (1970): 44. Brown here alludes to Thomas Fuller's famous account of the "wit-combates" between the two dramatists. See E. K. Chambers, *William Shakespeare: A Study of Facts and Problems*, 2 vols. (Oxford: Clarendon Press, 1930), 2:245.

11. This addition to Drummond's *Conversations* was inserted into an edition of Theophilus Cibber's *The Lives of the Poets of Great Britain and Ireland* (London, 1753), 1:241. Barish quotes it in his "Introduction," p. 3.

12. The question of when Shakespeare and Jonson became acquainted with each other, while it does not affect our understanding of their work, is a fascinating one. Certainly they were known to each other by 1598. It is at least possible that they were working in the same theatrical troupe in 1592, possible that they toured together during the plague year of 1593, possible that they acted in each other's very earliest works. The validity of this argument depends on whether Shakespeare was ever associated with Pembroke's Men and whether the "Mr. Johnson" who was a hireling member of the company was actually Ben Jonson. For the most cogent discussion of what is known and how it might be interpreted, see Mary Edmond, "Pembroke's Men," *RES,* n.s., 25 (1974): 129–36. David George doubts Edmond's conclusions in his own complicated, and at times highly speculative, essay concerning the development of the major troupes: "Shakespeare and Pembrokes's Men," *SQ* 32 (1981): 305–23. Scott McMillin also doubts the identity of this Mr. Johnson: see "Simon Jewell and the Queen's Men," *RES,* n.s., 27 (1976): 176, a rejoinder to Edmond's article.

13. In his *Life* of Shakespeare (1709), Nicholas Rowe claims that *Every Man in His Humour* had been rejected by the Lord Chamberlain's Men, but that Shakespeare came across the script, recognized its merit, and recommended its production.

14. Summary and discussion of these references are provided by E.A.J. Honigmann, *Shakespeare's Impact on His Contemporaries* (Totowa, N.J.: Barnes and Noble, 1982), pp. 100–103. The text containing the greatest concentration of allusions is *Every Man out of His Humour:* there are glances at Shakespearean characters (notably Falstaff), lines (two from *Julius Caesar*), and plots (Mitis's famous gripe that Jonson's play contains no "crosse-wooing" and no clown). The quarto text of *Every Man Out* (1600) contains "more than hath been publickely Spoken or Acted," and it may be that Jonson's break with the Lord Chamberlain's Men—perhaps he blamed the company for the play's failure—prompted him to supplement his text with swipes at his former fellows and their chief writer. Whether the Elizabethan theatergoers heard or read these statements, they would have been struck by Jonson's newfound confidence and independence of mind.

15. Jonson's jealousy of Shakespeare's popularity is accompanied by envy at the speed with which his colleague composed. The famous opinion that Shakespeare, who "never blotted out line," ought to have "blotted a thousand" (*Discoveries,* lines 649–50) should be read in this light. Honigmann points out that this charge reflects the sentiment found in the prefatory letter to *The Alchemist,* where Jonson distinguishes "between those, that (to gain the opinion of Copie) utter all they can, how ever unfitly; and those that use election, and a meane" (lines 27–29). See *Shakespeare's Impact,* pp. 98–100.

16. For commentary on these allusions, see Herford and Simpson, 1:333–35, 9:343–46; and Gabriele Bernhard Jackson's edition of *Every Man In* (New Haven: Yale University Press, 1969), pp. 186–88. Jackson presents a list of plays by other authors in which even more flagrant violations of the stated principles appear, and she cites similar statements of disapproval from Sidney, Whetstone, and Cervantes. Jonas A. Barish cautions against reading these references too specifically, complaining that from the eighteenth century onwards "the prologue to *Every Man in His Humour* was read not as a critical manifesto but as a savage diatribe (an 'insolent invective') against Shakespeare, wherein every rift was loaded with rancorous ore" ("Introduction," p. 2).

17. For example, an amusing reference to *Julius Caesar* is clarified by an awareness of this difference in point of view. At the denouement of *Every Man Out,* when Puntarvolo turns on Carlo Buffone and begins to seal his lips to silence his teasing, Carlo turns to Macilente, his comrade in raillery, and cries "*Et tu Brute!*" (v.vi.79). More than a gratuitous or envious dig at a momentous episode in a popular tragedy, this is probably a parodic comment on Shakespeare's tragic style, which Jonson regarded as morally indefinite and which he would seek to improve in *Sejanus.* For an extensive discussion of Jonson's opinion of *Julius Caesar,* see J. Dover Wilson, "Ben Jonson and *Julius Caesar,*" *SS* 2 (1949); 36–43.

18. See the Longer Note in Harold Jenkins's Arden edition of *Hamlet* (London: Methuen, 1982), pp. 470–73.

19. Elton notes the following parallels: Jonson was known early in his career as a braggart, and the friendly Drummond (among others less charitable) so describes him; Ajax's fame was as a soldier, and Jonson often made much of his military experience; Ajax's stupidity may be an ironic inversion of Jonson's self-proclaimed learning; Cressida's servant describes Ajax as "valiant as the lion, churlish as the bear, slow as the elephant, a man into whom nature hath so crowded humours that his valour is crushed into folly, his folly sauced with discretion" (1.ii.20–24), all traits associated with Jonson's public image; and the envy that Ajax cannot restrain is implicit throughout Jonson's comments on his peers. William Elton, "Shakespeare's Portrait of Ajax in *Troilus and Cressida*," *PMLA* 63 (1948): 744–48. Elton reflects the view of Roscoe Small, who attempts at length to show that Ajax is a detailed portrait of Jonson and that the purge is *Troilus and Cressida*. See *The Stage-Quarrel between Ben Jonson and the So-Called Poetasters* (Breslau, 1899), p. 170.

20. For the various points of view in this controversy, see J.B. Leishman's edition of *The Three Parnassus Plays* (London: Ivor Nicholson & Watson, 1949), pp. 59–60 and 370–71; E. K. Chambers, *The Elizabethan Stage*, 4 vols. (Oxford: Clarendon Press, 1923), 4:40; and Cyrus Hoy, *Introduction, Notes, and Commentaries to Texts in "The Dramatic Works of Thomas Dekker,"* 4 vols. (Cambridge: Cambridge University Press, 1980), 1:195–97.

21. See Kenneth Palmer's Introduction to his Arden edition of *Troilus* (London: Methuen, 1982), pp. 17–22.

22. One of the best commentaries on Jonson's use of the unities for the creation of meaning is R. L. Smallwoods's " 'Here, in the Friars': Immediacy and Theatricality in *The Alchemist*," *RES* 32 (1981): 142–60. See also Robert N. Watson, "*The Alchemist* and Jonson's Conversion of City Comedy," in *Renaissance Genres: Essays on Theory, History, and Interpretation*, ed. Barbara Kiefer Lewalski, Harvard English Studies, 14 (Cambridge: Harvard University Press, 1986), esp. pp. 338–39.

23. Ekbert Faas, in his recent *Shakespeare's Poetics* (Cambridge: Cambridge University Press, 1986), discusses Shakespeare's disregard for the unities in light of Jonson's professed commitment to them. Despite what seems to me a slightly condescending attitude toward Jonson, he makes some valuable remarks about the inconsistencies in Jonson's practice. See esp. pp. 58–60.

24. *Samuel Johnson: Rasselas, Poems, and Selected Prose*, ed. Bertrand H. Bronson (New York: Holt, Rinehart and Winston, rpt. 1971), p. 276.

25. Anne Barton speculates reasonably and informatively on Jonson's lost tragedies—*Page of Plymouth; Robert II, King of Scots;* and *Richard Crookback*—in *Ben Jonson, Dramatist*, pp. 9–13.

26. Nevill Coghill, "The Basis of Shakespearian Comedy," *E & S* 1 (1950): 15.

27. Ibid.

28. Madeleine Doran places these two different styles of comedy in their contemporary context: "The essential difference between the two models of English comedy is one of attitude and tone. The emphasis is on a different set of human motives—on the one hand, on poetic longings for love and adventure; on the other, on the grosser appetites for women, money, or power. The defining difference of tone is the difference between lyrical sentiment sympathetically expressed and critical satire." *Endeavors of Art: A Study of Form in Elizabethan Drama* (Madison: University of Wisconsin Press, 1954), pp. 148–49.

From the Preface to *The Dutch Lover* (1673)

APHRA BEHN

. . . Plays have no great room for that which is men's great advantage over women, that is Learning: We all well know that the immortal *Shakespeare's* Plays (who was not guilty of much more of this than often falls to women's share) have better pleased the World than *Jonson's* works, though by the way 'tis said that *Benjamin* was no such Rabbi neither, for I am informed his Learning was but Grammar high; (sufficient indeed to rob poor *Salust* of his best Orations) and it hath been observed, that they are apt to admire him most confoundedly, who have just such a scantling of it as he had; and I have seen a man the most severe of *Jonson's* sect, sit with his Hat removed less than a hair's breadth from one sullen posture for almost three hours at the Alchemist; who at that excellent Play of *Harry* the Fourth (which yet I hope is far enough from Farce) hath very hardly kept his Doublet whole. . . .

From "A General Prologue to all my Playes"(1662)

MARGARET CAVENDISH

Noble Spectators, do not think to see
Such Plays, that's like Ben Johnsons Alchemy,
Nor Fox, nor Silent Woman: for those Plays
Did Crown the Author with exceeding praise;
They were his Master-pieces, and were wrought
By Wit's Invention, and his labouring thought,
And his Experience brought Materials store,
His reading several Authors brought much more:
What length of time he took those Plays to write,
I cannot guess, not knowing his Wit's flight;
But I have heard, Ben Johnson's Plays came forth,
To the World's view, as things of a great worth;
Like Foreign Emperors, which do appear
Unto their Subjects, not 'bove once a year;
So did Ben Johnson's Plays so rarely pass,
As one might think they long a writing was.

As for Ben Johnson's brain, it was so strong,
He could conceive, or judge, what's right, what's wrong:
His Language plain, significant and free,
And in the English Tongue, the Mastery:
Yet gentle Shakespear had a fluent Wit,
Although less Learning, yet full well he writ;
For all his Plays were writ by Nature's light,
Which gives his Readers, and Spectators sight.
But Noble Readers, do not think my Plays,

From *Playes,* a 1662 Folio edition of Cavendish's work.

Are such as have been writ in former days;
As Johnson, Shakespear, Beamont, Fletcher writ;
Mine want their Learning, Reading, Language, Wit:
The Latin phrases I could never tell,
But Johnson could, which made him write so well. . . .

From *The History of the Worthies of English* (1662)

THOMAS FULLER

[Shakespeare] was an eminent instance of the truth of that Rule, *Poeta non fit, sed nascitur,* one is not *made* but *born* a Poet. Indeed his Learning was very little, so that as *Cornish diamonds* are not polished by any Lapidary, but are pointed and smoothed even as they are taken out of the Earth, so *nature* it self was all the *art* which was used upon him. Many were the *wit-combats* betwixt him and *Ben Johnson,* which two I behold like a *Spanish great Galleon,* and an *English man of War;* Master *Johnson* (like the former) was built far higher in Learning; *Solid,* but *Slow* in his performances. *Shake-spear* with the *English-man of War,* lesser in *bulk,* but lighter in *sailing,* could turn with all tides, tack about and take advantage of all winds, by the quickness of his Wit and Invention.

From *Theatrum Poetarum* (1675)

EDWARD PHILLIPS

Benjamin Jonson, the most learned, judicious and correct, generally so accounted, of our *English* Comedians, and the more to be admired for being so, for that neither the height of natural parts, for he was no *Shakesphear,* nor the cost of Extraordinary Education, for he is reported but a Bricklayer's Son, but his own proper Industry and Addiction to Books advanced him to this perfection: In three of his Comedies, namely the *Fox, Alchemist* and *Silent Woman,* he may be compared, in the Judgment of Learned Men, for Decorum, Language, and well Humouring of the Parts, as well with the chief of the Ancient Greek and Latin Comedians as the prime of Modern *Italians,* who have been judged the best of *Europe* for a happy Vein in Comedies, nor is his *Bartholomew Fair* much short of them; as for his other Comedies *Cynthia's Revels, Poetaster,* and the rest, let the name of *Ben Jonson* protect them against whoever shall think fit to be severe in censure against them: The Truth is, his Tragedies *Sejanus* and *Catiline* seem to have in them more of an artificial and inflated than of a pathetical and naturally Tragic height: In the rest of his Poetry, for he is not wholly Dramatic, as his Underwoods, Epigrams, &c. he is sometimes bold and strenuous, sometimes Magisterial, sometimes Lepid and full enough of conceit, and sometimes a Man as other Men are.

From the Preface to *The Works of Shakespeare* (1725–1726)

ALEXANDER POPE

I am inclined to think, this opinion proceeded originally from the zeal of the Partisans of our Author and *Ben Jonson;* as they endeavoured to exalt the one at the expense of the other. It is ever the nature of Parties to be in extremes; and nothing is so probable, as that because *Ben Jonson* had much the most learning, it was said on the one hand that *Shakespeare* had none at all; and because *Shakespeare* had much the most wit and fancy, it was retorted on the other, that *Jonson* wanted both. Because *Shakespeare* borrowed nothing, it was said that *Ben Jonson* borrowed everything. Because *Jonson* did not write extempore, he was reproached with being a year about every piece; and because *Shakespeare* wrote with ease and rapidity, they cried, he never once made a blot. Nay the spirit of opposition ran so high, that whatever those of the one side objected to the other, was taken at the rebound, and turned into Praises; as injudiciously, as their antagonists before had made them Objections.

Catiline

Anne Barton

Like *Epicoene, Catiline* was a play that flourished during the Restoration. It had been an unequivocal failure in 1611, when it was first performed by the King's Men, damned as it seems even by "the better sort" among the auditors, to whose more discriminating judgement Jonson usually felt able to appeal. A revival in 1635, two years before Jonson's death, in a more troubled political era, did elicit "great applause," justifying the second quarto edition in which this approval is recorded. But it was only under Charles II that Jonson's second Roman tragedy became, for a time, a staple item in the repertory. Even then, Samuel Pepys complained that although the play was "of much good sense and words to read . . . [it] doth appear the worst upon the stage, I mean the least divertising, that ever I saw any."[1] Interestingly, Pepys arrived at this verdict despite strenuous efforts on the part of the Theatre Royal to render *Catiline* visually more eye-catching. Pepys praises the splendid costumes, apparently provided by the king, and talks of a spectacular stage fight. The actor Hart presumably represented Catiline's death on stage, defying the original text in which Petreius, like a classical nuntius, merely reports how that death occurred. Yet despite such concessions to what Jonson, quoting Horace, had dismissed as the hollow delights of spectacle—in the Latin motto appended to the 1611 quarto—*Catiline* failed to retain its popularity. Abandoned by the theatre in the eighteenth century, it gradually lost its readers as well, to be relegated at last, like Addison's *Cato* and Johnson's *Irene,* to the category of frigid neo-classical mistakes.

There were reasons why *Catiline* should have appealed to Restoration audiences. In many ways, its affinities lie less with Jacobean tragedy than with the heroic plays of the 1660s and 1670s, works concerned to generate admiration and wonder more than pity and fear. Catiline's rant finds an echo in that of the hero/villains of the Restoration, Pordage's Herod, or Dryden's Maximin and Morat. The rhyming couplets of the four Choruses and the long descriptive or forensic speeches would not have disturbed playgoers who

From Anne Barton, *Ben Jonson, Dramatist* (Cambridge: Cambridge University Press, 1984), 154–69, 355–56. Reprinted with permission of Cambridge University Press.

relished the extravagant account of the bull-fight at the beginning of Dryden's *Conquest of Granada* (1670), or the debate on natural religion in his *Indian Emperor* (1665). The poetic justice of the ending, too, with its evasion of tragic feeling, must have recommended *Catiline* to audiences who applauded *Tyrannick Love* (1669), *Aureng-Zebe* (1675), or Congreve's *The Mourning Bride* (1697). There is little romance in *Catiline,* and Jonson ignored the love and honour conflict that was inherent in the Fulvia/Curius story, but in a number of other respects his tragedy might have been designed for the theatre which took shape under Charles II. Even the spectacle he so rigidly denied it could, on the evidence of Pepys, be smuggled in.

At least two plays dealing with Catiline's conspiracy existed before Jonson's, one by Stephen Gosson and the other a collaboration between Wilson and Chettle. Both are lost, but Jonson is unlikely to have been any more indebted to either than he was to Lodge's *The Wounds of Civil War* (?1588), a tragedy dealing with the excesses of Catiline's predecessor Sylla, whose ghost introduces Jonson's play. As with *Sejanus,* Jonson relied heavily on classical source material, drawn in this case mostly from Sallust and Cicero. Indeed, it seems to have been his scrupulous translation of most of Cicero's historic "First Speech Against Catiline" in Act Four that, more than anything else, exasperated the audience of 1611. Less predictably, he returned to Senecan revenge tragedy for the ghost of Sylla and (to some extent) for the troubled meditations of a Chorus which speaks for the average, right-thinking but fallible citizens of Rome. This ghost, and the Chorus, lend the tragedy at moments an oddly anachronistic Elizabethan quality absent from *Sejanus,* linking it superficially with old Inns of Court plays like *Gorboduc* (1562) or *The Misfortunes of Arthur* (1588).

Jonson's reasons for embarking on this play at all are far less obvious than those which led him to write *Sejanus,* his first classical tragedy. At the end of Elizabeth's reign, he felt with some reason that comedy had proved "ominous" to him, and that the time had come to see "If *Tragoedie* have a more kind aspect" (*P* "To The Reader," 223–4). *Every Man Out of His Humour, Cynthia's Revels* and *Poetaster* had made him famous, but they also created a furore, and a number of personal enemies. Even more important, their form was conditioned by an ephemeral vogue for dramatic satire. Jonson could not, in any case, have remained confined for much longer within so emotionally and theatrically restricted a mode. *Sejanus* broke decisively with that mode, and allowed him to create *Volpone. Catiline,* by contrast, followed immediately upon the resounding popular and artistic success of *The Alchemist,* one of the few Jonson plays which seems to have caused no trouble of any kind for its author. Even allowing for that stubborn streak in Jonson's nature which always led him after any rebuff or failure to repeat the original offence in an even more extreme form—as he did in writing *Poetaster,* and was still doing at the end of his life, in the quarrel with Inigo Jones—it seems puzzling that he should have chosen this moment to remember the debacle of *Sejanus,* and try once again to bully a London audience into liking what he conceived to be a proper classical tragedy. The second experiment was as catastrophic as the first. But what impelled Jonson in this direction at all, after *Volpone, Epicoene* and *The Alchemist,* when he seemed to be at the height of his power and renown as a writer of comedy?

Jonson of course was not to know that posterity would regard him as a great artist in comedy who was occasionally seduced, against the grain of his own talent, into perverse and disastrous experiments with the rival dramatic form. He had made his mark early as a tragic writer, and although he chose to disown and suppress those lost, popular Elizabethan plays, he probably felt that, in his maturity, he ought to be able to produce tragedies as distinctive and important in their own way as *Volpone* and *The Alchemist* were in theirs. *Catiline,* which precedes *Bartholomew Fair* by three years, was clearly not a forcing ground for the great comedy which came after it, as *Sejanus* had been for *Volpone.* On the other hand, it does introduce one theme—the coherence of the family as a social and personal unit—that was to prove central in the plays Jonson wrote later under Charles I. At the same time, it demonstrates why it was that after *Bartholomew Fair,* when he arrived for the second time at an impasse in his development as a writer of comedy, tragedy could not be for him—as it had been for Shakespeare at a similar point of crisis—a genuine artistic alternative.

Even more than *Sejanus, Catiline* is a play with persistent, and sometimes disruptive, inclinations towards comedy. Here, it was less certain in its appeal to Restoration taste. In his *Essay of Dramatick Poesie,* Dryden allowed Lisideius to compare both *Sejanus* and *Catiline* to an "oleo," because of their unnatural mixture of comedy and tragedy. But whereas Lisideius complains about only one scene in *Sejanus,* that between Livia and her physician Eudemus, he finds whole stretches of *Catiline* contaminated by comedy: "the Parliament of Women, the little envies of them to one another; and all that passes between Curio [*sic*] and Fulvia: scenes admirable in their kind, but of an ill mingle with the rest."[2] Lisideius draws his examples entirely from episodes involving female characters, from that realistic, psychologically and socially subtle area of the play which modern critics too have often found puzzlingly at odds with the melodrama, the fantastic, over-blown Senecan world of the conspirators. And indeed it is difficult not to feel that Lady Would-be, not to mention the collegiate ladies of *Epicoene,* would be perfectly at home in many scenes of *Catiline.*

When the young Ibsen embarked on a tragedy about Catiline, he hastily transformed the historical Fulvia, the Roman lady who betrayed the conspiracy to Cicero, into a demented vestal virgin called "Furia," who has the rape and suicide of a sister to avenge upon Catiline. Ibsen's *Catiline* (1850, revised 1875) is an atrocious play, but its tone is serious throughout as Jonson's is not. Jonson's Fulvia, chatting first with her maid Galla and then with Sempronia, mingles air fresheners and face-packs, tooth powder, hair styles, pearl earrings and adultery with "state-matters, and the *Senate*" (II.89) as though they were all of equal consequence. She restores her recently jettisoned lover, the conspirator Curius, to favour and her bed, because he promises to enrich her out of the spoils of Rome—but then reveals the whole plot to the authorities because even her greed takes second place to pique at discovering that Sempronia, an ageing beauty who pretends to learning in the attempt to retain male admirers, holds a place in it more prestigious than her own. This is to bring comedy dangerously close to the centre of the play, allowing it to undercut not only the dignity of Catiline and the other conspirators but that of a Cicero obliged to encounter Fulvia in her own terms. Shakespeare, in his tragedies, had allowed great latitude to fools and grave-diggers, fops, porters and clowns, but he never—not even in *Troilus and Cressida*—came as close as Jonson does in *Catiline* to allowing Thalia to push Melpomene off her throne.

Comedy invades even the heightened, masculine and ostensibly more tragic scenes of this play as well. Lisideius glides over this fact, but Dryden himself came close to pointing it out in another essay, "Of Heroic Plays," when he singled out Catiline's henchman Cethegus as a character who far outgoes his own hero Almanzor (*The Conquest of Granada*) in irrationality and absurdly inflated speech, "but performs not one Action in the Play."[3] Sallust says of Cethegus only that during the last stages of planning the conspiracy, he

> constantly complained of the inaction of his associates, insisting that by indecision and delay they were wasting great opportunities; that such a crisis called for action, not deliberation, and that if a few would aid him he would himself make an attack upon the senate-house, even though the rest were faint-hearted. Being naturally aggressive, violent, and prompt to act, he set the highest value on dispatch.[4]

Nothing here, or elsewhere in *The War With Catiline,* suggests that Cethegus struck Sallust as funny. It was Jonson who turned him into a comic thug, a man whose utterances throughout the play become so predictable, in a Bergsonian sense, as to arouse uneasy laughter. Whatever the situation, or the issue under discussion, Cethegus can be relied on to protest that his fellow conspirators are wasting time in talk when they should be hacking and hewing, slitting wind-pipes and crushing skulls. He is really a humour character, of a highly unpleasant kind. In him, according to Asper's definition, "one peculiar quality"—blood-lust—has become so dominant that it draws "All his affects, his spirits, and his powers, / In their conflluctions, all to runne one way" (*EMO* Induction, 105–8). Cethegus looks back wistfully to the "dayes / Of SYLLA's sway" (I.229–30) as other men hanker for the Golden Age. In this vanished ideal world

> Sonnes kild fathers,
> Brothers their brothers . . .
> Not infants, in the porch of life were free.

> The sick, the old, that could but hope a day
> Longer, by natures bountie, not let stay.
> Virgins, and widdowes, matrons, pregnant wives,
> All dyed. (I.232–3, 240–4)

What in Sallust had been a risky but essentially serious idea—with a "few" companions to "make an attack upon the senate-house"—becomes ridiculous in *Catiline:* "I ha' no Genius to these many counsells. / Let me kill all the *Senate,* for my share, / Ile doe it at next sitting" (IV.596–8). Whether insisting upon a second helping of the bowl of wine mixed with human blood ritually consumed by the conspirators (I.499), or enquiring querulously why the general slaughter has not yet begun, Cethegus is the caricature of a killer, too absurd to seem really dangerous.

Although sometimes terse to the point of self-parody—as when he informs his associates that, now he has personally undertaken to murder Cicero, the consul effectively no longer exists: "He shall die. / Shall,was too slowly said. He'is dying. That / Is, yet, too slow. He'is dead" (III.663–5)—Cethegus is also capable of extended flights of fancy. He longs to

> Swim to my ends, through bloud; or build a bridge
> Of carcasses; make on, upon the heads
> Of men, strooke downe, like piles; to reach the lives
> Of those remaine, and stand. (III.189–92)

Here, Jonson is consciously imitating Marlowe's *Tamburlaine.* Amyras, the Scythian shepherd's second son, had been eager, in part II, at a point where over-reaching verges upon comedy, to

> swim through pools of blood
> Or make a bridge of murdered carcasses
> Whose arches should be framed with bones of Turks,
> Ere I would lose the title of a king.[5]

There is something inherently silly about such conceits, especially when formulated by a boy of apparently frail and "womanish" appearance. Cethegus is an adult, not a stripling. But his rhetoric is just as preposterous as that of Tamburlaine's "lovely boy."[6] Moreover, as Dryden rightly observed, Catiline's ferocious lieutenant never actually *does* anything. He neither assaults the Senate, nor even tries to assassinate Cicero. When exposed at the end, he collapses into sullenness and bluster.

Jonson's Catiline is more frightening and intelligent than Cethegus, yet some of the savage comedy associated with the follower also adheres to his master. Although Catiline's confederates—the sluggish Lentulus, Bestia the pederast or the effeminate Curius—are patricians like himself, he has almost as low an opinion of them as of the upstart Cicero. They are expendable, to be cast aside in the moment of his success. Catiline's own motives are curiously diffuse. Sylla, whose ghost introduces the tragedy, had set out to be revenged on a single, hated opponent, whatever the cost in other Roman lives. Catiline, driven on by envy and aggression, wants to murder an entire population. A malcontent who has wasted his own fortune, he affects moral outrage before the dissipations and extravagance of Rome, a city relaxing after its conquests, where houses are built of gold, and harlots wear pearls that are the spoils of nations in their ears. Like Epicure Mammon, he would rather see the world destroyed than have to endure the sight of other people's prosperity. Sallust called Catiline a "madman," whose "disordered mind ever craved the monstrous, incredible, gigantic."[7] Jonson makes him both more calculating than this, and more petty. As his plots successively fail him, first through his unexpected defeat in the consular election, then with the intelligence which so mysteriously keeps Cicero informed of the plans of the conspirators and allows him to escape their swords, Catiline gradually loses control. In the culminating Senate scene of Act Four, his rage becomes almost pathetic, like that of a child in the grip of a tantrum, unable to articulate its fury. Neither here, nor anywhere else in the play, does he look like a tragic hero.

Jonson's treatment of Cicero is equally idiosyncratic—and anti-tragic. Sallust called Cicero the "best of consuls"[8] but he did not allow him the commanding position in *The War With Catiline* that he assumes in the second half of Jonson's play. Between Sallust and Jonson there lay, of course, many centuries of veneration of Cicero as a moralist, and also as the greatest orator, rhetorician and prose stylist of the ancient world. His reputation, though by no means unassailed, was especially high in Elizabethan and Jacobean England. There is no way of knowing how he was presented in the lost Catiline tragedies of the period, but he is likely to have played a prominent part. Even the anonymous author of *Caesar's Revenge* (1595), and Shakespeare in *Julius Caesar* (1599), insisted on dragging him into the story of Caesar and Brutus, less as it seems because his presence contributed anything to the action than out of a conviction that audiences would feel cheated if so celebrated a contemporary Roman were to be left out.

Cicero had a particular and very personal importance for Jonson. Like Jonson, he was a "new man" who had made his way to fame entirely through his own efforts and abilities, from a socially inferior position. No one in *Catiline,* least of all Cicero himself, ever forgets that he is "A meere upstart, / That has no pedigree, no house, no coate, / No ensignes of a family" (II.119–21). He is, in fact, a low-born but enterprising comic hero who has to rely on a combination of virtue, intelligence and cunning to justify his marriage to the noble matron Rome. Cicero seems to have infuriated his contemporaries, just as Jonson infuriated his own, by being "a great lover and praiser of himself" (*Conv.* 680). Both men suffered from a dread of being underestimated, of having their abilities misprised. Like Jonson too, Cicero was a conservative in his own time, a man urging return to a vanished social order, the traditionalism of which he not only idealized but saw, unrealistically, as the only possible cure for present ills. Most important of all, he was (as Quintilian said) an artist in politics, an orator who used language to influence individual lives, and shape the course of history. He seems to have believed of orators, as Jonson passionately wished to believe of poets, that it was impossible to excel without being, at the same time, a good and virtuous man. Yet this conviction did not restrain him from exercising his creative artistry, on occasion, purely for its own sake, in defence of causes he knew to be dubious, or flagrantly bad.

Like the Horace of *Poetaster,* Cicero does not appear on stage until Act Three. When he does, it becomes clear almost at once that he has personal weaknesses from which Horace, and his predecessors Criticus and Asper in the comical satires, were free. It is hard not to sympathize with Caesar and Crassus, unattractive though they are as Jonson portrays them, when Cicero persists in congratulating himself so fulsomely at having been raised to the consulship against all the odds: "Now the vaine swels . . . Up glorie" (III.28). Nor is the newly elected consul a man of physical courage. Caesar is derisive of the throat armour which he sees peeping out over Cicero's gown in the Senate (IV.92), and it is clear that the consul recoils hastily and with alarm in the same scene, when Catiline "turnes sodainly on Cicero" (*s.d.* 491–2), fearing a blow. A flexible, even a compromised, statesman, adept at bestowing flattery, gifts and bribes, ready to use informers and spies, Cicero is an exponent of politics as the art of the possible. He is even a little like Catiline in the way he despises such necessary human instruments of his will as Fulvia, Curius or his fellow consul Antonius. Whatever he may believe privately, in his actions as consul he espouses a doctrine of expediency and moral relativism more often found in comic than in tragic protagonists. But then, in the context of *Catiline* as a whole, nothing else would do.

Like his successor Justice Overdo in *Bartholomew Fair,* Cicero sets out to uncover and correct "enormities." They are real enough in this society, and they involve the consul in forms of subterfuge and play-acting far more complex and sophisticated than Overdo's childish disguise. A kind of benevolent Tiberius, an intriguer for good in an immemorial comic line, Cicero relies in the end on the persuasive power of words to annihilate his chief adversary. Jonson's original audience became restive and finally rebellious during the nearly three hundred lines of Cicero's speech against Catiline in Act Four. As an experienced man of the theatre, Jonson ought indeed to have known better. There was nothing to prevent him from abbreviating his translation of Cicero's historic speech, and also allowing Catiline, hitherto a man anything but tongue-tied, some rhetoric of his own. Chettle and Gosson, in their lost Catiline plays, surely made accommodations of this kind. For Jonson, however, the absence of real conflict—or even contact—between Cicero and Catiline at this climactic moment of the play was essential to his oddly anti-tragic purpose.

Catiline sneers at Cicero as a "boasting, insolent tongue-man" (IV.161), but the "prodigious rhetoricke" (465) he despises cuts him down more effectively than a sword. When Cicero has finished speaking, Catiline not only has no answer, he finds it difficult even to formulate a complete sentence of his own. Catulus is obliged to prompt him, as he would a man suddenly afflicted with an incapacitating stammer: "Speake thy imperfect thoughts" (509). But, as Crassus acknowledges, "H'is lost, there is no hope of him" (512). Catiline flees from the Senate he thought to master. The entire confrontation has seemed less like a tragic agon than like those almost effortless triumphs in Jonson's masques when Fame's trumpet sounds, the palace of the Fays opens, or Pallas appears and, at the sound of her voice, the creatures of darkness and disorder "change, and perish, scarcely knowing, how" (*GAR* 69). After it, Catiline's off-stage defeat and death in battle come as a kind of coda, a reported incident to be assimilated into the pattern of judgements passed upon Cethegus, Lentulus, Statilius and Gabinius, and the re-establishment of tranquility in Cicero's Rome.

In his account of Catiline's end, the nuntius Petreius carefully dehumanizes his subject:

> CATILINE came on, not with the face
> Of any man, but of a publique ruine:
> His count'nance was a civil warre it selfe. (V.642–4).

According to Petreius, Catiline fought bravely, "like a *Lybian* lyon" (672). When he saw that the day was lost, he sought death by charging into the midst of his opponents, and fell fighting. Sallust had recorded that "Catiline was found far in advance of his men amid a heap of slain foemen, still breathing slightly, and showing in his face the indomitable spirit which had animated him when alive."[9] It was Jonson who made Petreius imagine that Catiline simply turned to stone, as the giants did before Medusa's head, "at the sight of *Rome* in us" (684). He also chose to ignore Sallust's grim conclusion that Rome "gained no joyful nor bloodless victory, for all the most valiant had either fallen in the fight or come off with severe wounds," so that the entire army was torn between "rejoicing and lamentation."[10] Even at the end, he deflects attention away from individual tragic experience towards the things *Catiline* is really about: public ruin, civil strife, Rome as a living, suffering mother. He seems to have been determined that Cicero's achievement, that of a dutiful son whose sagacity and skill have, for a time, preserved a parent from death, should not be darkened by what in Sallust is a pyrrhic victory.

It has been argued that the Roman republic, not Catiline, is the real protagonist of Jonson's play. And that this emphasis explains why the work is, after all, tragic. Although it escapes the holocaust plotted by the conspirators, the republic is doomed to succumb to Caesar, and this ineluctable future should be seen as darkening a denouement which is only superficially optimistic.[11] It is true that Jonson does depart radically from Sallust by incriminating Caesar in the conspiracy. Cicero is more merciful than wise when he chooses to ignore Caesar's guilt at the end. And yet, open though it is, the ending of *Catiline* nonetheless feels far more positive than that of *Sejanus*. At the price of only five characters' lives, all of them irredeemably bad, a society teetering on the brink of total destruction has been miraculously preserved. What lies ahead, outside the limits of the play, seems less important than the fact that Cicero has purged the most immediately dangerous ills of a community. Rome is indeed more central than either the man who would annihilate or the man who saves it. But its fortunes in the play follow the familiar comedic path from darkness and disorder to the comparative sanity of what Cicero finally sums up as "this glad day" (V.698). Even in his corrective Elizabethan comedies, Jonson had never pretended that an entire social order could be permanently cleansed, and he does not do so here. Caesar has had a fright, but he is no more likely to change his spots than Bobadilla or Subtle. In Rome, as in contemporary London, the sorting out of one imbroglio cannot protect a city from the next.

The comedic quality of *Catiline* is further enhanced by the unusual stress Jonson places on family relationships, a concern visible less in the action of the play than in a network of images and allusions. All the conspirators are associated with the perversion or violation of ordinary domestic ties. From scattered sources, Jonson painstakingly amassed every literal transgression of this kind of which Catiline himself was either known or rumoured to be guilty: his murder of a wife, a brother and a son, his incest with his sister and a daughter. Cicero, Catulus and the ghost of Sylla all refer to him as a "parricide." They mean only that he is a man who has killed his close relations, but the word cannot help but associate Catiline, however unfairly, with that most terrible of crimes for Jonson: the murder of a father by his son. A different, but even more powerful metaphoric link establishes him as a matricide as well. Rome is for everyone in the play a powerfully maternal presence. But Catiline repudiates this natural bond: "I will, hereafter, call her step-dame, ever" (1.91). This promise he not only keeps but ceremonially reaffirms when he drinks from the bowl of blood and wine (I.495). Yet the step-mother he means to attack is a real mother too. He will in Rome's "stony entrailes / Dig me a seate: where, I will live, againe, / The labour of her wombe" (I.93–5) to emerge as a twice-born monster. Catiline paints for the conspirators a glorious future in which husbands will freely hand over their wives, and parents their boys and nubile daughters, to be prostituted to the lusts of the new rulers. Meanwhile, Cethegus, the man who takes particular pleasure in the violation of family bonds, significantly claims Catiline as "my parent" (I.289).

In sharp contrast to the conspirators, Cicero upholds the normalities of family life. Jonson emphasizes his reliance on his brother Quintus, a somewhat colourless individual in himself, and prone to think that Cicero exaggerates the peril in Rome, but fraternally loyal and dependable. In a society where many patricians are no longer scandalized by adultery, even when it carries murder in its train, where Catiline has "remov'd a wife, / And then a sonne, to make my bed, and house / Spatious, and fit t'embrace" his new love Orestilla (I.115–17)—as though it were a minor act of domestic re-decoration—Cicero's marriage is presented as a model of old-fashioned fidelity. He is merely playing with Fulvia, for his own political purposes, when he assures her that her virtues are such, "I could almost turne lover, againe: but that / TERENTIA would be jealous" (III.343–4). Fulvia is a married woman who lives openly on the gifts and money she extracts from her lovers, abandoning them as their means decline. Cicero's show of respect for a useful spy is counterfeited, but it cannot prevent his automatic recourse to an ideal of constancy in marriage which, to Fulvia's sophisticated eyes, must look strangely outmoded. Caesar goes out of his way to sneer at Cicero's esteem for Terentia when he suggests that Quintus Cicero, entering the Senate in Act Four with tribunes and guards, is doubtless conveying to his brother "Some cautions from his wife, how to behave him" (105). He attacks Cicero's adherent Cato in a similar fashion, later in the play, when he tries to frighten him out of intercepting and opening a letter addressed to Caesar from the conspirators, by insinuating that it is really "a love-letter, / From your deare sister, to me" (V.576–7). Predictably, Cicero characterizes Rome throughout as a kind and bounteous, if threatened, mother, with inalienable claims to the support of her offspring:

> Thinke but on her right.
> No child can be too naturall to his parent.
> Shee is our common mother, and doth challenge
> The prime part of us; doe not stop, but give it. (III.364–7)

At the end, Cato salutes Cicero as "Great parent of thy countrie" (V.610), around whom her old men, matrons, youths and maids ought to gather in a symbolic family group, reaffirming the sureties of that domestic order imperilled by the conspiracy.

So pervasive is the play's identification of evil with a desecration of family ties, that it even enforces a radical reinterpretation of the story of Romulus and Remus, legendary founders of Rome. The Chorus shies away from the fact that the city about which it cares so much originated through a fratricide: the slaying of Remus by his brother. Remus was said to have quarrelled with Romulus because the latter received more auspicious signs from Jove when the two were disputing which should have the honour of being patron of the new city. But the Chorus insists upon exonerating Romulus from any responsibility for shedding his brother's blood. It tells Jove firmly, in its prayer, that Romulus "strove / Not with his brother, but your rites" (III.366–7). This is scarcely a very convincing excuse. But in the world of *Catiline,* where any abrogation of family bonds is synonymous with wickedness, there is no other way in which the patriotism of the Chorus can be sustained.

Jonson was proud of this Chorus. It was one of the features of *Catiline* which made it "a legitimate Poeme" (Dedication to Pembroke, H. & S. vol. V, p. 431), as even *Sejanus* was not. Although certainly performed in the theatre by a single actor (like the Chorus in Shakespeare's *Henry V*), it nonetheless employs the first person plural, and without displaying any awareness of the presence of a theatre audience. Here, as with the quarto "stage" direction calling for sudden, thick darkness, or a mysterious fiery light above the Capitol, Jonson appears to be distinguishing between the text as acted, and as read. He knew better than to try and persuade either his audience or the King's Men to accept a group of actors speaking and moving in unison, in some approximation to the proper classical manner, but he could at least suggest the corporate nature of his Chorus, and rely on "the Reader extraordinary" to imagine it correctly on the page. Neither chauvinist and partial, like Shakespeare's commentator in *Henry V,* nor thumpingly didactic and personally distanced, like the Chorus of *Gorboduc,* the *Catiline* Chorus does in fact reach back sensitively even beyond Seneca to the complex, communal consciousness of ancient Greek choruses like that of Aeschylus's *Agamemnon,* or Sophocles' *Oedipus Tyrannos.* Apart from its formal appearances at the end of acts, it is present and speaks in the two crucial public scenes of the play: after the election of Cicero as consul in Act Three, and again in the Act Four Senate which results in the exposure and banishment of Catiline. It intervenes twice on the first occasion, to lend its support to Cicero's ally Cato (60), and then to endorse the sentiments of the new consul and ceremoniously attend him home (83). On the second, it registers alarm when Catiline seems about to offer physical violence to Cicero, and calls for help (IV.492). In its more extended utterances, it speaks as the sometimes perplexed, even suffering, but responsible voice of traditionalist Rome. Troubled by the new vices and manners which have infiltrated the city, it prays after Act Two for the forthcoming election to pick out consuls who will preserve Rome in her ancient ways, "Excluding such as would invade / The common wealth" (II.374–5)—and is rewarded by the surprise victory of Cicero. Despite an initially favourable impression, it does not entirely trust the behaviour of its defender. The final Chorus, following Act Four, confesses to having believed in the innocence of Catiline, and listened to slanders of Cicero, far longer than it should. Events have demonstrated how "in our censure of the state, / We still doe wander" (IV.875–6), but it aspires to clearer judgement in future.

Paradoxically, this Chorus, on which Jonson congratulated himself, and which ought to move the play closer to classical tragedy, ends by emphasizing its affinities with comedy. This is partly because, unlike most of its ancient prototypes, it avoids association either practical or emotional with any tragic individual or group of individuals. The comments it offers are general, concerned with the well-being of the city, and with the tenor of ordinary life there, not with the particular fortunes of Catiline, Cicero or even the conspirators at large. The effect is to stress the extent to which this is a play about the rescue of a community threatened with the overthrow of all its political institutions, rather than an account of exceptional people suffering in an extreme situation. (Aeschylus, arguably, did something a little like this in his *Eumenides,* but the play is unusually dependent upon the first two tragic dramas in the trilogy, and its Chorus of Furies, partisan and violent, could scarcely be more unlike Jonson's.) By refusing to make either Catiline or Cicero a focus of tragic attention, burlesquing Cethegus, handling Fulvia, Sempronia and the other women in much the way he had the collegiate ladies in *Epicoene,* and generalizing the Chorus, Jonson consistently undercut and dissipated the tragic potential of his material. *Catiline* is something more than the icy neo-classical mistake it has often been thought to be. On the other hand, it reveals the extent to which Jonson, by 1611, was temperamentally committed to comedy. Particularly indicative here is his handling of some of the proper names he inherited from his sources, by comparison with those in *Sejanus,* his first Roman tragedy.

Comedy as a form has always allowed writers greater control over proper names than tragedy. This is partly because comedy tends to invent its characters, as opposed to inheriting them from history, myth or epic. There are obvious exceptions here—the recurring types of *commedia dell'arte,* the characters in Lyly's mythological plays, or Caesar Augustus and the circle of Golden Age Latin poets in Jonson's *Poetaster*—but, for the most part, the comic dramatist enjoys godlike power in his fictive world. Like Adam in paradise, he is privileged to give the creatures their names as they walk by him, and also to decide how important and "true" those names should be. Comic writers who insist upon conjuring their plots and characters out of the air have total control over the designations they assign, and sometimes invent: "Peithetairos," "Trygaeus," "Fastidius Brisk," "Mosca" or "Morose." Those who avail themselves of pre-existing stories are, in theory, more restricted. In practice, they have always claimed much the same liberty. Plautus and Terence, although they re-used the plots of Greek New Comedy, and pretended that these events were still happening in Greece, had no scruple about changing the characters' names. Shakespeare, for his part, felt free to re-christen Plautus's brothers Menaechmi in *The Comedy Of Errors,* just as he did to transform Lodge's "Rosader" into "Orlando" when he wrote *As You Like It,* or Greene's "Pandosto" and "Fawnia" into the "Leontes" and "Perdita" of *The Winter's Tale.*

The power to give names is an index to the artistic freedom of the comic dramatist, and also to his ability to control the play's view of life. He can, if he chooses, bestow names which (usually because they are common in literature, or in his own society) are as neutral and uncommunicative as any proper name can be: "Sosia," "Palaestra," "Maria," "Antonio," "Rachel" or "Chamont." Alternatively, he can draw attention to a character as "Trygaeus" (from the Greek word for a vine-prop), "Armado" or "Phoenixella," names gently but not insistently suggestive of personality and fate. More usually—although Shakespeare's predilection for the first two methods has tended to obscure recognition of this fact—he can construct a more deterministic world: one in which strongly defining names like "Pyrgopolinices," "Lusty Juventus," "Simplicity," "Parolles," "Aguecheek," "Fungoso" or "Mammon" delimit character and imply destiny. There are several reasons why comedy, in all ages, should tend to gravitate towards this third class of clearly expressive, "speaking" names. One of the most important is comedy's innate interest in the risibly predictable: in the fun to be derived from what Bergson defined as "something mechanical encrusted upon something living."[12] The comic individual thinks of himself as unique, someone flexible, spontaneous and self-aware in the way he conducts his life. But in the eyes of others, including the theatre audience, he is laughable in his rigidity, his bondage to habit and unconscious approximation to a type. The fact that a man called "Pyrgopolinices," "Simplicity," "Aguecheek" or "Mammon" is likely to be quite deaf to the obvious implications of his own name, the extent to which it sums up or fixes his nature, restricting his development and mocking his aspirations, is part of the dramatist's joke.

Tragic dramatists are only infrequently or peripherally inventors of names. Some of the characters they take over from myth and history come equipped with names which can be seen to offer some statement about their owners. "Oedipus" ("swellfoot" in Shelley's unlovely translation) derives from the spike driven through the feet of Laius's son when he was abandoned in infancy. "Ajax" (Aias) is, prophetically, a cry of woe. In Plato's *Cratylus,* Socrates amused himself (and astonished his interlocutors) by tracing "Atreus" back to a cluster of related Greek words meaning "the stubborn," "the fearless" or "the destructive one," and claimed to find "man of the mountains" in "Orestes."[13] But most of the names in Aeschylus, Sophocles (or Homer) refuse to speak in a genuinely revelatory fashion. They are accidental, opaque, or communicate in ways that would defeat even the etymological ingenuity of Socrates to find appropriate to the personalities of their bearers. Significantly, even with a name like "Oedipus," given to the supposed son of Polybus, king of Corinth, because of an observable physical trait, tragic writers have never wanted to dwell on its construction, let alone suggest that it provides a key to the way this man behaves. To do so would be to risk introducing the wrong sort of determinism into the story. Whatever the gods, his parentage, his circumstances or his previous actions may have pre-ordained for him, a tragic character cannot be deprived of that small, but crucially important space in which his destiny, through his individual and unpredictable way of confronting it, becomes inalienably his own. To permit his name to curtail or abolish this space is to threaten him with comic diminution.

There is not very much tragic experience of this kind in Jonson's *Sejanus.* And yet, despite his emphasis on the satiric and grotesque in this play, Jonson nonetheless conformed to tragic orthodoxy in his treatment of the characters' names. Agrippina's son Nero, the one who believes that the shortest way with informers is to pluck out their tongues and eyes as soon as they cross the threshold, arguably displays a disposition "black" as his name, but the correspondence goes entirely unremarked. In the case of his brother Caligula ("Baby-boots," a nickname attached to him when he was very young by the army), the opportunity for onomastic play must have been particularly tempting, but Jonson decorously let it pass. *Sejanus* is filled with characters—"Macro," "Eudemus," "Regulus," "Tiberius" or "Sejanus" itself, with its entirely appropriate reference to the two-faced god—whose names might have been made to "speak." All are handled quite neutrally.

In *Catiline,* by contrast, although Jonson restrained himself from tampering with the names of the two principal adversaries, Cicero and Catiline, he exercised considerable ingenuity in demonstrating how the characters of Fulvia, Curius, Lentulus and Bestia are all implicit in their names, names which become guides and source material almost as important as the accounts given of these people by Sallust. Gabriele Bernhard Jackson has pointed out acutely that although Sallust says of Fulvia only that she was of noble birth, Jonson made her "outstandingly beautiful and outstandingly greedy" because he recognized in her name "a feminine variant of *fulvus,* deep yellow, a stock epithet of gold."[14] Fulvia's lover Curius is aware, like the dramatist, that his mistress has a "speaking" name. Unfortunately, he grasps only its flattering connotations. "Why, now my FULVIA lookes, like her bright name! / And is her selfe!" (II.348–9). What he fails to grasp in his infatuated state is the mercenary nature of this woman, the extent to which her mind runs continually on the acquisition of wealth. The character of Curius himself (the "care-full or troubled one"), a man of weakness and vacillation, craving emotional dependence, Jonson also seems to have extracted from his name. As for Lentulus, few of his fellow conspirators can resist punning on the meaning "slow," "heavy" or "immovable." There is no suggestion, historically, that Lentulus was like this, that his associates and opponents constantly remarked "the sloth / And sleepinesse of LENTULUS" (V.380–I), or accused him of being "too heavy, LENTULUS, and remisse" (III.224). Nor, as Jonson's Oxford editors comment, was there any real justification in classical sources for Bestia, another of the conspirators, to be shown sexually assaulting one of Catiline's young page-boys (H. & S., vol. x, p. 130). With all four of these characters, he has insisted upon a similarity between name and nature, even though by doing so he threatens to reduce them to automata, to render their actions predictable and even ludicrous in the manner normally associated with comedy rather than tragedy. Not even *Poetaster,* the comical satire Jonson wrote a decade earlier, had subjected the names of its historical characters to this kind of belittling interpretation. The etymologies of *Catiline* are part of the anti-tragic bias to be felt almost everywhere in this play. As such, they occupy a special and somewhat isolated position in what, by 1611, had already become the complex development of Jonson's attitude towards proper names.

Notes

In this article's parenthetical citations, *P* stands for *Poetaster, Conv.* for the *Conversations with Drummond, EMO* for *Every Man Out of His Humour,* and *GAR* for the masque "The Golden Age Restored."

1. *The Diary of Samuel Pepys,* ed. Robert Latham and William Matthews (London, 1970–83), vol. IX (1668–9), p. 395.
2. Dryden, *An Essay of Dramatick Poesy, Works,* vol. XVII, p. 38.
3. Dryden, "Of Heroic Plays," *Works,* ed. J. Loftis, D. S. Rodes, V. Dearing, G. Guffey, A. Roper and H. Swedenberg, Jr. (Berkeley, Los Angeles and London, 1978), vol. XI, p. 17.
4. Sallust, *The War With Catiline,* trans. J. C. Rolfe (Loeb Classical Library, London, 1921), p. 75.
5. Christopher Marlowe, *Tamburlaine the Great,* ed. J. S. Cunningham (The Revels Plays, Manchester, 1981), part II, I.3.92–5.
6. *Ibid.,* 1.3.96.
7. Sallust, *The War With Catiline,* pp. 27, II.
8. *Ibid.,* p. 73.
9. *Ibid.,* p. 127.
10. *Ibid.,* p. 129.
11. Joseph Allen Bryant, Jr., "Catiline and the Nature of Jonson's Tragic Fable," *PMLA,* 69 (1954), pp. 265–77.
12. Bergson, *Laughter,* p. 57.
13. Plato, *Cratylus,* in *The Dialogues of Plato,* trans. B. Jowett (London, 1892), vol. I, p. 185.
14. Gabriele Bernhard Jackson, *Vision and Judgement in Ben Jonson's Drama* (New Haven and London, 1968), pp. 63–6.

To his worthy friend Mr. Ben Jonson (1611)

JOHN FLETCHER

He, that dares wrong this Play, it should appear
Dares utter more, than other men dare hear,
That have their wits about 'hem: yet such men,
Dear friend, must see your Book, and read; and then,
Out of their learned ignorance, cry ill,
And lay you by, calling for mad *Pasquill,*
Or *Greene's* dear *Groatsworth,* or *Tom Coryate,*
The new *Lexicon,* with the errant Pate:
And pick away, from all these several ends,
And dirty ones, to make their as-wise friends
Believe they are translators. Of this, pity,
There is a great plague hanging o'er the City:
Unless she purge judgement presently.
But, O thou happy man, that must not die
As these things shall: leaving no more behind
But a thin memory (like a passing wind)
That blows, and is forgotten, ere they are cold.
Thy labours shall outlive thee; and, like gold
Stamped for continuance, shall be current, where
There is a Sun, a People, or a Year.

This poem appeared in the front matter of the 1611 Quarto edition of Jonson's *Catiline.*

Preface to *Sejanus* (1605)

BEN JONSON

First, if it be objected, that what I publish is no true *Poem,* in the strict Laws of *Time.* I confess it: as also in the want of a proper *Chorus,* whose Habit, and Moods are such, and so difficult, as not any, whom I have seen since the *Ancients,* (no not they who have most presently affected Laws) have yet come in the way of. Nor is it needful, or almost possible, in these our Times, and to such Auditors, as commonly Things are presented, to observe the old state, and splendour of *Dramatic Poems,* with preservation of any popular delight. But of this I shall take more seasonable cause to speak; in my Observations upon *Horace* in his *Art of Poetry,* which (with the Text translated) I intend, shortly to publish. In the meantime, if in truth of Argument, dignity of Persons, gravity and height of Elocution, fullness and frequency of Sentence, I have discharged the other offices of a *Tragic* writer, let not the absence of these *Forms* be imputed to me, wherein I shall give you occasion hereafter (and without my boast) to think I could better prescribe, than omit the due use, for want of a convenient knowledge.

The next is least in some nice nostril, the *Quotations* might savour affected, I do let you know, that I abhor nothing more; and have only done it to show my integrity in the *Story,* and save myself in those common Torturers, that bring all wit to the Rack: whose Noses are ever like Swine spoiling, and rooting up the *Muses'* Gardens, and their whole Bodies, like Moles, as blindly working under Earth to cast any, the least, hills upon *Virtue.*

Whereas, they are in *Latin* and the work in *English,* it was presupposed, none but the Learned would take the pains to confer them, the Authors themselves being all in the learned *Tongues,* save one, with whose English side I have had little to do. . . .

Lastly I would inform you, that this Book, in all numbers, is not the same with that which was acted on the public Stage, wherein a second Pen had good share: in place of which I have rather chosen, to put weaker (and no doubt less pleasing) of mine own, than to defraud so happy a *Genius* of his right, by my loathed usurpation.

Fare you well. And if you read farther of me, and like, I shall not be afraid of it though you praise me out.

From *A Short View of Tragedy* (1692)

THOMAS RYMER

Ben Johnson, knew to distinguish men and manners, at an other rate. In *Catiline* we find ourselves in *Europe,* we are no longer in the *Land of Savages,* amongst Blackamoors, Barbarians, and Monsters.

The Scene is Rome and first on the Stage appears *Sylla's* Ghost.

Dost thou not feel me, Rome? Not yet?

One would, in reason, imagine the Ghost in some public open place, upon some Eminence, where Rome is all within his view: But it is a surprising thing to find that this rattling Rodomontado speech is in a dark, close, private sleeping hole of *Catiline's.*

Yet the *Chorus,* is of all wonders the strangest. The *Chorus* is always present on the Stage, privy to, and interested in all that passes, and thereupon make their Reflections to Conclude the several *Acts.*

Sylla's Ghost, Though never so big, might slide in at the Keyhole; but how comes the *Chorus* into *Catiline's* Cabinet?

Aurelia is soon after with him too, but the Poet had perhaps provided her some Truckle-bed in a dark Closet by him.

In short, it is strange that *Ben,* who understood the turn of Comedy so well; and had found the success, should thus grope in the dark, without any rule or proportion, without any reason or design.

This passage, pp. 158–60, follows Rymer's attack on *Othello.*

"He may be our father, perhaps": Paternity, Puppets, Boys, and *Bartholomew Fair*

KRISTEN MCDERMOTT

In 1603, as "the Pest was in London," Ben Jonson joined his old schoolmaster William Camden at the country estate of Sir Robert Cotton. He "saw in a vision" one night, "his eldest sone (then a child and at London) appear unto him with ye Marke of a bloodie cross on his forehead as if it had been cutted with a suord, at which amazed he prayed unto God." After confiding the dream to Camden and receiving his mentor's comforting opinion that it was "but ane appreehension of his fantasie," Jonson received notice from his wife, Anne, that seven-year-old Benjamin had died of the plague. Jonson also recalled, as he was relating this tale to William Drummond some 15 years later, that the boy had appeared in the dream "of a Manlie shape & of that Grouth that he thinks he shall be at the resurrection" (*Conversations,* 261–72).

This anecdote not only provides insight into Jonson's guilt complex over his children, which David Riggs explicates at length in his biography,[1] but also provides a striking introductory image to anyone interested in the relationship between the child actor and childhood vulnerability. This vision of Benjamin, appearing to Jonson in a dumb-show reenactment of the Resurrection and (most tellingly) as an adult, offers an eerie counterpart to the spectacle of the child actor in a typical revenge tragedy of the turn of the century: out of his natural place, marked with blood, silently accusatory, and prematurely adult.

The English Renaissance is by no means the only culture fascinated by the Platonic metaphor equating procreation and poetic creation; however, dramatic poets of this time enjoyed the unique privilege of regularly seeing their poetic labors brought to life by professional companies of boy performers.[2] By 1603, Jonson would have been connected with the children's companies for at least three years; that his anxious vision of his son is so overtly theatrical is not surprising. But was there an intersection between the issues of

This essay is published for the first time in this volume, and appears by permission of the author.

sexuality and identity implied by the presence of the children's companies and by Jonson's own ambivalence about his identity as a parent of his own children, as a surrogate parent to the boy actors, and as a poetic parent to the fictional progeny of his poems and plays?

More specifically, I wonder whether Jonson was affected by his culture's struggle to define sexual "otherness" (which would include both homosexuality and the sexuality of children) and whether such anxieties might be expressed in the childlike world of *Bartholomew Fair.* We must remember that Jonson created this world for the repertoire of the Princess Elizabeth's Men, which had just incorporated a number of child actors from the Children of the Queens's Reveals. This could have created a larger-than-usual number of boys in the company, a novel situation and therefore possibly an unstable one.

The boys' presence would matter less if Jonson's own poetry and drama were not so frequently concerned with the fate of children's bodies. Riggs believes the deaths of Jonson's children generated an important motif in the drama and poetry of his most productive period, during the first decade of James's reign. The "latent empathy with the dead child" that we see in his 1602 epitaph for his daughter extends through his revisions of *The Spanish Tragedy,* his epitaph for Benjamin, and finally into *Sejanus* (88). Riggs ends his investigation into the "dead child" motif at this point but acknowledges that the poems and the plays of subsequent years reveal not only a concern but an obsession with questions of parentage and procreation. I will argue that this obsession was in many ways a predictable response to personal tragedy but in other ways an intensely idiosyncratic reaction to a set of anxieties and assumptions about the nature of childhood, reaching far beyond the responses of a bereaved parent.

Bartholomew Fair appears at the culmination of a process in which Jonson discards the traditional forms of consolatory literature in favor of a more effective coping mechanism: an apparent substitution, metaphorically and in real life, of the relationship between teacher and pupil for that of natural father and son. This substitution becomes, in the course of Jonson's career, inextricably linked with the relationship between the playwright and his young actors because (ironically) his own lack of a university education denied him a position like that of his own teacher William Camden. Jonson's only known pupils were either rakehells like young Wat Ralegh or the child actors of the Children of the Queen's Chapel. Therefore, except in the idealized atmosphere of the *Discoveries* and his poems, Jonson was forced to move from his failed real-life parenting into his idealized pedagogical parenting by way of the child actors, specifically Nathan Field and Salomon Pavy.

The status of these children, to whom he was probably closer than to his own, was ambiguous on a variety of levels and a potential source of real anxiety for Jonson. His plays reveal that he was concerned not only about the boy actors' educational upbringing but also about their sexual innocence and physical safety; this anxiety is clearly present in plays up to and including

Bartholomew Fair. The play's Smithfield—Jonson's mirror of the London stage—is a world without real children, and the puppets are "children" only figuratively; they become substitutes for the child actors in much the same way that Jonson's protégés were substitutes for his own offspring. Riggs suggests that, beginning with the murdered children of *Sejanus,* Jonson removed his own dead children to successive levels of metaphoric distance in order to mitigate his own guilt for their deaths and his abandonment of them before their deaths (102). I suggest that this systematic distancing also extended to his young pupils; his characterizations of boy actors onstage; his creation of comic worlds of childlike, impotent adults; and finally to the puppet-substitutes for children in *Bartholomew Fair.* All of these removals allowed Jonson the distance not only to evade or mitigate his own feelings of guilt, regret, and grief but also to engage in his culture's exploration, acknowledgment, and reinvention of the very concept of childhood.

Historical theories developed a generation ago about early modern family life and childhood argued that parents rarely developed emotional attachments to children before they emerged from their vulnerable childhood years.[3] Indeed, Jonson's frequent elegies for dead children invite such a reading; they are conventionally philosophical, expressing the Boethian Stoicism that advised sufferers to place individual deaths and losses in a broader perspective. Epigram XXII, "On My First Daughter," expresses this convention, as does his rather dispassionate elegy for the first Charles II, who died on the day of his birth in 1629 (*Underwood* LXIII). In "An Epigram Consolatory," Jonson advises Charles I and Mary not to "grutch" at the payment of "first fruits" owed to the Almighty—the same meager consolation he had offered to his wife on the death of their daughter.

But contemporary social theorists believe that historians like Ariès overstated the incidence of parental indifference. These theorists argue that well before the eighteenth century, the loss of a child appears frequently in literature not just as physical death but also as the death of identity and is therefore tragic in a way perceptibly different from the death of an adult.[4] Given such an assumption, the tone in Jonson's most famous epitaph, "On My First Sonne" (Epigram XLV), is not (as critics have traditionally suggested) one of unemotional egotism but the more complex expression of loss and terror.

In this poem, Jonson momentarily resurrects his son, as he did in his dream-vision; unlike the silent dream-Benjamin, however, the poetic Benjamin speaks for his grief-stricken father. As Riggs points out, the dream-Benjamin appeared to Jonson in the adult form he would never physically attain, but that his soul would bear at the end of time, perhaps an indication that Jonson had already begun to put some affective distance between himself and his child.[5] Therefore, when Benjamin speaks as an adult alter ego from the tomb (as he had no chance to do in life), he describes himself as Jonson's "best piece of poetrie," stressing not the finality of his own death but the continuing life of his father's career. Of course, the Stoic sentiment of the other child-epitaphs is present in this poem, as is the Christian commonplace that death is a desirable gateway to salvation, but Robert Watson notes that this poem, like other Jacobean consolatory poems, also expresses an explicit anxiety over the possibility that the death of the body includes the death of the soul.[6]

The crucial line, ". . . here doth lye / BEN. IONSON his best piece of *poetrie,*" has long interested both reader-response and deconstructionist critics for its syntactic ambiguity, which blurs the separation between father and son.[7] The son has become an apologist for the father, inverting the expected order and focusing attention on poetic immortality, a less traumatic topic than that of a child's mortality. It is certainly clear that Jonson cannot this time completely separate himself from the dead child.

Jonson's anecdotal version of his tragic loss (which probably included the death of his other son, the infant Joseph, in the same pestilence) seems remarkably dispassionate to modern audiences. When we add to our understanding of Jonson's reaction his formal meditation on his son's death in Epigram XLV, in which he protests, "[M]y sinne was too much hope of thee, lov'd boy," we can either condemn Jonson for his selfishness or, in our psychoanalytic era, assume that the poet is repressing (even after 15 years) the grief and guilt any father would have felt after choosing to doom his family to a perilous urban summer while removing himself to rural safety and comfort. Also, by identifying the emotion as "sinne," Jonson displaces responsibility for it to God, the ultimate patriarch.

Moreover, we are not invited to *hear* Benjamin's words; instead, we are figuratively reading his headstone. Not even Benjamin's nonverbal communications are his own: when he speaks symbolically, marked with the bloody cross, it is still within Jonson's own mind. The child is eloquent in the way signs are eloquent, but he generates no language himself. So, even as Jonson conveniently admits to being a too-doting parent (again, perhaps to deflect his feelings of guilt), he immediately transfers his parental overachievement to his poetry (and any parental unkindness implicitly to God). He ruefully resolves not to become too attached to any of his individual "pieces of poetry," which may not survive their initial exposure to the world, but rather to love them impersonally for what they represent: the material of his potential literary immortality.[8]

Jonson equates the boy with his own monument in the same way he conflates his child with his poetry—and the same way he confuses his own role as father with that of son when he cries, "O, could I loose all father now," lamenting the end of his fatherhood, possibly expressing a wish to have no more children, and perhaps in the same line mourning the memory of his own fatherlessness. For Jonson, the paternal function and the poetic function are so inseparable that he blurs the distinctions between father and son, author and reader, objective observer and grieving parent, poet and poem. Even the emotions he reveals waver between gratitude that he had a son at all and bitterness that he has lost him, implying a wish that he had never had a son in the first place, thereby avoiding any dread of the wronged boy's judgment.

Perhaps Jonson transforms his dead boy's moral judgment into critical judgment in order to deflect (again) some of its horror. Gabriele Bernhard Jackson suggests that Jonson's "peculiar metamorphosis of the real into the ideal" goes beyond the normal scope of Metaphysical literature to create a "drama of revelation," a precise ritual of insight arriving at "reality." If, as Jackson argues, "Jonson's perfect poet is simultaneously visionary and judge,"[9] then here in Jonson's "best piece of poetry," the poem/Benjamin is superior because it/he has transformed the horrific ritual of death-vision, burial, and mourning into an opportunity to judge. For Jonson, such opportunities enabled him to control himself and, through language, his world.

Jonson's child becomes, then, not a sentimental gift from God but a version of the *puer senex,* the child wise beyond his years. Shakespeare's characteristic versions of the *puer senex* are, unlike Benjamin's silently judgmental ghost, models of eloquence and an expression of the desire to control the chaotic nature of childishness: they speak as intelligently as adults while retaining the candor and innocence of childhood. MacDuff's son and the young princes of *Richard III* are only two examples of childhood perspicacity and prophecy; discounting our post-Romantic tendency to think of Puck as a child, we never see children acting or speaking in a sense of pure playfulness in Shakespeare. Even the Boy who attends the hopelessly puerile Bardolph, Nym, and Pistol in *Henry V* comments on his surroundings with mature gravity.[10]

By privileging the *puer senex* model over that of the newer, more sentimental view of the affectionate bond between parent and child while simultaneously depriving the *puer* of his eloquent wisdom, Jonson may also have been replicating the characteristics of his own childhood. Psychoanalytical critics have commented on the developmental effect of losing his biological father and enduring an unsatisfactory replacement.[11] Jonson's response seems to have been, in part, to create intellectual fathers for himself to take the place of his absent father and laborer stepfather. Camden, his first teacher and mentor, seems to have filled such a role for Jonson (Epigram XIV), as did Esmé, Lord Aubigny (Epigram CXXVII), and James I himself. In a similar action, Jonson also creates spiritual and artistic sons for himself, such as Lucius Cary (*Underwood* LXIX) and the "Sons of Ben," whose self-adoption the poet was pleased to ratify. These father-son relationships were invariably pedagogical in nature. His dramatic colleagues were, to him, friends and brothers; his noble female patronesses were muses; the vast majority of his acquaintance were rivals; but the paternal bond was reserved for those men who shared his love for and knowledge of classical literature, poetry, and teaching.[12] This again implies an effort on Jonson's part to create and inhabit a Golden World in which the formal discourse of pedagogy replaces the unruly dynamic of the flesh-and-blood family.

Jonson is explicit in *Discoveries* about his notions (based largely on received classical commonplaces) of proper education. Again, it is important to note the conventionality of Jonson's opinions. Following Quintilian, he recommends to "your Lordship" (probably the Earl of Newcastle) that education for the young should be mixed with delight, that "the Schoole it selfe is call'd a Play, or Game: and all Letters are so best taught to Schollers." Moreover, young scholars do best away from home, for "[t]o breed them at home, is to breed them in a shade; where in a schoole they have the light, and heate of the Sunne." That nourishing sun, presumably, is the patronage of an enlightened teacher. Further, in a proper school, their models and acquaintance would be worthy of emulation, whereas children forced to study at home, as Jonson was, were likely to be distracted by the stresses of dealing with blood- (or step-) relations. Jonson likely transferred his own youthful preference for his school life over his home life to his theories about the education of noble boys and, based on his own failures at home, recommended "no private breeding" (*Discoveries,* 1657–85).

Lacking a university education himself, Jonson was in no position to become officially one of the scholarly father-teachers he so revered. In fact, his idealized picture of the schoolmaster aside, he seems to be chewing some sour grapes when he describes rival (and internationally successful) epigrammist John Owen as "a pure Pedantique Schoolmaster sweeping his living from the Posteriors of little children" (*Conversations,* 223–25).

Jonson's tutoring of the boy actors in the private theater companies was therefore informal, and his students included his "Schollar" (Nat Field) and other boys who, according to Gerald Bentley, were (with royal permission) abducted or "impressed" as choirboys by Nathanial Giles, choirmaster of the Children of the Queen's Chapel (*Conversations,* 164).[13] Hardworking and usually lower or middle class, the boy actors may have been good students, but the busy tiring-rooms of the private theaters were hardly the pastoral home away from home that Jonson envisioned as the ideal educational environment for his hypothetical aristocratic scholars in *Discoveries.* He did seem to take some pains with these boys, who would likely have been intelligent and quick studies (and more motivated than the privileged sons of the court). Nat Field, at least, went on to a successful (if brief) career as a playwright himself; Richard Brome, also a successful playwright, is remembered as Jonson's "man" rather than his pupil, but he was of the right age to perform with the children in their heyday and possibly to study with his employer.[14]

Jonson's association with the boy actors also produced the one child-epitaph that differs—crucially—from the rest. Salomon Pavy, also a Child of the Queen's Chapel, may or may not have been one of Jonson's occasional "Schollars," but his special genius for naturalistic portrayals is immortalized in Epigram CXX:

> [He] did act (what now we mone)
>   Old men so duely,
> As, sooth, the *Parcae* thought him one,
>   He plai'd so truely.
>
> (13–16)

The poem's conceit is that Heaven reclaimed Pavy out of the mistaken belief that he was a literal *puer senex*—that he had somehow metamorphosed into the elderly man he so often played, a hazard of the acting life that probably wouldn't have occurred to even the most antitheatrical commentators.[15] More important, Jonson here reveals (still obliquely but more vividly than in his other epitaphs) his anxieties about the type of relationships available between children (even the quasi children of the theater) and adults.

Although Jonson had yet to experience the crushing loss of Benjamin when he wrote Pavy's epitaph, he was keenly aware how much more vulnerable than aristocratic children the boy actors were to a wide variety of threats: to the ordinary physical dangers of disease and accident that threatened all children (intensified, perhaps, by exposure to the reputedly disease-ridden atmosphere of the playhouses); to exploitation as sex objects and laborers; to the spiritual danger all actors were believed to endure whenever they put on a role; and, perhaps worst of all, to anonymity after death not often compensated by fame in life.

This poem, simultaneously an epitaph and a commentary on the stage, offers a transition from Jonson's verse treatments of children to his dramatic ones. Pavy becomes a figurative offspring of the page, his physical being subordinated to other people's words and his very fate determined in actions circumscribed by the stage that is his only real home. He cannot argue with the fates that have mistaken him for an old man; he has no language of his own. He has, in fact, given up his language to Jonson in much the same way Benjamin's potential words are sacrificed and with as little say in the matter. No matter how accomplished a mouthpiece for Jonson's dramatic poetry, Pavy ultimately is as dependent on the poet as any of Jonson's other mute dead children to have his "little story" preserved in verse.

Moreover, the playwright is like the teacher in that he bestows language (and at times even the ability to use language) on his students. This gift can be double edged, as we see in examples ranging from Genesis (in which Adam becomes subject to God's law at the same time he receives the ability to name) through Shakespeare, whose Prospero simultaneously frees and enslaves Caliban with the gift of language and self-awareness. The teacher, in a way, enjoys greater power even than the poet because he not only creates the Golden World of language but enjoys a fellowship with other young minds that is far more intimate than that of poet and reader. For someone like Jonson, in fact, the intimacy of the act of feeding knowledge to young minds could have transcended even fatherhood and reached the mystery of motherhood—without, of course, the mitigating physical aspects that made motherhood (as we see in Epigram XXII) the lesser of the two parental experiences.[16]

Here the implied intimacy of the pedagogical relationship begins to create problems for Jonson. The boy actors possessed not just waiting minds and voices but bodies as well. And these bodies, unlike those of his dead children, were present on a day-to-day basis in Jonson's life. Like his contemporaries, he probably believed (and could well have had ocular proof of) the conventional wisdom that the boy actors performed more than just lip service for their masters and spectators. There is little hard evidence of the sexual exploitation of the boy actors, but implied anxiety about it runs throughout Jonson's (and his contemporaries') plays and bears closer investigation here. Michael Shapiro argues that a crucial aspect of the child actors was their sexuality, or their lack thereof.[17] Various critics, especially R. A. Foakes, have argued that plays like *Antonio and Mellida* influenced the sex-and-violence excesses of Senecan revenge tragedy in the public theaters not a little because of the prurient attractions offered by the performing boys (along with their inferred harmlessness) in the first place.[18] And Lisa Jardine argues that the boy actors' contemporaries explicitly equated transvestism with eroticism.[19] In both theatrical and antitheatrical literature, there is an implied assumption that the children were sexual as well as dramatic players, available to gallants offstage in the way that actresses in Restoration England were assumed to be.[20] As far back as 1569, an anonymous pamphleteer had complained,

> Plaies will never be supprest, while her majesties unfledged minions flaunt it in silkes and sattens . . . profan[ing] the Lordes Day by the lascivious writhing of their tender limbs, and gorgious decking of their apparell, in feigning bawdie fables gathered from the idolatrous heathen poets.[21]

And Jonson himself—along with other playwrights—commonly referred to boy actors as "enghles" or "ingles," which, according to the O.E.D., meant "catamite" or "boy-favourite (in a bad sense)."

As Marcus points out in *Childhood and Cultural Despair,* although Jonson's peers were well aware of the facts of childhood sexuality, seventeenth-century literature operated within the *conventions* of sexual innocence in children (203). However, the comment by one of the child actors in the induction to *Cynthia's Revels*—"I'lde crie, a rape, but that you are children (102–3)"—simultaneously reinforces and subverts this convention, as does the speech of the little page in *Epicoene* (specifically called an "ingle" by Truewit) who boasts about the female gallants' unsuccessful efforts to meddle with him. In the case of the page, as Jardine points out, there is an irony in his pride in resisting the women when he punningly admits he is "the welcom'st thing under a man" (1.1.8).[22] She also investigates the aspects of sadism and fetishism inherent in the presence of child actors, adding support to the notion that myths of childhood innocence were as misleading in the seventeenth century as they are now, in an age when child molestation—and recent evidence that those molested sometimes victimize still younger children—challenges our own assumptions about sexual function in children as young as three or four years.

There was obviously something both unsettling and appealing about seeing young boys go through the motions of lovemaking and murder on stage. The children's companies seemed to be trying to have it both ways: simultaneously claiming innocence of theatrical mayhem based on the boys' supposed real-life impotence and a scandalously attractive reputation based on their supposed sexual charms. Such an arrangement was necessarily unstable and, as it turned out, short-lived. Less than a decade after going public, the children's companies were effectively shut down by a combination of censorship, behind-the-scenes recruiting scandals, and competition from the public theaters.

Elsewhere in his plays, Jonson emphasizes the physical limitations of the child actors and also mentions their susceptibility to exploitation. In *Poetaster,* when Histrio offers to employ the two Pyrgi in his company for a week, Tucca objects, "No, you mangonizing slave, I will not part from 'hem; you'll sell 'hem for enghles, you" (3.4.275–76). Ovid Senior in the same play also worries about Ovid Junior's involvement with plays: "What? shall I have my sonne a stager now? an enghle for players?" (1.1.15–16). Moreover, the "honest women" of Jonson's comedies—for example, Celia in *Volpone,* Dame Pliant in *The Alchemist,* and the Dames Overdo and Purecraft in *Bartholomew Fair*—are invariably rescued just before the point in the play at which they are to suffer ravishment. No matter how prurient or crude the language of their wooing, Jonson seems to stop short of portraying actual physical harm to ladies.[23] The reason could be the conventional gallantry typical of Jonson's epigrams addressed to noblewomen, or a comedic convention that precludes harming sympathetic or helpless characters. Also, because both playwright and audience were fully aware that female sexuality could never be shown explicitly, such plays participated in a mutually acknowledged, unfulfillable fantasy. Still, Jonson could have been expressing a subconscious reluctance to exploit, via his dramatic inventions, the young boys who would have been playing these women any further than he already has linguistically. Or he may have been simply expressing a wish to "rescue" the boys onstage from the type of sexual use he could not prevent offstage.[24]

This fatherly concern would complement the paternal/pedagogical (but not pederastic) relationship we have already seen Jonson expressing in his poems, particularly if we transfer Jonson's anxieties—as he often did—from sexuality to language.[25] He seems to have found linguistic exploitation (other poets', at least, if not his own) of the children as distasteful as their physical exploitation. At one point in the induction to *Cynthia's Revels,* the "Second Child" remarks of "their author,"

> [W]ee are not so officiously befriended by him, as to have his presence in the tiring-house, to prompt us aloud, stampe at the book-holder, sweare for our properties, curse the poore tire-man, raile the musicke out of tune, and sweat for everie veniall trespasse we commit, as some Author would, if he had such fine engles as we. Well, tis but our hard fortune. (160–66)

In other words, although Jonson must give his child actors words to speak, he seems to claim that he does not, like his rival playwrights, wring the words out of the boys by main force. Jonson thus conveniently removes himself from the more exploitive aspects of the playwright's role: he uses the "ingles" as vessels but stops short of penetrating them himself. This is not an indictment of Jonson as would-be molester but a recognition of the centuries-old tradition of tutor-as-seducer of which the poet must have been aware. The Greek philosophers on whom Jonson's classical studies centered were, to the Elizabethan mind, notorious pederasts. By translating Sall Pavy into an old man, by transforming Benjamin into an adult, Jonson may have been protecting them from the physical vulnerability of the child to adult desire and objectification.[26]

When the Third Child (played originally by Sall Pavy) insists on "reveng[ing him]selfe on the Authour" by giving away the plot of *Cynthia's Revels,* the other two children, wisely realizing that the production (and the players) will suffer for such a strategy more than the author, try to restrain the rebel physically. He hollers, "What, will you ravish mee? . . . I'lde crie, a rape, but that you are children" (99, 102–3). Here he claims to be protected only by his fellow actors' sexual immaturity, inviting though not speaking the assumption that he could be ravished by someone else.

This induction is certainly focused more anxiously on the disruptive power of the boys than on their own vulnerability; still, the reference to rape evokes a hidden "primal scene" (in Freudian terms) that implies by its concealment an unspeakable act. As Arthur Little has suggested, it is possible to translate Freud's *Urzene,* or the "moment when a child imagines or (by accident) actually sees his parents engaged in sexual intercourse," to other loci of cultural anxiety and to pre-Freudian contexts.[27] The boys' explicit reminder that they can be raped provides a similar dislocation given that (as we have seen in the rescued gentlewomen as well as in the symbolic rapes in plays such as *Othello*) such an expectation can never be fulfilled onstage. Ultimately, Jonson seems to have suspected that the boys should not have been on that stage at all.[28]

In *Epicoene,* Jonson's last comedy for a company comprised solely of children, the playwright carries the ambiguity of the boy actors' effect to an extreme.[29] The point made earlier about Jonson's "rescue" of his noble female characters takes on some interesting implications in this play in which the "heroine" is not just played by a boy actor but is a disguised boy in the context of the play as well. Transvestism in the Jacobean theater was a common comedic strategy inspired in part by the physical advantages of having a large supply of androgynous young actors. *Epicoene* is unique, however, in that the title character's true sex is revealed simultaneously to the audience and to the other characters in the play.[30] Jonson may well have manipulated the audience's perceptions of the character's sex in part as a comment on the ethical difficulties presented to both the playgoer and the playmaker by the physical nature of the boy actors.

Epicoene, like Scheherazade, escapes the indignity of Morose's love by means of a loquacity imposed on her by her employer, Truewit (and ultimately by her author, Jonson), but it is only when "her" true masculinity is physically revealed that "he" is rescued from homosexual consummation.[31] However, Jonson has changed the ending of the source story, in which the old man is glad that he has married a boy, and a future happy sexual relationship for the pair is clearly indicated.[32] Jonson seems here to be taking advantage of the theatrical self-consciousness offered in other plays by the framing device to reject, at least for himself, a theatrical style that must inevitably involve the physical exploitation of children.

This rejection seems to be confirmed in *The Devil Is An Ass* when Jonson's adult hero takes the place of the famous child actor whom Meercraft wishes to employ to counterfeit a woman. Upon learning that the boy actor is "every jot" as tall as the adult amateur (an occupational hazard that had begun afflicting the children's companies almost as soon as they reached their prime), Meercraft avers, "I had rather / To trust a Gentleman with it, o' the two" (3.1.14–16). Robert Watson and Peter Womack are among the readers who have noticed that this play appears to be, on its self-consciously theatrical level, Jonson's epitaph for the festive native theater traditions: Tudor morality plays, which seemed to be a product of the university and civic mystery plays.[33]

If this is the case, then the play that immediately preceded *The Devil Is An Ass*—*Bartholomew Fair*—may contain within its theatrical boundaries a transitional exploration of the reasons for the demise of at least one aspect of the festive English theater. It seems likely that part of Jonson's purpose in devising the puppet play in *Bartholomew Fair* was to comment on the then mostly defunct and apparently unlamented children's companies.

Here we find a play in which there are scarcely any juvenile characters but rather a number of adult characters who conform to Renaissance models of childishness. One of the characters, Cokes, is described by everyone as a child in an adult's body; ironically, most of the Fair visitors themselves possess certain childish qualities. In the play as a whole, Jonson takes many opportunities to confine childish impulses and personalities in adult bodies. Such a mismatch of physical and emotional selves creates hybrid characters that reflect and symbolize the similar hybrid nature of the Jacobean stage at precisely the transitional moments in which Jonson was writing *Bartholomew Fair*.

Early characterizations of children and childhood read like specific "characters" of Bartholomew Cokes. The thirteenth-century commentator (and, coincidentally, Cokes's namesake) Bartholomaeus Anglicus observed:

> [Children] love plays, game, and vanity, and forsake winning and profit. And things most worthy they repute least worthy, and least worthy most worthy. They desire things that be to them contrary and grievous, and set more of the image of a child [i.e., a puppet], than the image of a man, and make more sorrow and woe, and weep more for the loss of an apple [or a basket of pears], than for the loss of their heritage [or a marriage-warrant]. And the goodness that is done for them, they let it pass out of mind. They desire all things that they see, and pray and ask with voice and with hand. They love talking and counsel of such children as they be, and void company of old men [like Wasp]. They keep no counsel, but they tell all that they hear or see.[34]

The Renaissance heritage also included the medieval view that children "shared something of the vague aura of sanctity surrounding the fool," to the extent that fools and children were often described in the same way; however, by the seventeenth century, fools were enjoying somewhat less sufferance for their social, mental, and moral shortcomings and children somewhat more.[35]

In *The Court Of Conscience: or Dick Whippers Sessions* (London, 1607), Nathanial West characterizes a number of disreputable types to be found at the average urban fair; he describes "*Fooles and Flattering Maple-Faces*":

> Thou like a foole with coxcome, motley coat,
> Ladle and pudding and a thousand toyes:
> Goest like a cokes an noddy and a sot,
> Derided by a hundred little boyes.
>
> (n. pag.)

Cokes's name is, of course, a commonplace for fool, but Wasp's image of his charge chasing wondrous parrots and monkeys around London, "with all the little-long-coats about him, male and female," and our own observance of Bartholomew's circuit of the Fair as the boy picks up toys and sweets, losing his prized coat and hat in the process, create a strong affinity between West's vision of this type of fair-goer and Jonson's (1.4.115–16).

To further emphasize Cokes's childishness, Jonson offers the contrasting figure of the mad Trouble-All. Renaissance culture distinguished between fools and madmen chiefly in the sense that madmen were diseased and fools merely arrested in their development—literally children in their minds. "Fools are not mad folks," Imogene insists in *Cymbeline* (2.3.99), and Feste in *Twelfth Night* distinguishes the fool at "one draught above heat" from the madman at two (1.5.131). Madmen could be depraved and sexual (as we see in *The Changeling*), but fools rarely were; madmen were characterized by inarticulate, broken, or repetitious language whereas fools (including Shakespeare's clowns) often offered rich word-hoards if little actual matter (Littlewit shares this characteristic);[36] and fools were usually costumed in "motley" or layer upon layer of brightly colored clothing whereas madmen were often pictured nearly naked (cf. *Lear*'s Poor Tom). Likewise, poor shabby Trouble-All, with his meaningless, monotonous demands for Overdo's warrant, is the victim of a sudden, pathological, Lear-like onset of madness and not, like Cokes, of merely a failure to mature. Trouble-All's losses—his job, family, and sanity—are tragic (although Overdo makes an attempt to correct them); Cokes's losses—some toys, some money and clothes, some sweets, and a fiancée he didn't want anyway—are minor and temporary. In general, the madman suffers from want and the fool tends toward excess, the very afflictions that characterize, respectively, old age and childhood.[37]

With the exception of Trouble-All (and possibly Wasp), every one of the city fair-goers is at one time or another, in some small way, classically and foolishly childish. Busy is described as "ever . . . i' the state of Innocence, though; and childhood . . . and what discretion soever, yeeres should afford him, it is all prevented in his *Originall ignorance*" (1.3.143–46). Grace, perhaps the most overtly poised and mature character, nevertheless chooses her husband in a game of chance. Win and Dame Overdo dutifully follow their men into the Fair and, like the hapless children who never instigate mischief but are always the ones caught and blamed, bear the brunt of the physical punishment in the forms of incontinence (a common childhood mishap) and near-violation (again hinting obliquely at the child actors' vulnerability). Littlewit's longing to "see some Hobby-horses, and some Drummes, and Rattles, and Dogs, and fine devices" is virtually identical to Cokes's (3.6.6–7).[38] Even Quarlous and Winwife nearly forget their friendship in quarreling over Grace; Bartholomaeus reminds us that children are "lightly and soon wroth, and soon pleased, and lightly they forgive."[39]

Unlike the visitors to the fair, the fair workers participate in this childish world while remaining curiously unchildlike themselves. The boys of the Fair—Mooncalf (clearly a youth, although his age is unclear) and Edgeworth—are mature in their responsibilities and illegal talents; Ursula is suffering prematurely the infirmities of age; Haggis and Bristle, the watchmen, are not bullies but rather fairly reasonable men who demand respect for authority; and the distinct lack of childishness on Trouble-All's part I have already pointed out.

The relative maturity of the fair-folk is important to note because of the curious aura of sterility in a setting normally associated with plenty and sexual increase. R. B. Parker has commented at length on this in "Themes and Staging of *Bartholomew Fair*," and, although I do not agree that Win's pregnancy is feigned, it does seem clear—and odd—that there are no literal parent-child relationships portrayed in the play except for that of Win and her mother.[40] And in this case, that both are equally scatterbrained levels their relationship; that the daughter is married while the mother is seeking a husband inverts it. Grace is the ward, not the daughter of Overdo; Bartholomew is Dame Overdo's brother, not her son; Wasp is Bartholomew's tutor, and not—to his vast relief—his father. Like Jonson himself, *everyone* in the play lacks a father. Littlewit's excuse for allowing Winwife to fondle Win—he "may be our father, perhaps," if he succeeds in wooing Win's mother—begins to sound like a wistful desire for a complete family (1.2.10).

In fact, the relationships in the play that most resemble the traditional parent-child relationship are those between fair-folk and their apprentices. Womack comments on the privileging of economic relationships over class and blood relationships in the play: Mooncalf seems to dote on his grotesque mistress, Ursula, and Edgeworth and Nightingale have quite a fruitful master-journeyman relationship; the two seem to regard Ursula with filial affection as well. We have, in the prospect of these relationships, a picture much closer to Jonson's ideal of a pedagogical fatherhood, where the transfer of knowledge takes the place of shared blood, and therefore much closer to that ideal than the supposedly pedagogical relationships between Wasp and Cokes, or Busy and Dame Purecraft. The festive setting of the play inevitably perverts normal social relationships; Jonson further emphasizes the "world upside down" by translating the lessons taught by affectionate Fair "parents" into discourses on larceny and greed rather than Latin and Greek.

For example, Ursula instructs Mooncalf in the art of adulterating tobacco and ale:

> . . . 6 and 20. shillings a barrell I will advance o' my Beere, and fifty shillings a hundred o' my bottle-ale; I ha' told you the waies how to raise it. Froth your cannes well i' the filling, at length, Rogue, and jogge your bottles o' the buttocke, Sirrah, then . . . drinke with all companies . . . ; you'll mis-reckon the better, and be lesse ashamed on't. (2.2.94–100)

Mathematics, pricing, customer relations, and ethics are covered in this short speech. Later, Edgeworth carefully coaches Nightingale: "And i' your singing, you must use your hawks eye nimbly, and flye the purse to a marke still . . . that you may gi' me the signe with your beake" (2.4.42–45). Here Jonson seems to be attempting to replace—or at least infuse—commerce with the kind of cooperative, affectionate relationships absent in, for instance, *Volpone* or *The Alchemist*. As in his relationship with his stepfather, Robert Brett, Jonson would likely have been as ambivalent about the master-apprentice relationship as he was about father-son relationships anyway. The confusion of parental ties with economic ones informs Jonson's life and pedagogy; therefore, similar confusion in *Bartholomew Fair* may not be merely an ironic strategy but may also reflect an unavoidable and deeply ingrained association on Jonson's part.[41]

As we are led inexorably through the dissolution of conventional blood ties and the increasing childishness of the visitors, we end up at the semiotically freighted puppet show, where the childlike adults convene to watch the performance of the eerily lifelike "pretty youthes . . . all children both old and young" (5.3.51). We are offered a number of textually explicit opportunities to compare the puppets with the acting boys, some of whom would have been working onstage in the play's first two performances, watching this parody of their own work.[42] Like the boys, the puppets are "players minors," but Cokes commends them because unlike the boys, they "offer not to fleere, nor geere, nor breake jests, as the great *Players* do" (5.3.75, 97–98). The boys were, of course, "great" only in relation to puppets but were castigated in comparison to the adult companies for their reliance on raillery and improvisation.

Implicitly, the similarities of the boy actors to puppets is equally rich. Like the puppets, the boys are mere mouthpieces onstage, manipulated by the text as the adult actors are. Unlike the adult players, they are manipulated and owned by their producer-owners offstage almost as completely as Leatherhead controls his dolls. When Jonson makes a point of the puppets' sexlessness, we are reminded of his insistence that the children of *Cynthia's Revels* are equally sexless and harmless—the puppets could no more commit a rape than could little Sall Pavy. However, Cokes's oft-expressed affection for the puppets (and his desire to own or keep them) might echo for Jonson the desire for physical possession inflicted on the children by their managers and perhaps by the gallants who may have been able to hire them for illicit purposes. Cokes mentally transforms the "actors" into "fairings," inanimate pieces of property, and strips them of the little anthropomorphism they possess. And later, Cokes must be restrained from joining the puppets on their stage in a bit of business that is surely evocative of the gallants' presence on the private stages, as well as of *The Knight of the Burning Pestle.*

In "*Bartholomew Fair* and Its Puppets," Barish writes,

> Everything [in the Fair] comes in families and diminuitives. . . . The world shrinks to a Lilliputian array of dolls and baubles in which children play at being grown up. . . . The puppet play, written in the jog-trot couplets of the old interludes . . . shrinks literature as well as life into the tiny compass of a peep show and decomposes it into the grossness of its baser elements.[43]

The puppet play mirrors and multiplies the implications of such childishness. The notoriously extreme level of scatology in the play takes on even more resonance when it is linked to issues not only of social shame and transgression but also of the boys' precarious hold on their identities.

The moment of genital nonrevelation by the puppets is comic not only in its own childish way but also in the extreme discomfort it causes Busy. And it echoes the Third Child's snide reminder that anyone who imagines that the induction to *Cynthia's Revels* might include a rape scene is worse than obtuse. Busy's consternation at the childishly hilarious gesture surely resonates with Jonson's own anxiety about the dirty thoughts he and his colleagues have been provoking in their audiences by making the boys mouth obscenities before adult spectators.[44] Jonson makes it clear that the puppet play would have none of this power were it not for the essential childishness of the watching characters and the underlying ability of the game of theater to fascinate adult audiences.[45]

It is worth noting here that the childish chaos of the *Cynthia's Revels* induction, and its accompanying indictment of audience taste, is mirrored by *Bartholomew Fair*'s induction. Where the *Cynthia's Revels* induction is multivocal (with the author's words subversively interpreted through the boys' "unwritten" dialogue), the *Bartholomew Fair* induction is univocal (with the author's words carefully presented as a binding—and written—contract). Also, *Cynthia's Revels* ends with a formal, balanced masque (a "Palinode," in fact) that carefully lists (as does *Bartholomew Fair*'s induction) the crimes against taste that will no longer plague the theater; *Bartholomew Fair* ends with not only an antimasque of childish chaos that indicts by lampoon (as does *Cynthia's Revels*' induction) its own audience but also a threat that the play will escape the boundaries of the stage and follow the spectators home. *Cynthia's Revels* ends where *Bartholomew Fair* begins (a logical if not chronological progression, as the new public companies have by then replaced the boys' companies); however, *Bartholomew Fair* ends with the ghosts (and in Sall Pavy's case, this is meant literally) of those little boys monstrously parodied before us. Is this progress or an admission of defeat on Jonson's part?[46]

If this careful inversion implies that Jonson is satirizing the ability of the private (boys') companies to influence audience taste, then the puppet play is clearly meant to be a microcosmic representation of the private theater tradition in general.[47] By using the puppets to represent the boy actors, Jonson has finally created "children" who cannot be sexually exploited, who cannot die, and who can (though only in collusion with the will of the playwright) shout down and control the destructive forces of misplaced childishness. This creation is terribly ironic, however, because it is so transparently a fantasy. In "Nobody's Perfect," Orgel reminds us, "Fantasies of freedom in Shakespeare tend to take the form of escapes from the tyranny of elders to a world where the children can make their own society, which usually means where they can arrange their own marriages. . . . the crucial element is the restrictive father, not the sex of the child" (10). In Jonson's fantasy world, the "children" do not escape but are kept in tiny baskets and only taken out to be forced to speak by a man who holds them firmly by the nether parts.

This appalling fantasy proves that some griefs defy conventional modes of comfort. The best Jonson can achieve, as he reveals this nexus of ambiguity and anxiety, is the masochistic comfort of self-inflicted punishment. Such self-disgust, in fact, becomes oddly comforting for a number of reasons: it is a reminder that the sufferer is, after all, still alive and sensible; it can act as punishment for unrevealed sins; and it can deflect attention from the sufferer's worse interior pain.

The Fair puppets thus become Jonson's own masochistic reminder of his dead babies. The fact that the puppet also represents a bizarre embodiment of a dead theatrical style becomes almost moot in the face of the tremendous psychic impact the sight of puppets tucked into a basket to sleep must have had on a man who, through his own neglect, missed the opportunity to "cover gently" with earth, in the imperative Western ritual of burial, his own dead son.[48] The induction may have lulled us into a feeling of security about the playwright's control not only over his own play but over himself; the experience of the play, however, becomes a symbolic pilgrimage through all the fears and anxieties to which any intelligent parent is vulnerable. The relics at the end of this pilgrimage are not venerable bones but pseudocorpses. The absolution they offer is far from absolute.

The play's overtly festive ending is not negated by this reading; rather, by calling our attention to a multileveled version of parent-child relationships, Jonson demonstrates the gap between how a play functions for its audience and how it functions for its maker(s). The audience may well take away the image of a happy family reunited; still, by offering so bland a fantasy to his audience, Jonson invites closer attention to that fantasy's inadequacy on an individualized level. Jonson may have designed the "forgiveness" offered by *Bartholomew Fair*'s ending to mock his own inability to forgive himself for the breakup of his own family. There is certainly precedent for such self-mockery in Jonson's comedy; the connections between Jonson and Morose, for example, have been extensively noted.

Little wonder that when faced with the void implied by the naked lifelessness of the puppets, Jonson encourages us to "ha' the rest o' the play at home"—to escape the receding layers of identity displayed through the distorted lens of the stage—and return to the mundane comfort of family and hearth, where every member's role is well known and well played. Jonson's home, of course, was the source of—not a refuge from—his tragedy, bitterness, and loss. Did the playwright put those words into the mouth of the play's greatest baby in a spirit of deep sarcasm or of nostalgic hope? Or is the theater—replicating as it does all Jonson's core issues of appetite, aggression, vulnerable childishness, and frustrated artistic ambition—Jonson's true home? Jonson is suggesting, when he creates a world in which there are no natural fathers, that it is perhaps better to be a Leatherhead, a pseudofather who not only owns his children outright and animates them directly by the workings of his own hands and mouth, than it is to be a natural father. Not coincidentally, Leatherhead is a playmaker.

Even though it was possible for poets in Jonson's time to imagine a maternal mode of poetic generation, it was probably impossible for the father-obsessed, son-haunted Jonson to do so. Thus, there are no actively parental couples in *Bartholomew Fair;* and thus, there are no real children but only pseudochildren. By manipulating his audience into accepting such a "home," Jonson here is like Milton's Satan or Shakespeare's Prospero: defiantly isolated at first but ultimately desirous of ordinary empathy and human company. When *Bartholomew Fair*'s pseudochildren take control of the play, Jonson reveals the strain of sharing his life with poetic demons and tiny ghosts.[49] *Bartholomew Fair,* then, may be the conciliatory play so many critics wish it to be, but the community it creates is one of mutual escape from the fear of death through a conspiracy of denial. "Be converted," Jonson tells us when he holds up the puppet mirror; "Be obedient; be witty; be ideal. Be my children."

Notes

1. David Riggs, *Ben Jonson: A Life* (Cambridge: *Harvard University Press,* 1989), 86–102.

2. The issues involved in the presentation of the transvestite child on the Shakespearean stage are a recent focus of Renaissance drama studies. A *partial* list includes J. W. Binns, "Women or Transvestites on the Elizabethan Stage?" *Sixteenth Century Journal* 5 (1974): 95–120; Steve Brown, "The Boyhood of Shakespeare's Heroines: Notes on Gender Ambiguity in the Sixteenth Century," *SEL* 30 (1990): 243–63; Jackson Cope, "Marlowe's *Dido* and the Titillating Children," *ELR* 4 (1974): 315–25; James Hill, "What, Are They Children?" *SEL* 26 (1986): 235–58; Peter Hyland, "A Kind of Woman: The Elizabethan Boy Actor and the Kabuki *Onnagata,*" *Theatre Research International* 12 (1987): 1–8: Lisa Jardine, "Boy Actors, Female Roles, and Elizabethan Eroticism," in *Staging the Renaissance: Reinterpretations of Elizabethan and Jacobean Drama,* ed. David Scott Kastan and Peter Stallybrass (New York: Routledge, 1991): 57–67; Richard Levin, "The Acting Styles of the Children's Companies," *American Notes and Queries* 22 (1983): 34–35; Kathleen McLuskie, "The Act, the Role, and the Actor: Boy Actresses on the Elizabethan Stage," *New Theatre Quarterly* 3 (1987): 120–30; Stephen Orgel, "Nobody's Perfect; or, Why Did the English Stage Take Boys for Women?" *South Atlantic Quarterly* 88 (1989): 7–30, Phyllis Rackin, "Androgyny, Mimesis, and the Marriage of the Boy Heroine on the Renaissance Stage," *PMLA* 102 (1987): 29–41; Michael Shapiro, "Lady Mary Wroth Describes a 'Boy Actress,' " *Medieval and Renaissance Drama in England* 4 (1989): 187–94; and Shapiro, *Gender in Play on the Shakespearean Stage: Boy Heroines and Female Pages* (Ann Arbor; University of Michigan Press, 1995).

3. Phillipe Ariès's; *Centuries of Childhood: A Social History of Family Life* (New York: Random House, 1962) and Laurence Stone's *The Family, Sex and Marriage in England, 1500–1800* (London: Harper and Row, 1977) are much-quoted and now much-challenged examples. More recent sociological studies such as Linda Pollock's *Forgotten Children* (London: Cambridge University Press, 1983) indicate that everyday relations between children and their parents in the Renaissance were not radically different from today's.

4. See Richard DeMolen, "Erasmus on Childhood," *Erasmus of Rotterdam Society Yearbook* 2 (1982): 25–46, and "Childhood and the Sacraments in the Sixteenth Century," *Archiv für Reformationsgesicht* 66 (1975): 49–71. David Bergeron bases much of his study of James I, *Royal*

Family, Royal Lovers: King James of England and Scotland (Columbia: University of Missouri Press, 1991), on the assumption that the loss of children created lasting trauma within a family.

5. Riggs argues that, at the very least, Jonson had apparently already begun to imagine his son outside the generational split, to de-emphasize his own son's childishness in favor of an imagined adulthood. Ben had already hypothetically taken on the responsibilities of an adult as he was, in his father's absence, the oldest male in the household (95).

6. Robert Watson, *The Rest Is Silence: Death as Annihilation in the English Renaissance* (Berkeley: University of California Press, 1995), 36. Watson goes on to cite the "psychoanalytic commonplace" developed by D. W. Winnicott that "suggests that a compulsive interest in death reflects the early death of the self that was not acknowledged as such, leaving the adult to search continuously for some objective correlative to that repressed experience of personal erasure" (177).

7. Patrick Mahoney's meticulous comparative deconstruction of the two "genetic companion" epigrams, concludes (among other things) that the less intimate relationship implied in little Mary's epitaph represents a "defense of distanciation against the father's oedipal desires towards the daughter" ("Ben Jonson's 'best piece of *poetrie*,' " *American Imago* 37 [1980]: 68–82, 75). This is the type of reading that gives psychoanalytic criticism a bad name; however, it is plausible that some of Jonson's motivation in the case of Benjamin's epitaph is a "defensive" strategy.

8. Jonson, possibly aware of Francis Bacon's characterization of children not merely as legacies but as "hostages to fortune," may have seen his poetry the same way ("Of Marriage and Single Life," in *The Essays,* ed. John Pitcher [London: Penguin, 1985], 81). The pitfalls of this strategy, of course, continued to haunt Jonson; we revisit his struggle with the notion of posterity a quarter century later in his "Ode to Himself."

9. Gabriele Bernhard Jackson, *Vision and Judgment in Ben Jonson's Drama* (New Haven: Yale University Press, 1968), 1–2.

10. We should not, however, assume that Shakespeare's stage children lacked any resemblance to real children. Leah Marcus comments, "Shakespeare's young princes were not monstrous aberrations, but accurate reflections of the best that sixteenth-century education could accomplish," in *Childhood and Cultural Despair: A Theme and Variations in Seventeenth-Century Literature* (Pittsburgh: University of Pittsburgh Press, 1978), 7. The fact that poets could choose between a wide range of real-life examples of childhood personality lends further importance to choices they did make.

11. See Judith Gardiner, "Infantile Sexuality, Adult Critics and *Bartholomew Fair,*" *Literature and Psychology* 24 (1974): 124–32; Joseph Loewenstein, "The Jonsonian Corpulence: Or, the Poet as Mouthpiece," *English Literary History* 53 (1986): 491–518; E. Pearlman, "Ben Jonson: An Anatomy," *English Literary Renaissance* 9 (1979): 364–94; and Edmund Wilson, "Morose Ben Jonson" (1938), in *Ben Jonson: A Collection of Critical Essays,* ed. Jonas Barish (Englewood Cliffs, N.J.: Prentice-Hall, 1963): 60–74.

12. This bond extended to his studious monarch, the "best of poets" (Epigrams IV). William Blisset characterizes James as "a better uncle to his favourites than father to his sons. Like an avuncular dominie, King James was well-known for taking a pedagogical and sentimental interest in likely-looking young men" in "Your Majesty Is Welcome to a Fair," *The Elizabethan Theatre* 4 (1972): 80–105, 86.

13. Gerald Bentley, "A Good Name Lost: Jonson's Lament for S.P.," *Times Literary Supplement,* May 30, 1942: 276. Jonson also alludes, in *Christmas His Masque,* to the lucrative traffic in talented boys, when Venus, "a deaf tire-woman" offers her son Cupid for Christmas's production: "I could ha' had money enough for him, an I would ha' beene tempted, and ha' let him out by the weeke, to the King's Players: Master *Burbage* has beene about and about with me; and so has old Mr. *Hemings* too" (ll: 133–37).

14. Even if Brome was not himself an actor, he was probably part of the company that performed *Bartholomew Fair,* and would, through his close association as servant to the didactic

Jonson, have qualified as one of his unofficial "Schollars." See Alwin Thaler, "Was Richard Brome an Actor?" *MLN* 36 (1921): 88–91; and R. J. Kaufmann, *Richard Brome: Caroline Playwright* (New York: Columbia University Press, 1961), 35–46.

15. Jonas Barish notes in *The Anti-Theatrical Prejudice* (Berkeley: University of California Press, 1981) that concerns about the protean nature of acting and its dangers to the soul—based on the Platonic belief that you can become what you act—were common (80–131).

16. Katherine Eisaman Maus also notes the quotation that heads this chapter, from *Poetaster,* in which the unappreciated poet threatens to consign his poetic offspring to the fire ("To the Reader," 212–13) and argues that we should not mistake this metaphor for "womb envy;" it is "a claim that [Renaissance poets] are already possessed of the real thing" (*Inwardness and Theater in the English Renaissance* [Chicago: University of Chicago Press, 1995], 186). Watson suggests that Donne's lyrics and letters addressed to Magdalen Herbert, which imagine her as the "womb nurturing his poetry," reflect his attempt to counteract a morbid obsession with the mortality conferred on all men by their mothers (*The Rest Is Silence,* 243). Both metaphors—the possessive and the transcendant—seem present in Jonson's insistence that he mourns the boys as lost pieces of lyric or dramatic poetic progeny.

17. Michael Shapiro, "Audience vs. Dramatist in Jonson's *Epicoene* and Other Plays of the Children's Troupes," *ELR* 3 (1973): 400–417.

18. R. A. Foakes, "Tragedy at the Children's Theatres after 1600: A Challenge to the Adult Stage," *The Elizabethan Theatre* 2 (1970): 37–59.

19. Jardine, "Boy Actors, Female Roles, and Elizabethan Eroticism," 57.

20. In *Comic Theaters* (Athens: University of Georgia Press, 1986), William Gruber supports his argument that "the audience must have been contemplating the actor . . . as a sexual object," by relating an anecdote in which the sexually notorious Restoration actress Mrs. Barry provoked audience laughter as Cordelia with the line "Arm'd in my Virgin Innocence" (2). He assumed this to be a representative incident, and we may assume the same type of reactions may have occurred in the audiences of a mere generation earlier.

21. Cited in E. K. Chambers, *The Elizabethan Stage,* 4 vols. (Oxford: Oxford University Press, 1923), 2:34.

22. Another epigram of Jonson's (XC) presents a foolish lady-in-waiting (Mill) who uses her mistress's page as a "schoole" for lovemaking, but knows no better than to continue the affair into the boy's adulthood. "His face growing worse . . . both his body and face blowne up," notwithstanding, Mill has the poor taste to marry the page, "[a]nd it is hop'd that shee, like MILO, wull, / First bearing him a calfe, beare him a bull." The commonplace that boys are preferable to men for the sexual pleasure of both men and women is explicated; so, too, is the availability of subordinate boys to the sexual predations of adults. The pun on "bear" and "bull," too, evokes (as does *Epicoene*'s Tom Otter) the common equation of the public playhouses (often the site of bear- and bull-baitings) with sexual play, and with sex as an aggressive, animalistic act.

23. Watson, *Ben Jonson's Parodic Strategy: Literary Imperialism in the Comedies* (Cambridge: Harvard University Press, 1987), 201.

24. Such a reading need not deny the simple effect of suspenseful titillation: the audience enjoys the experience of indulging in erotic speculation about what would happen were such creatures actually to be sexually assaulted (and therefore exposed) onstage, while it is morally protected by the knowledge that such a spectacle will not happen. The *Bartholomew Fair* puppets offer similar (though probably more comic than erotic) titillation.

25. Peter Stallybrass argues in "Reading the Body and the Jacobean Theater of Consumption" that the transference of the genital to the oral was a Jacobean commonplace (*Renaissance Drama* 18 (1987): 121–48).

26. If we are to see Jonson as the benign protector of children, we must, of course, ignore George Chapman's later accusation: ". . . didst thou not put out / A boies Right eye that Croste thy mankind poute?" ("Invective . . . against Mr. Ben Johnson" [1624], *The Poems*

of George Chapman, ed. Phyllis Brooks Bartlett [New York: Modern Language Association, 1941]: 374–78, 29–30). Herford and Simpson believe most of the "Invective" is the result of envy and thus manufactured or exaggerated (10:692–97). An accusation of maiming a defenseless child would be in keeping with Chapman's frequent use of the poetic-progeny metaphor throughout "Invective," and also with the overkill that characterizes the poem in general. This is the only suggestion I have found that Jonson did not restrict his famous violent temper to physical equals.

27. " 'An essence that's not seen': The Primal Scene of Racism in *Othello,*" *SQ* 44 (1993): 304–24, 305.

28. I have found no historical references to notable failures by child actors onstage, but the anxieties expressed by theatrical pieces like this induction and by Cokes's inquiry to Leatherhead, "Do they [the puppets] use to play perfect? Are they never fluster'd?" (5.3.94–5), imply that the child actors were as prone to incompetence as the adults. Jonson's *Christmas His Masque,* Beaumont's *The Knight of the Burning Pestle,* Chapman's *The Gentleman Usher,* and Heywood's *The Four Prentices of London* also feature unruly child actors.

29. Shapiro's "Audience vs. Dramatist in Jonson's *Epicoene*" reads the play in the context of the history of the children's companies, not in the context of Jonson's career.

30. The element of surprise, of course, applies only to the play's spectators; the folio "Persons of the Play" lists Epicoene as "a young gentleman suppos'd the silent woman."

31. Of course, the actor playing Morose would also have been a boy, but Jonson emphasizes only Epicoene's protean aspects, and we have already seen how the boys were capable of highly naturalistic characterizations, particularly, we presume, in the case of old men. And in the play, the boy-character who "plays" Epicoene is "a gentleman's son" (5.4.205) and, as such, shares a class-based right to sexual rescue with the gentlewomen of the other plays.

32. Barish, *Ben Jonson and the Language of Prose Comedy* (Cambridge: Harvard University Press, 1960), 185.

33. Watson, *Ben Jonson's Parodic Strategy,* 172 ff; Peter Womack, *Ben Jonson* (London: Basil Blackwell, 1986), 43–47; see also Anne Barton, *Ben Jonson, Dramatist* (New York: Cambridge University Press, 1984); 222–24; and Leah Marcus, *The Politics of Mirth: Jonson, Herrick, Milton, Marvell, and the Defense of Holiday Pastimes* (Chicago: University of Chicago Press, 1986).

34. Bartholomaeus Anglicus, *Medieval Lore from Bartholomaeus Anglicus,* ed. Robert Steele (London: Chatle and Windus, 1907), 51–52, quoted in Marcus, *Childhood,* 11.

35. Marcus, *Childhood,* 14. We see a vivid reminder of the privileging of the childlike fool in the recent enthusiasm (and multiple awards) for a film about a childlike and preternaturally lucky retarded man, *Forrest Gump.*

36. The repetitious nature of early childhood speech would seem to evoke the "mad" rather than the foolish style; however, most happy children, while repetitious, are also loquacious in amusing and highly original ways that offer none of the unsettling pathos of a madman's monotony. Unhappy children, of course, are another matter.

37. In the various contemporary tracts that compare the body to the state—Edward Forset's *A Comparative Discourse of the Bodies Natural and Politique* (London, 1606), Andrew Boorde's *A Compendyous Regement or A Dyetary of Helth* (London, 1542), and Robert Underwood's *A New Anatomie. Wherein the Body of Man is Very Fitly and Aptly (Two Wayes) Compared: 1. To a Household; 2. To a Cittie* (London, 1605), for example—or that discuss the body as microcosm, excess as a state of being or type of disease is almost always considered preferable to want, more easily corrected, and less severely debilitating.

38. John Earle, in his *Microcosmographie* of 1628, praises children for the very qualities we laugh at in the adults of *Bartholomew Fair:* "His hardest labour is his tongue. . . . and he is best company with it when he can but prattle. . . . his game is our earnest: and his drummes, rattles and hobby-horses, but the Emblems, & mocking of mens businesse. . . . The older he grows, he is a stair lower from God" (quoted in Marcus, *Childhood,* 74).

39. Bartholomaeus Anglicus, quoted in Marcus, *Childhood,* 11.

40. R. B. Parker, "Themes and Staging of *Bartholomew Fair*," *University of Toronto Quarterly* 39 (1970): 293–309.

41. Given the frequency with which Jonson's poetic rivals threw his bricklayer past in his face, we can imagine that the poet felt more than ordinary resentment for the youthful *doppelgänger* that, like Cokes's "little long-coats," dogged his every career step.

42. One of the most blatant moments of theatrical self-reference occurs when Bartholomew Cokes visits the puppet stage, asking, "Which is your *Burbage,* now? . . . Your best actor. Your *Field?* (5.3.79–82)" Field is, of course, Nathan Field, who made a successful transition to the adult companies. Although we don't know which role he played, Field was certainly one of the actors in *Bartholomew Fair.* The joke would have been even funnier had Cokes been played by Field; since Field "presumably played Humfrey" in *The Knight of the Burning Pestle* six years earlier, it is plausible to think he played the similarly clueless, unlucky-in-love Cokes for the Lady Elizabeth's Servants (Chambers, *Elizabethan Stage,* 2:316).

43. Barish, "*Bartholomew Fair* and Its Puppets," *Modern Language Quarterly* 20 (1959): 11–12.

44. I'm reminded of the schoolyard game (probably now defunct in the current time of unisex dressing) in which one invited a clueless playmate to play "Dress-Up" and then flipped her skirt unceremoniously over her head. It was a ritual probably more annoying to any observing adults than to the participants and one that sounds considerably more perverted in the retelling than it actually was. Even in this era of child-abuse paranoia, children themselves still universally find hilarious the sight—and even the mention—of underpants.

45. Johan Huizinga's *Homo Ludens* is the most influential study of the play-element in culture (and specifically drama) and its roots in childhood (New York: Roy Publishers, 1950).

46. History itself offers a macabre coda to the questions of *Bartholomew Fair*'s farewell to the children's company: Frances Teague mentions in *The Curious History of* Bartholomew Fair (Lewisburg: Bucknell University Press, 1985) that the Hope Theater managed to remain open several years into the interregnum but closed at last in 1655 when, during an illegal bear-baiting, one of its bears killed a child (55).

47. The transition from *Bartholomew Fair,* which is ambivalent about festivity, to the unambiguously antifestive *The Devil Is An Ass* becomes clearer in this context.

48. It is safe to assume that Benjamin ended up in a mass plague grave and had no formal funeral, or at least none that Jonson could have attended.

49. The puppets are like Jacques Lacan's "Void" in that they remind us of "the ghost, that image which can catch the soul . . . unawares when someone's departure from this life has not been accompanied by the rites that it calls for." See *The Four Fundamental Concepts of Psychoanalysis,* ed. Jacques-Alain Miller, trans. Alan Sheridan (New York: Penguin, 1981), 38.

From *The Reformer* (1748)

EDMUND BURKE

Ben Jonson, of all the Comic Writers is the only one in whom unite all the Graces of *true Comedy* without the monstrous Blemishes that stain and disfigure the Merit of the others. He has Wit sufficient, Humour in abundance, and a Judgment not to be matched by any, since or before him; his Morals are sound, and the way he takes to attack Vice, and Folly, the most efficacious that can be thought to overcome them. In short, had this Man lived in the times of *Grecian* Learning, he might have stood up for the Laurel against the most excellent of them; but his Writings, instead of doing Honour to our Age, will always be a Proof of its Degeneracy, that could neglect such delicious Feasts as his happy Muse has provided for us, to feed on the Garbage of vile, and uninstructive Authors.

This passage appears in issue number 2 of the young Burke's periodical, dated February 4, 1748.

Impotence and the Satirist's Vocation

KATHARINE EISAMAN MAUS

In the fourth act of Ben Jonson's *Volpone,* Celia and Bonario complain in court of Corvino's attempts to prostitute Celia to Volpone, and of Volpone's attempted rape. Initially the *avocatori* empaneled to judge the case are inclined to believe their tale despite its strangeness since they are both "of unreproved name" while Corbaccio and Corvino are more dubiously regarded. As the scene proceeds, however, the lawyer Voltore skillfully demolishes their credibility. To their accusations of secret sexual sin he opposes a counteraccusation: Celia and Bonario are adulterous lovers, guilty of the outrages they wish to fasten upon others.

To support his claim, Voltore produces several witnesses. Corvino testifies to Celia's lasciviousness in lurid detail. She is, he announces, "a whore / Of most hot exercise, more than a partridge" who "neighs like a jennet" (4.5.116–18). Although the judges express shock at Corvino's graphic language, his vividness strengthens the plausibility of Voltore's claims, as does Lady Politic's apparently spontaneous deposition immediately following. Then Voltore submits his most telling piece of evidence.

Volpone is brought in, as impotent.

VOLTORE: Here, here,
The testimony comes that will convince,
And put to utter dumbness their bold tongues!
See here, grave fathers, here's the ravisher,
The rider on men's wives, the great imposter,
The grand voluptuary. Do you not think
These limbs should affect venery? Or these eyes
Covet a concubine? pray you mark these hands;
Are they not fit to stroke a lady's breasts?
Perhaps he doth dissemble!

From Katharine Eisaman Maus, *Inwardness and Theater* (Chicago: University of Chicago Press, 1995), 128–57, and adapted by the author for this volume. Reprinted with permission of the University of Chicago Press.

BONARIO: So he does.
VOLTORE: Would you have him tortured?
BONARIO: I would have him proved.

(4.6.23–30),

Volpone's invalid body, Voltore insists, constitutes evidence to which Bonario and Celia cannot possibly reply. In this drama of accusation and counteraccusation, something finally seems decisively to favor one side over the other. The fact that Volpone himself does not speak enhances the credibility of his testimony, which seems to transcend or precede mere rhetoric in its physical factuality and obviousness. The judges, who have become increasingly impatient with Celia and Bonario in the course of the trial, are thoroughly won over. Without further delay they commit Celia and Bonario to custody and request that "the old gentleman be returned with care" (4.6.60).

The trial scene sets up a rhetorically competitive situation conventionally imagined in terms of phallic rivalry. In *Volpone,* however, triumph is ironically achieved by a move that seems to overturn the implicit terms upon which antagonism takes place: by ceding the very grounds that would normally be in question. When a reputation for sexual mastery is relinquished to Bonario, he loses his case rather than winning it. The audience knows, of course, that the outcome of the trial is wrong, and that the "testimonies" Voltore offers are fraudulent. But Jonson has gone to some trouble to emphasize the coherence and plausibility of Voltore's arguments. When Corvino confesses himself a cuckold, or Volpone presents himself to the court as impotent, they enact an abdication of masculine power and privilege so astonishing that unless they are telling the truth their behavior seems inexplicable.

Not surprisingly, the *avocatori* fail to realize that they are witnessing a bizarre charade. They believe that Volpone's decrepitude is "right before their eyes," and that physical evidence is a better guide to truth than mere argument. Of course, Voltore is only pretending to abandon the indefiniteness of rhetoric for the certainties of brute physical facts. Not the sight of Volpone's body but Voltore's accompanying speech, with its rhetorical questions and leaden ironies, creates the appearance of irrefutability. Bonario attempts to bring the case back into the domain of the arguable by answering one of Voltore's sarcastic rhetorical questions in the affirmative.

Perhaps he doth dissemble!
BONARIO: So he does.
VOLTORE: Would you have him tortured?
BONARIO: I would have him proved.

The surfaces of the body are always capable of being theatricalized, so that while they can be made to seem absolutely trustworthy, they are never actually so. Unlike, say, Anne in *Richard III,* Bonario remains aware of, and continues to insist upon, the possibility of fakery.

Since torture could not be applied to those presumed crippled or infirm, Voltore risks a sarcastic rhetorical question, designed to make Bonario's zeal for truth appear sadistic. In fact, Bonario replies, he wishes only that Volpone be "proved." Yet Voltore has succeeded in discrediting Bonario, and the judges ignore his request. Thus it might seem pointless to dwell upon what Bonario's "proof" might involve, were it not that similar scenarios recur in Jonson's later plays. The entire last act of *Epicoene* is a mock divorce proceeding in which Morose, like Volpone, finds it in his interest to admit the inadmissible.

> MOROSE: I am no man, Ladies.
> ALL: How!
> MOROSE: Utterly unabled in nature, by reason of frigidity,
> to perform the duties or any of the least office of a
> husband.
> (5.4.38–41)

Like Bonario, Epicoene insists that Morose's confession is an act of language, and therefore falsifiable, rather than the "manifest frigidity" he pretends.

> EPICOENE: Tut, a device, a device, this! It smells rankly,
> ladies. A mere comment of his own.
> TRUEWIT: Why, if you suspect that, ladies, you may have
> him searched.
> (5.4.46–48).

Finally, at the climax of *Bartholomew Fair,* Dionysius Puppet seems triumphantly to provide undeniable evidence of the deficiency to which Volpone and Morose had laid claim.

> BUSY: . . . my main argument against you is that you are
> an abomination, for the male among you putteth on the
> apparel of the female, and the female of the male.
>
> PUPPET DIONYSIUS: It is your old stale argument against the players, but it will
> not hold against the puppets, for we have neither male nor
> female amongst us. And that thou may'st see, if thou wilt,
> like a malicious purblind zeal as thou art!

The puppet takes up his garment.

EDGEWORTH: By my faith, there he has answered you, friend, by plain demonstration.

(5.5.101–14).

It seems worthwhile to ask, therefore, what is at stake when Bonario asks that Volpone be "proved": what would constitute the proof of Voltore's assertion and how that proof would be obtained.

In fact, Bonario is requesting, in vain, a regular procedure for ascertaining impotence in court cases. Although an individual's impotence might well become an issue in a rape trial, like Volpone's, in early modern Europe sexual dysfunction more commonly came under official scrutiny in the context of a divorce proceeding. Such proceedings were under the purview of the ecclesiastical court system, which dealt with all kinds of sexual and marital irregularities:[1] actionable offenses included conceiving a child in advance of a wedding ceremony, indulging in sex outside of marriage, choosing to live apart from one's spouse even for the most pressing economic reasons, and impugning another person's sexual reputation. Incurable sexual incapacity that predated the wedding concerned the ecclesiastical court because the impotent individual could provide his or her partner neither with "solace," defined as penetrative sex, nor with the children that would result from that penetration. Since these two goods were imagined to be the main benefits of marriage, the unimpaired partner could bring suit claiming that an agreement he or she had entered into in good faith could not be performed.

In England, impotence was the only ground upon which a validly contracted marriage might be annulled. Thus the policing of the marriage bond required the development of a definition of impotence, and ways of confirming it in particular cases. According to canon law, "impotence" in women meant neither the inability to experience sexual pleasure, nor infertility, but a physical abnormality that rendered penetration impossible. Jonson attributes this kind of impotence to Queen Elizabeth when he tells William Drummond that "she had a membrana on her that made her incapable of man, though for her delight she tried many."[2] In men, "impotence" could refer either to a genital malformation or to an inability, even in the absence of obvious deformity, to sustain an erection, vaginally penetrate a woman, and emit semen. One consequence of these definitions was that impotence was charged far more commonly against men than against women. The condition was presumed to be permanent if married persons had cohabited for three years without being able to consummate their union.

Claims of impotence were often contested, since the party accused of the disability was normally prohibited from remarrying, and often became a subject of ridicule. When the assertion was undisputed, on the other hand, judges might suspect collusion—an effort between two warring spouses to uncouple themselves by any means possible. In either case, some evidence was required to establish the truth or falsity of the charge. The nature of the proof varied. In France, where accusations of, and anxiety about, impotence seem to have become extremely common in the sixteenth and seventeenth centuries, the courts developed ever more baroque procedures, the most notorious of which was the "trial by congress."[3] This test required husband and wife to lie in a curtained bed together for an hour or two, while court officers waited in an adjoining room. Afterwards the curtains were opened and the couple was investigated for signs that sexual intercourse had taken place. Unsurprisingly, few men successfully proved their virility under such circumstances, especially since their partners had no reason to cooperate and often actively resisted their advances.

In England, trials by congress, or any other procedure to make a man demonstrate his potency in the courtroom, were considered uncanonical and obscene.[4] Usually English ecclesiastical courts relied upon "compurgation": the accused might clear himself by bringing seven "oath-helpers"—friends, relatives, or neighbors—to swear to the truth of his deposition. Since the English procedure, unlike the French one, threw the burden of proof heavily upon the plaintiff, English impotence cases were extremely rare. Both in England and on the Continent, however, judges could insist that both a man accused of impotence and his wife undergo physical examinations by qualified physicians or midwives: to assess whether and to what degree the man was impaired, and to ascertain the woman's continued virginity.

This, then, is what Bonario means when he asks that Volpone be "proved." Although Bonario and Voltore are opponents in the courtroom, Bonario's request participates in the same assumptions about the nature of evidence that Voltore uses to persuade the judges. Both men maintain that there is an undeniable fact-of-the-body that can somehow be made publicly manifest, and that the discovery of this fact will provide the resolution of the case. The difference between what Voltore offers the court, the display of Volpone's limp body, and what Bonario demands, the display of Volpone's limp penis, is only a difference of procedural stringency, not a logical difference or a disagreement about what "truth" might entail.

In practice, however, supposedly irrefutable bodily facts were exceedingly difficult to establish. Tests of impotence were notoriously liable to error. The physical examination of supposedly deficient men usually yielded ambiguous results, except in cases of gross abnormality. Even then, they could be untrustworthy. Jonson may well have known about "Bury's case," which generated a minor scandal and a number of ribald jokes at the end of the sixteenth century. In 1561, a John Bury of Devon had been accused of impotence by his wife, Willmott. Prior to the marriage a horse had kicked Bury in the testicles, so that "nothing but a little one of them remained . . . of the size of a small bean" (State Trials, 2.850). Later both parties remarried—in Bury's case, apparently despite the terms of the annulment, since impotent persons were supposed to be debarred from marrying again. Bury's second wife then gave birth to a son, while his original wife was still alive. In 1599, the son's right to his father's estate was challenged by one Webber, next in line to Bury's inheritance. Webber did not argue that the second wife must have conceived the son with someone other than Bury, for English common law customarily considered all children born during a marriage to be the offspring of their mothers' husbands. Instead he claimed that the production of issue showed that "the holy church was deceived in its first judgment."[5] Since the sentence of divorce was based on spurious evidence, Webber maintained, Bury actually remained wedded to Willmott, and the later marriages of both Bury and Willmott were invalid. In consequence, Bury's son was a bastard, excluded from the line of inheritance. Webber's conundrum occasioned "many arguments and great deliberations." Eventually Bury *fils* won the case on appeal, on the grounds that although his father's second marriage was "voidable"—that is, it could have been declared invalid during Bury's lifetime—it had not actually been annulled, and "remaineth a marriage until it be dissolved."[6]

If these kinds of complications could ensue even when the defendant was virtually a eunuch, they were all the more likely in the more common situation, in which the man was apparently *aptus ad generandum* but seemed incapable of intercourse with his wife. The evidence in the case of women was just as questionable. Wives who claimed that their marriages had never been consummated needed to verify their virginity. Renaissance physicians disagreed, however, over whether that fact could be discovered by physical examination. Some authorities claimed that in virgins, the hymen was always intact. But other influential experts pointed out that all kinds of accidents short of sexual intercourse—including the physical examination itself—could rupture a delicate membrane. A few physicians, notably the important obstetricians Ambroise Paré and Jacques Guillemeau, insisted that the hymen was a mere fiction, declaring that they had never encountered one in the course of dissecting thousands of female corpses.[7]

The inquiries that accompanied annulment proceedings compared in their indignity and invasiveness, with the bodily searches for the "devil's teat" commonly conducted in witchcraft trials, the place where the witch was supposed to have given suck to her demonic familiar. In both cases, the crucial events were unwitnessed or unwitnessable, known with certainty only by the accused and by supernatural agencies that could not participate in court.

AVOCATORE 1: What witnesses have you, to make good your report?
BONARIO: Our consciences.
CELIA: And heaven, that never fails the innocent.
AVOCATORE 4: These are no testimonies.

(*Volpone* 4.6.15–19)

As a way out of this dilemma, physical evidence was sought with the idea that it would provide clear, conclusive answers to difficult questions. In both cases, the accused's secrets were supposed to have stamped themselves unequivocally on the material of his or her body: silently proclaiming themselves in a misplaced or supernumerary nipple, a flaccid member, a torn or missing hymen. In both cases, that definitiveness turned out to be illusory, as supposedly stolid flesh evanesced and transmuted before the investigators' very eyes.

Nonetheless, the relationship between the material proof and the question being investigated differed significantly in the two kinds of case. In the witchcraft trial, the "witch's teat" was merely a sign that referred to a wicked intention hidden further within. In the impotence trial, by contrast, the body was a subject of inquiry for its own sake. The less the mind was likely to have involved itself in the body's vagaries, the better the "proof." In the 1613 Essex divorce case, for instance, the Earl claimed that he was unable to consummate his union with Frances Howard, although he had "oftentimes felt motions and provocations of the flesh, tending to copulation" with women other than his wife (*State Trials,* 2.787). When asked why he thought he suffered so specific a disability, he ascribed it to his dislike of Frances:

> when they were alone, she reviled him, and miscalled him, terming him cow, and coward, and beast; and he added, that she was as bitter a woman as any in the world: which things so cooled his courage, that he was far from knowing, or endeavoring to know her (*State Trials,* 2.819).

Because such remarks suggested that "*vitium animi non corporis*" [the defect was of the spirit, not of the body] (*State Trials,* 2.814), the ecclesiastical authorities balked at granting an annulment. The undoubted fact that Essex and his wife loathed one another was irrelevant to the question of whether they ought to be allowed to dissolve the marital bond. Only King James I's aggressive interference secured the divorce, over the strenuous objections of George Abbott, Archbishop of Canterbury.

The popular nickname for the ecclesiastical tribunal, the "bawdy court," resentfully captured what was seen as the habitual prurience of its procedures. In *The Court and Character of King James,* Anthony Weldon complains that the Essex trial generated "a learned discourse in the science of bawdry . . . wherein were so many beastly expressions, as for modesty sake I will not recite them."[8] Weldon's delicacy seems rather disingenuous, given the scurrilous details he lavishly proffers in the paragraphs immediately following. Yet his curious combination of voyeurism with compunctions about privacy and decorum is in fact entirely characteristic of the proceedings he describes. The scopophilia of the annulment trial was carefully circumscribed. Even in France, the warring couple was sequestered in a curtained bed. In the Essex trial, Weldon reports, when Frances Howard needed to prove a long-lost virginity, she claimed to be overwhelmed by feminine modesty. This demureness seemed only natural to the court, which permitted her to veil her face during the examination: a subterfuge that enabled her to send a substitute to endure the examination in her place. A similar squeamishness is suggested by the English courts' reliance upon compurgation, in cases in which the seven oath-helpers—usually male friends and neighbors of the accused husband—were patently unqualified to testify.

Thus impotence proceedings restricted their territory in two controversial respects. Their first self-limitation was to define sexual inadequacy in a purely physical way, despite the acknowledged tendency in these matters for the state of one's mind to impinge upon the state of one's body. Their second self-limitation was a refusal fully to display even this restricted "truth." These proceedings gestured toward, but at the same time recoiled from, a public revelation of the "privates," and hindered their own inquiry by failing to follow through upon their initial voyeuristic impulse.

This halfhearted inquisitiveness, and the insurmountable impracticalities of obtaining clearcut confirmation, compelled a dependence upon hearsay that was made to seem more blatant by the initial insistence upon decisive material evidence. Obscurely motivated by loyalty, hope of gain, or desire for revenge, servants offered the court their inferences about their masters and mistresses:

> she and the lady's chamber-maid turned down the bedclothes, and there they saw the places where the earl and lady had lain, but . . . there was such a distance between the two places, and such a hill between them, that this deponent is persuaded that they did not touch one another that night. (*State Trials,* 2.791)

Siblings and cousins likewise took their turns speculating about the sex lives of their kin, even while plainly acknowledging their ignorance of the facts. In the Essex divorce trial, George Abbott worried over a report he heard from "a good friend" outside the courtroom:

> that my lord of Essex, on that Sunday morning, having five or six captains and gentlemen of worth in his chamber, and speech being made of his inability, rose out of his bed, and taking up his shirt, did shew them all so able and extraordinarily sufficient matter, that they all cried out shame on his lady. (*State Trials,* 2.822)

Essex brandished his "extraordinarily sufficient matter," but not where its display could count as evidence, so that for Abbott, "matter" was frustratingly displaced into the elusiveness of an anecdote overheard.

The impotence trial thus began to resolve itself into a structure also familiar in treason and witchcraft inquisitions: there was an accusation abroad, but the hidden location in which responsibility actually lodged seemed frustratingly difficult to specify. In the ecclesiastical courts, accusations of sexual misbehavior typically attracted countersuits of "defamation," a word that significantly could refer either to the formal charge of misconduct itself—the court's indictment—or to a malicious slur irresponsibly cast upon a neighbor. In the sixteenth and early seventeenth century the number of defamation suits skyrocketed both in the ecclesiastical and the common-law courts, as innocent parties pursued cases, sometimes at considerable cost, as a way of publicly clearing their names. The hypersensitivity of early modern English men and women to social perceptions was exacerbated not only by the practical importance of a good reputation for transacting business or living in peace with one's neighbors, but by an acute sense of how easy and at times how expedient it could be to accuse others of secret sexual sin. In *Volpone,* as we have already seen, the only way for the guilty to evade punishment is to slander Celia and Bonario. Likewise in *Epicoene,* Morose's desperate desire to be rid of his wife encourages the groundless degradation of Epicoene's character by Daw and LaFoole.

On the one hand, then, reputation was dangerously detachable from fact, as Jonson had reason to know from personal experience. "Every accusation doth not condemn," he writes from prison in 1605, in trouble for his collaboration on *Eastward Ho.* "And there must go much more to the making of a guilty man, than rumor."[9] On the other hand, despite every precaution, the ecclesiastical courts often had nothing but "public fame" to rely upon in assessing the guilt of the parties that came before it; moreover, public fame was essential to their usual punishments, shaming rituals of the kind Corvino is eventually sentenced to undergo at the end of *Volpone.* If Jonson is more interested in a relatively uncommon annulment proceeding than in the much more frequent prosecutions of bigamy and bastardy, it is perhaps because the evidentiary problems intrinsic to the "discovery" of sexual secrets are especially acute here, far more so than in cases where two living wives or an infant bastard might be presented in the courtroom. In the impotence proceeding, what advertised itself as a straightforward inquiry into hidden truths, insisting upon the most definite material evidence, almost inevitably became an exercise in the construction of reputation. What advertised itself as a discovery of what was not externally perceptible turned out actually merely to depend upon and elaborate conjecture and surmise. In such cases the difference between fact and reputation was obscure; so that fact seemed nothing more than a particularly convincing form of reputation.

Both the procedures for ascertaining impotence and the dilemmas posed by those procedures were, in their general form, of persistent interest to Ben Jonson. To an unusual degree, Jonson's authorial tactics are closely concerned with the way reputation—his own and other people's—could be controlled and manipulated. Ambitious for personal fame, desirous of associating his own eminence with the unquestioned "fact" of his literary merit, Jonson simultaneously recognized and excoriated the sordid, contingent means by which reputation could be established: by flattering the powerful, by pandering to the taste of undiscerning audiences, by stealing other people's ideas. Like the judges in the ecclesiastical courts, who insisted upon the unreliability and the trustworthiness of reputation at the same time, the want of an alternative seems to have forced Jonson into a self-contradiction.

In the epigrams and in the comedies, Jonson favors the conventional image of the satirist as one who "discovers" a hidden truth by peeling off layers of obscurity or deceit. Asper, his mouthpiece in *Every Man Out of His Humour,* promises that

> with an arméd and resolvéd hand
> I'll strip the ragged follies of the time
> Naked as at their birth.
> (induction, lines 16–18)

The purpose is not always to shame the person or thing thus denuded: in his prefatory letter to *Volpone* Jonson promises to "raise the despised head of poetry again, and stripping her out of those rotten and base rags wherewith the times have adulterated her form, restore her to her primitive habit, feature, and majesty." But all such passages offer the uncovered body, whether degraded or glorious, as a model of truth, just as it was in the Renaissance divorce court. The satirist, in other words, is a literary equivalent of the judicial examiner, expertly stripping the body of the accused. At the same time, the nature of this revelation, in the playhouse as in the courtroom, is uncertain. In the final lines of *Volpone,* the hero announces to the stymied judges that "the fox shall here uncase," removes his disguise, and flatly informs them of his own and his associates' wrongdoing (5.12.85). On the one hand, this resolution seems to provide the kind of "proof" Bonario had originally demanded and Voltore had pretended to offer, an unanswerably veracious exposure of the criminal body.

> AVOCATORE 1: The knot is now undone by miracle.
> AVOCATORE 2: Nothing can be more clear.
> (5.12.95–96)

On the other hand, Volpone's divestiture is a metaphor for confession, not a replacement for it: he reveals a plot that does not primarily reside in the material of the body and that could not have been discovered without his cooperation.

Considered as striptease, moreover, Volpone's unmasking hardly satisfies. Early in his career, Jonson virtually invented ways to translate satire from a nondramatic to a dramatic form: he *staged* satiric exposure. But this exposure was performed in a medium associated not with undressing but with an amplification of the importance of attire, the covering of the actor's body with the costume that indicated his dramatic identity. Moreover, Jonson could not literally strip and exhibit the bodies of fools and knaves, because

English Renaissance standards of theatrical decorum, more stringent than our own, did not permit genitalia to be displayed on the public stage. The recognition scenes at the end of *Epicoene* and of *Bartholomew Fair,* and perhaps at the end of *Volpone* as well, jokily conflate satiric revelation with obscene exhibition, but at the same time they shy away from that exhibition, metonymically removing a jacket or a wig, hoisting a garment only when there is nothing to see. The self-limiting voyeurism of Jonson's satiric comedy resembles and shares its rationale with that of the ecclesiastical courts, simultaneously violating and insisting upon the boundary between public and private domains, displaying and concealing secrets by the same theatrical gestures.

As in the impotence trial, the body cannot be fully shown, and even if it could be, what that display could "prove" would be open to dispute. Thus the physical model of revelation-by-making-naked seems inadequate even at the moment at which it is melodramatically evoked. On other grounds as well its very irresistibility continues to raise troubling questions. Throughout his career Jonson was deeply interested in the way human beings helplessly revealed themselves in their bodily demeanor. "Do we not see, if the mind languish, the members are dull?" Jonson writes in *Discoveries.* "Look upon an effeminate person: his very gait confesseth him" (950–53). The word "confesseth" suggests that the sissy's body, like the body of the impotent, testifies involuntarily and therefore utterly reliably to its shameful secrets. Yet the relation between the "confession" and the "secret" is, typically, peculiar. Since the man's gait is what attracts Jonson's contemptuous attention, allowing him to classify the man as effeminate in the first place, it is logically circular to see that gait as *revelatory* of anything. Rather the man's gait *constitutes* his effeminacy, which does not need to be discovered because it is already on display. The effeminate person is so, that is, "all the way down": there is no discrepancy between surface and depth. In the world Jonson provisionally imagines here, in fact, inwardness as we have seen it elaborated by other writers would not exist. There would be no difference between what is true about a person and what is socially discernible through the material of the body: through manifest tics, gestures, tones of voice, unconscious habits.

In this wholly transparent or legible social world, deception would seem to be an impossibility. But of course, Jonson's comedies exhibit worlds in which deception is not only feasible but rampant, worlds inhabited by men and women who have learned to profit from the fissure between truth and what is thought to be true. How can this be the case? Often Jonson reconciles his ideal of transparency with the fact of opacity by attributing the success of his frauds to the greed, egoism, or stupidity of their victims. Thus Mosca and Volpone wonder at the success of their endeavor:

> Too much light blinds 'em, I think. Each of them
> Is so possessed and stuffed with his own hopes,
> That anything unto the contrary,

Never so true, or never so apparent,
Never so palpable, they will resist it.
(5.2.23–27)

In *The Alchemist* the creakiness of the scheme is even more blatant: the "venter tripartite" succeeds by so efficiently colluding with the gulls' wishful narcissism that they are willing to ignore its flagrant implausibilities. The responsibility for deception, then, partly shifts from the Machiavellian deceiver to the persons he swindles, whose desperate collusion with their own victimization becomes an important subject of Jonsonian satire.

Even while the satirist claims to be stripping the targets of his scorn, then, he simultaneously insists that, like Hans Christian Andersen's emperor, they were always wholly visible. What the satirist effects is less an actual exposure than an adjustment in interpretive perspective. If the nakedness of the satiric object is located in the eye of the beholder, its "uncasing" is a kind of optical illusion. But so too, then, may be the apparent truthfulness thus achieved. Jonson is continually accused of libel, of maliciously defaming rather than guilelessly divesting his satiric objects. When Dekker, for instance, replies to Jonson's *Poetaster* in *Satiro-mastix,* he does so by mocking Jonson's outlook and motives. What Jonson represents as self-evident and impartial, Dekker represents as self-promoting and tendentious. Dekker strips Jonson of his pretensions just as Jonson had tried to strip Dekker: the subtitle of Dekker's counterblast is *The Untrussing of the Humourous Poet.*

In his combination of truculent authorial self-assertiveness with a scarcely concealed nervousness about the sources of his authority, Jonson resembles the religious polemicists I earlier associated with the development of the stage machiavel. He claims to be uncovering brute material facts, but discoverer and discovered, prestigious examiner and denuded examinee, always seem perilously close to switching places. In such a world, all the normal appurtenances of respectability, simply because they are inevitably mere appurtenances, have the potential suddenly to convert into their opposites.

AVOCATORE 2: The young man's fame was ever fair and honest.
VOLTORE: So much more full of danger is his vice,
That can beguile so, under shade of virtue.
(*Volpone* 4.5.60–62)

Certainly Jonson's manipulative protagonists participate in the same complex of epistemological uncertainties that other "machiavels," like Shakespeare's Richard III or Kyd's Hieronimo, learn to exploit and must endure.

What distinguishes Jonson from Thomas Kyd, or from the Shakespeare of *Richard III* (though not, perhaps, from the Marlowe of *Jew of Malta*) is his interest in the economic conditions that enable such uncertainties; in particular, in the relationship between material prosperity and the possibility of bodily secretiveness. Acquisitiveness, unlike other forms of self-assertion, does not necessarily demand an audience; nor do the sensuous pleasures of consumption need to be witnessed in order to be actual. Kyd imagines worthy underlings challenging a decadent ruling class for the right to various forms of publicly acknowledged power and prestige. Shakespeare's Richard struggles for, and wins, England's preeminent public role. By contrast, Jonson imagines people of various class origins recognizing that if they were rich enough, they could live a life of carnal pleasure that could remain entirely apart from public acknowledgment. The courtroom scam in *Volpone* works because the *avocatori* rely, probably without fully realizing it, upon the intuition that it is normally in one's interest to protect one's reputation, even while Volpone's scheme ingeniously ruptures the connection between social status and personal gratification, both for himself and for his gulls.

In fact, the distinction Volpone makes between a private bodily truth and a publicly accepted version of bodily truth is so counterintuitive that he cannot himself keep it securely in mind. When he attempts to seduce Celia, his phallic pride erupts incongruously and disastrously. He assaults her at the moment when he becomes convinced that she will "Think me cold, / Frozen and impotent, *and so report me*" (3.7.259–60; my italics). He forgets at this heated juncture that his entire charade depends upon presenting himself as frozen and impotent, and that if Celia were to inform Corvino or anyone else of his sexual prowess, his profitable game would be up. Volpone cannot bear to think of others condescending to his bodily incapacity, even though that incapacity works to his advantage. He cannot help but attempt to dazzle a real or imagined onlooker: Mosca, Celia, "the great Valois," even when bidding for their admiration works against his own best interests. His theatrical gifts are rooted as much in a love of self-display as in a penchant for deception, and thus his very triumphs bear the seeds of his eventual downfall.

Nonetheless, the possibility of a life of cloistered self-indulgence, a possibility upon which Volpone inconsistently capitalizes, interested Jonson deeply.

> What should I do,
> But cocker up my genius, and live free
> To all delights my fortune calls me to?
> (*Volpone* 1.1.70–72)

Almost alone among his contemporaries, Jonson considers how the possession of wealth provides not merely competitive, novel ways to impress others (what Jonson in *To Penshurst* calls "envious show"), but the means to "live free," to opt out of the activities of a community altogether. Against this kind of threat to social cohesion, even the most pointless forms of conspicuous consumption seem almost reassuring: reassuring because conspicuous, because therefore socially available and responsive to the opinions of other people. Egotistical and fundamentally gregarious, Volpone cannot finally bear the disgraceful solitude to which his own acquisitive logic condemns him. His impotence may not be "true," bodily impotence, but it is its social equivalent. At the same time, the very gratuitousness of Volpone's self-betrayal suggests that another person of different temperament—more shameless, more misanthropic, or more insensitive—might succeed where he fails: *Sejanus's* sinister Tiberius, perhaps, or *Epicoene*'s chilly Dauphine.[10]

Perhaps such entirely private characters, able to indulge themselves in nameless unsupervised pleasures, fascinated Jonson so persistently because they are so deeply subversive of his literary endeavor. To the extent that someone might wholly rebuff another's scrutiny, wholly disregard another's censure, satire becomes impossible. The effectiveness of satiric excoriation, like the effectiveness of the ecclesiastical courts, depends upon a consensus about what is shameful, and a collective fear of being publicly humiliated. Ideally, in fact, this consensus should be so unquestioned, so automatic, that it seems not to be a social artifact at all, but a natural truth or brute fact about human beings. A shameless person, defying such unanimity or even devising ways to exploit it for gain, challenges the inevitability of consensus, insinuating the contingency and fragility of a given social arrangement.

Thus it is not surprising that *Epicoene,* a play about a recluse, should become Jonson's fullest treatment of the implicit, troubled analogy between the satirist's revelatory theater and the ecclesiastical judge's revelatory courtroom. I shall argue that Jonson makes the conundrum of Morose's marital fitness a kind of metonymy for far more general problems of sexual identity and theatrical representation in Jacobean London. The setting and plot of the play encourages Jonson to confront not merely the relatively limited epistemological problems attendant upon the impotence trial, but the difficulty of establishing any kind of ground for sexual supervision or discipline, and hence for the satirist's endeavor, in a heterogeneous urban world.

Epicoene stages a conflict between two ways of imagining the marriage bond and, by extension, of imagining sexuality generally, each of which receives some institutional support from early modern English marriage customs. Morose's assumption that marriage is compatible with seclusion was theoretically endorsed both by canon and common law, which required for a valid marriage merely a promise passed between a couple, followed by sexual consummation. No public ceremony, no consent of kin, and no witnesses were necessary. At variance with this private conception of the marital relationship, both in *Epicoene* and in early modern England generally, is a conception of marriage as a social institution of interest to, and subject to regulation by, the larger community.[11] Ian Donaldson has suggested that the middle acts of *Epicoene* stage one such method of social regulation: the influx of noisy wedding "guests" constitutes, he claims, a *charivari* or social expression of comic outrage at an ill-suited match.[12] Of course, the parodic ecclesiastical proceedings with which the play concludes invoke another, more elaborately ceremonious, way in which the community systematically exercises its authority over the marital household.[13]

These two conceptions of marriage, at odds with one another throughout the play, are also occultly related. Anne Barton has remarked that it is strange that Morose, who affects to hate noise and people, should live in the bustling commercial center of Europe's biggest city. But where else would Morose live? Early seventeenth-century London, as Jonson recognized, provided at least for the well-to-do not merely the possibility of manipulating one's social *persona,* but the possibility of simply dispensing with it altogether. Morose's possession of a modest fortune enables him to indulge peculiarities unthinkable in the limited confines of a village. The labor pool is large enough, for instance, that for the right price one might conceivably obtain a silent barber, a servant willing to converse in sign language and wear tennis-court socks, construction workers capable of building a room with double walls and treble ceilings. At the same time, for a person of Morose's independent means, the city diminishes pressures for social participation and conformity. In a large, heterogeneous community, the opinions of one's neighbors are likely to be far less intimidatingly uniform than in a small village. Thus in seventeenth-century London, social historians have found, *charivari* was a distinctly rustic survival: when urbanites became the butt of such humor, they were more likely to file suit for defamation than blushingly to reform their ways. For similar reasons, the effectiveness of the ecclesiastical courts' regulation of sexual behavior varied inversely with the size of the communities over which the courts attempted surveillance.[14] Procedures and sanctions dependent upon "common fame" fail when the community grows so large that nothing is common to all of it. The rituals of compurgation, which depend upon people's unwillingness to risk manifestly perjuring themselves before their friends and neighbors, break down in London: dubious personages lurk outide the courtroom, offering to serve as oath-helpers on any matter whatsoever, for a price. Ecclesiastical punishments, shaming rituals designed to be intensely humiliating in the intimate context of village life, are less vividly experienced in the looser urban setting, not to mention easier to evade altogether.

Morose's constantly frustrated desire for silence and solitude is hardly shared by the rest of the cast of *Epicoene,* who form overlapping, interconnected pairs or groups: the Collegiate Ladies, the Otters, the wits, Daw-and-LaFoole. Nonetheless, his particular form of absurdity constitutes both an opportunity and a caution for his sometimes obsessively sociable colleagues.[15] *Epicoene* concerns itself, as P. K. Ayers notes, with members of an urban gentry class deracinated from their original rural power base and responsibilities, whose moral code "owe[s] little to traditional social patterns or sources of value."[16] Like Morose, profoundly dependent upon the community from which he withdraws, "polite society" requires the resources of the large indiscriminate and undiscriminating population against which it may then define itself. The same breakdown of public discipline that permits Morose's idiosyncratic withdrawal likewise allows the flowering of contingent, voluntarily assumed statuses and social affiliations that prove at least as significant as formal, publicly ascertainable institutions for the production of the characters' various identities. Affection and loyalty seem to have become unmoored from the ties of kinship; spinsterhood is no guarantee of virginity; marriage fails to indicate who cohabits with, sleeps with, or dominates whom.

This failure, of course—this chasm between private experience and public institution—is just what the traditional regimen of the ecclesiastical courts was meant forcibly to close: censuring shrewishness in women, prohibiting spouses from residing apart from one another, punishing fornication, ensuring that husbands controlled their households and properly penetrated their wives. But even as the urban world enables Morose's eccentric repudiation of normal social intercourse, it disables the traditional public means of inhibiting eccentricity. In the absence of community consensus, any punishment of the individual eccentric must itself be egregious. When Truewit invades Morose's house, a stranger who purports to be "careful after your soul's health," his phrasing recalls the rationale of the ecclesiastical courtroom. But Morose exclaims indignantly:

> Have I ever cozened any friends of yours of their land?
> Bought their possessions? Taken forfeit of their mortgage?
> Begged a reversion from 'em? Bastarded their issue?
> What have I done that may deserve this?
>
> (2.2.37–40)

Even as Morose spurns Truewit's meddling, his language clarifies how peculiar Truewit's mission actually is: an attempt at enforcement warranted neither by comprehensible family allegiances nor by recognized governmental function. The inclination to discipline has become a private whim, merely a new form of eccentricity: the illegitimate, self-promoting churlishness of which Dekker accuses Jonson in *Satiro-mastix.*

Rather like Volpone, Morose often seems to resist his own supposed objectives. While he pretends to concern himself with no one but himself, he is in fact obsessed with his nephew's every minor misstep; by idiosyncratically withdrawing from the world, he makes himself a public laughingstock. Nonetheless, in Morose as in Volpone Jonson plays with the tantalizing possibility of keeping oneself, or at least aspects of oneself, wholly unknown. Critical private facts about Morose remain obscure. By marrying, he threatens to belie the presumption of sexual quiescence implied by his age, oddity, and reclusiveness. In the early part of the play, Morose's phallic fantasies seem merely foolish: he is sublimely unaware of his unprepossessing demeanor when asking Epicoene whether she feels love "suddenly shot into you, from any part you see in me" (2.5.24–25). Likewise when Truewit pretends to ascribe Morose's omission of wedding festivities to the pressure of exorbitant sexual desire, the joke depends upon Truewit's knowledge, and ours, that lust is hardly a credible motive. When Morose assures himself that "this night I will get an heir," he seems likely to be deluding himself or cheering himself up, or both. On the other hand, if Morose really were impotent, and known to be so, then Dauphine's elaborate plot would be virtually beside the point. And as the play proceeds, moments of comic exorbitance as well as of deficiency accumulate around Morose. In 2.1 he is introduced with a "trunk" or long-speaking tube; in 4.3 Mistress Otter complains that "he came down with a huge, long, naked weapon in both his hands"; in 4.7 he enters bearing the two "naked weapons" confiscated from Daw and LaFoole in a ceremony of symbolic castration. Morose seems simultaneously insufficient and excessive, judged rather like the Earl of Essex to be lacking despite "extraordinarily sufficient matter." Clerimont characterizes old men by their "gray heads and weak hams, moist eyes and shrunk members" (1.1.38–39); but Morose's example seems to jeopardize this casual extrapolation from visible head and eyes to unseen hams and members.

Neither we, the theater audience, nor any of the characters swirling about the stage know, as Jack Daw puts it, "what's what" with Morose. As an interpretive conundrum, Morose suggests the slipperiness of the conventional signifiers of sexual prowess. For the virility of all the male characters, not merely of Morose, is constantly at issue in this play,[17] requiring us to wonder how one is supposed to assess that capacity. The more a man talks about his conquests, the less likely he is to have had them, as Daw and LaFoole demonstrate; but silence could as well indicate inexperience as propriety. Thus oblique forms of "proof" must be made to serve: skill in physical, verbal, or wit combat substitute for the proscribed public display of "extraordinarily sufficient matter." The sheer stupidity of Daw and LaFoole seems to convict them of a corresponding sexual ineptitude; certainly when the Collegiate Ladies are brought to believe that Dauphine has engineered their humiliation, they incontinently abandon the losers for the victor. At the same time, an ability to write clever poems, or to play aggressive practical jokes, or to skewer an opponent in a duel, is obviously only remotely related to the ability the Collegiate Ladies most desire to assess. It is as if the men in this play were all on trial for impotence, required to marshal "proofs" that never seem entirely adequate or convincing.

The social construction of femininity is at least as remote from bodily fact as is masculinity. The most conventionally "feminine" individual in the play, shy virgin and assiduous housewife, is not genitally a woman at all. Moreover, the urban breakdown of institutional consensus affects women's social representation even more than men's. Women's social and moral status is traditionally established in reference to their marital status, but in the world of *Epicoene* marriage indicates nothing about the hidden truths of sexual conduct or of gender identity. In the absence of a uniform, obvious standard of assessment, women must establish a *persona* by an improvisatory assembly of incongruous elements. Clerimont deplores Lady Haughty's "pieced beauty"; and Tom Otter announces of his wife that "all her teeth were made i' the Blackfriars, both her eyebrows i' the Strand, and her hair in Silver Street" (4.2.81–83). Conventionally the signifiers of prostitution—"every part of the town owns a piece of her," the apparently cuckolded Otter equivocally complains—cosmetics might seem dependably to reveal interesting facts about sexual availability even as they conceal blemishes of the bodily surface. But as the traditional distinctions between wife and whore are blurred, so the marks of the professional harlot lose their stigma, and become everywoman's property. The debate about cosmetics in *Epicoene* exploits, as a number of critics have pointed out, common misogynist *topoi;*[18] but *Epicoene*'s variety of misogyny hardly lets men off the hook, since they perforce participate in the same epistemologically troubled social arena as the women do.

When the surfaces of the body conceal rather than reveal—when the signs of gender difference are externally applied, rather than an emanation from or a guide to a hidden truth—all heterosocial interaction contains the potential for trickery. Morose's *error personae* instantiates risks everyone runs. On the other hand, the intelligent can attempt to minimize those risks, remaining mindful of the chasm between visible exterior and invisible interior. The need to guard against sexual duplicity puts a premium upon *knowingness.* Secrets thus become a supremely valuable commodity. The silly Otter attempts to curry favor with his drinking companions by advertising what he claims to be the mysteries of his wife's dressing table (who knows whether he is telling the truth?). Daw and LaFoole, even more desperately, invent and ascribe secret improprieties to Epicoene, resorting to sheer defamation. The garrulity of these informants is not merely amusing but useful to the wits, who cultivate their company even while condemning their inability to keep their mouths shut. The wit's intelligence, in the sense of sagacity, requires intelligence, in the sense of information.

The individual who would be knowing, therefore, tends to find himself in a partially compromised position, like the canon lawyers spying on the secrets of the marriage bed even while veiling their eyes and disclaiming their voyeurism. Truewit, for instance, insists high-mindedly that men should not inquire what women do in their dressing rooms: "Is it for us to see their perukes put on, their false teeth, their complexion, their eyebrows, their nails?" (1.1.104–5). But having "followed a rude fellow into a chamber" where a woman was dressing, he is nonetheless able to provide an authoritative account of the counterfeiting he labels as privy and inscrutable: separating himself, typically, both from importunity and naiveté.

In *Gender Trouble,* the feminist theorist Judith Butler writes of the transvestite Divine:

> His / her performance destabilizes the very distinctions between the natural and the artificial, depth and surface, inner and outer through which discourse about genders almost always operates. Is drag the imitation of gender, or does it dramatize the signifying gestures through which gender itself is established? Does being female constitute a "natural fact" or a cultural performance, or is "naturalness" constituted through discursively constrained performative acts that produce the body through and within the categories of sex?[19]

In *Epicoene* Jonson formulates remarkably similar questions, toying with the possibility that virility is a facade and with the corresponding possibility that femininity is merely a matter of *appliqué.*

At the same time, he cannot quite accept the morally corrosive implications of the radical conception that there is nothing "real" underneath, no *substance* to the illusions of masculine or feminine identity. A thoroughgoing constructivist like Butler, who thinks there is no alternative to the theatrical production of gender identity, is in some ways in a more comfortable position than Jonson, the framer of theatrical fictions who nonetheless requires real or natural gender difference to provide the satiric standard by which all his characters may be judged and found lacking. Both the obsolescence and the residual power of that standard are suggested in the final scene, in Otter's broken Latin.

> OTTER: . . . So your *omnipotentes*—
> TRUEWIT: Your *impotentes,* you whoreson lobster!
> OTTER: Your *impotentes,* I should say, are *minime apti ad*
> *contrahenda matrimonium.*
> TRUEWIT: *Matrimonium?* we shall have most unmatrimonial
> Latin with you. *Matrimonia,* and be hanged!
> DAUPHINE: You put them out, man.
>
> (5.3.164–70)

Confusing omnipotence with impotence, Otter rehearses the conflation of exorbitance and inadequacy associated throughout the play with Morose, who after all is the individual whose plight is under discussion here. Significantly Otter stumbles, too, over the gender of his Latin words, making the feminine *matrimonia,* marriage, into a neuter noun. The wits, characteristically, recognize Otter's incompetence in comprehending and manipulating gender categories, but cannot afford simply to disown his ineptitude: Truewit's indignant insistence upon "correctness" merely threatens to derail an improvisatory *tour de force.* Rather like Jonson himself, Truewit fuses a proficiency in colorful colloquial idiom—"whoreson lobster"—with a commitment to decorum almost too punctilious for his own good.

The Latin language is surprisingly prominent in *Epicoene:* the wits and would-be wits effortlessly quote Juvenal, Ovid, Horace, Catullus, and Seneca; and even a lowborn drunkard and a barber are able to manage a fractured approximation of an academic debate. In Latin, gender is often obvious from the terminations of nouns and adjectives. Even here, of course, the category of the neuter disturbs a binarism of masculine and feminine, and words designated as *epicoene* are ambiguously gendered. But the unclarities pale in contrast to the vernacular, in which, Jonson claims in *The English Grammar,* there are six genders, none of which can be discerned from the configuration of the words themselves. In his attempt to describe the structure of English, Jonson does not, significantly, merely dispense with gender as a grammatical category, as modern linguists do.[20] Rather he insists upon assigning gender to nouns and adjectives despite their lack of distinguishing characteristics. In *The English Grammar* as in *Epicoene,* the effect is both to imply a certain defectiveness in the material to which the laws of gender so imperfectly apply, *and* to call into question the appropriateness of the laws being invoked. The standard of the silent woman permits Jonson's satiric critique upon actual chatterers and gossips, who break the rule enjoining female silence. At the same time, the fact that silent women do not exist in Jacobean London suggests that the rule is moot; therefore, Morose's insistence upon a silent wife is likewise a butt of satire.

In *Epicoene*—the title itself simultaneously designates an ambiguity of bodily sex and a grammatical uncertainty[21]—Latin stands in the same relation to English that normatively gendered behavior stands in relation to the behavior of seventeenth-century Londoners. In the archaic language, most words indicated their gender plainly. Once upon a time, Jonson imagines, men's and women's socially obvious features—their marital status, valor, wit, freshness of complexion—were likewise dependable guides to their truth. In the contemporary world of *Epicoenes,* however, those indicators are no longer reliable, and gender becomes invisible, just as it is in the vernacular tongue. Like knowing Latin, understanding the disregarded decorum of sexual difference is at once superfluous, the mastery of an obsolete signifying system, and prestigious, a sign of the knowingness to which everyone aspires. But the prestige thus attained is of a problematic kind. As we have already seen, the outrageousness with which *Epicoene*'s characters all violate what are supposed to be the "natural" rules of sexual conduct necessarily reflects not only upon them but upon the adequacy of the rules themselves. Similarly a satirist finds it easier to chastise individual offenders against a commonly accepted standard, than to reform an entire society in which that standard is nowhere instantiated.

As Jonson becomes less interested in individually grotesque humors characters, and more interested in the shared failings of large groups, the increasing ambitiousness of his satiric project inevitably endangers his authority. For increasingly his effectiveness, like the effectiveness of the ecclesiastical court judge, seems to depend not upon the sheer conspicuousness of vices, shortcomings, and anomalies, but upon an agreement by the larger society to regard them as vices, shortcomings, and anomalies in the first place. Moral policing thus appears to be less the discovery of material facts it pretends to be than a way of manipulating opinion, an attempt to force others into an attitude of disapproval. Jonson finds both threatening and irresistible the possibility that neither satire nor the impotence trial really display self-evident material facts, but rather constitute occluded forms of persuasion that depend, like all persuasion, upon highly fluid standards of plausibility and obviousness. Jonson's satire, in other words, relies upon its claims to a factual material basis even while persistently undermining those claims.

The critical debate about *Epicoene* has turned largely on whether the wits are meant to be surrogates for the author-satirist, or satiric targets themselves.[22] Critics on both sides of this discussion have assumed that if the wits are in some measure self-portraits, Jonson must have intended them to be viewed in a positive light; and that therefore, to whatever extent he was able to see them as cruel or exploitative, he must have desired to distance himself from them. But perhaps Jonson is not so self-protective. Clerimont's suspicion that "all is not sweet, all is not sound" with Lady Haughty does not assuage his sexual hunger for her, and Dauphine's contempt for the pretensions of the Collegiates does not prevent him from falling "in love" with all of them at once. The wits fully comprehend how they are implicated in and tainted by the rules of the game, but they do not for that reason opt out of the game. If Jonson eventually came to view his own satiric activity as compromised or epistemologically insecure, as dependent upon the exorbitance it attacks, and as unable to achieve a fixed and absolute perspective, then he may have thought of his authorial endeavor in *Epicoene* in a similarly bleak, clear light. Certainly this disillusion or sense of limitation would help account for what many critics have noticed in the plays between *Volpone* and *Bartholomew Fair:* a progressive easing of the unself-conscious disciplinary zeal that pervades the earlier comical satires.[23]

And if Jonson does not let himself off the hook, neither does he reassure his audience about their motives or their capacity to judge. *Epicoene* opens upon "Clerimont, making himself ready": a liminal scene that hovers between a private nakedness that cannot be exhibited onstage, and the fully public self-presentation that Clerimont seems to prepare himself for here, but that, of course, he is already undergoing in the eyes of the theater audience. We are allowed to congratulate ourselves that we are "privy" to these characters' secrets, that they bare themselves to us. For after all, as spectators since Aristotle have reassured themselves, theatrical maskings are paradoxically undertaken to the end of revelation; deception is put in the service of making truth visible. Actually, even in other Jonson plays there are limits upon what we know about his characters: who can tell whether Volpone is actually "as hot, and high, and in as jovial plight" as he claims to be in his interview with

Celia? The end of *Epicoene,* however, in a move unprecedented and rarely imitated in English Renaissance theater, roughly and unmistakably disabuses the spectators of any complacent assumption of omniscience. Epicoene's male identity is at least as much a surprise to us as to his fellow-characters: probably more of a surprise, since we have justifiably imagined that the playwright would let us in on such a secret earlier. At the same time, we recognize with some chagrin that we have known all along that Epicoene, like every female character on the Renaissance stage, was played by a boy. Like the typical Jonson gull, we have collaborated in our own deception.

What sort of pleasure or interests has our wilful forgetting served? *The Silent Woman* was, of course, written for a company of boy actors, and the play's skeptical qualms converge on the highly ambiguous body of the cross-dressed adolescent boy.[24] Boys are not marriageable, we learn from Tom Otter, because they are "*impotentes,*" incapable of "rendering the debt." But the boys on Jonson's stage, hovering on the edge of puberty, beg precisely that question. Clerimont wonders in the opening scene over the reasons for his page's popularity at Lady Haughty's house; Truewit suggests that the boy serves as Clerimont's "ingle" or homosexual pet; Dauphine claims that the "metamorphosed" Epicoene "is almost of years, and will make a good visitant within this twelvemonth." Are these boys presexual or sexual beings? Phallic subjects or nonphallic objects? In a binary sexual system, are such liminal creatures classified with men, because they will be so eventually, or with women, because they apparently lack the potency which is the male's defining trait? Much as *Othello* encourages the audience to imagine Desdemona in bed with Othello, but leaves unclear what if anything is happening offstage, *Epicoene* eroticizes its epistemological quandaries, and in so doing makes qualms a site of pleasure. Pedophilia—captivation by what is not yet visible or clear-cut, by what straddles or evades the lines of gender difference—seems a sexual analogue to the intellectual vertigo induced by the vagaries of the impotence trial. The titillating equivocations of boy theater make it an ideal vehicle for exploring the *aporias* of Jonsonian satire.

Notes

1. The strict regulation of the marriage bond is the more striking because of the apparent indifference of Renaissance courts to deviations that to a modern sensibility might seem more flagrant. Sodomy, for instance, made a capital crime under common law in 1533, was almost never prosecuted in Elizabethan and Jacobean England. The most common view is that this infrequency suggests "a probable low incidence of sodomy" (Richard Wunderli, *London Church Courts and Society on the Eve of the Reformation* [Cambridge, Mass.: Medieval Academy of America, 1981], 84.) More recently, gay-affirmative critics have claimed just the opposite, that sex between men was so frequent and ordinary that it went unnoticed and unclassified as "sodomy" unless some other social taboo was simultaneously breached (Alan Bray, "Homosexuality and the Signs of Male Friendship in Elizabethan England," *History Workshop Journal* 19

[1990]: 1–19; Jonathan Goldberg, *Sodometries* [Stanford: Stanford University Press, 1992]). Bray and Goldberg, following Foucault, have tended to be suspicious of identifying the domain of the sexual with the domain of the private in the early modern period, regarding such an identification as an anachronistic application of post-Enlightenment categories. I shall argue, on the contrary, that in both Jonson and Shakespeare sexual experience becomes a *topos* of unknowable inwardness.

The argument about the frequency of male/male sex correlates with an older disagreement among historians about the effectiveness of the ecclesiastical courts: how widely their strictures were flouted, what the relation was between moral and legal strictures on behavior, and so forth. For an account of the argument, see Martin Ingram, *Church Courts, Sex and Marriage in England, 1570–1640* (Cambridge: Cambridge University Press, 1987), 6–17. Ingram himself argues that the ecclesiastical courts' regulation of sexual conduct was quite effective and was widely supported by the populace. Of course this debate, replacing the stymied ecclesiastical court judge with the baffled historian, participates in the same difficulties about the unknowability of sexual "facts" that I shall be addressing in this essay. I am less interested in whether ecclesiastical court procedures were efficient and fair than in what their professed aims reveal.

2. *Conversations with Drummond of Hawthornden,* lines 342–44.

3. For a lively discussion of the French situation, see Pierre Darmon, *Damning the Innocent: A History of the Persecution of the Impotent in Pre-Revolutionary France,* trans. Paul Keegan (New York: Viking, 1986). The same book was published in England under the title *Trial by Impotence: Virility and Marriage in Pre-Revolutionary France* (London: Chatto and Windus, 1985).

4. George Abbott, the Archbishop of Canterbury who resisted granting Frances Howard a divorce from the third Earl of Essex, discusses the differences between English and French practice in William Cobbett and Thomas Howell, *Cobbett's Complete Collection of State Trials* (London, 1809), 2.851–53, hereafter referred to as *State Trials.* In *Marriage Litigation in Medieval England* (Cambridge: Cambridge University Press, 1974), 88–90, R. H. Helmholz discusses a medieval English case in which an allegedly impotent man was "tested" by a group of women who attempted to give him an erection, but there are no records of this procedure being employed after 1450.

5. James Dyer, *Reports of Cases in the Reigns of Henry VIII, Edward VI, Queen Mary, and Queen Elizabeth* (Dublin, 1794), 179–80.

6. *The Reports of Sir Edward Coke,* V.98.b, 2d ed. (London, 1680), 344. The common-law judges supported their opinion by the novel suggestion that Bury might have been impotent during his first marriage but not during his second, a possibility at odds with the ecclesiastical requirement of permanent incapacity. Bury's precedent became important in the Essex divorce case, in which the earl admitted a specific but not a general disability

7. The hymen is much discussed in sixteenth- and early-seventeenth-century France. Writers who consider the presence of the hymen a sign of virginity include Jacques Duval, *Traité des hermaphrodits, parties, génitales, accouchements des femmes* (Rouen, 1612), and Séverin Pineau, *De integritatis et corruptionis virginum notis* (Paris, 1598); doubters include Ambroise Paré, published in England as *The Anatomy of Mans Body,* in *The Workes of that famous chirurgeon Ambrose Parey,* trans. Thomas Johnson (London, 1649), and Jacques Guillemeau, trans. as *Child-birth, or, the Happie Deliverie of Women* (London, 1612).

8. Anthony Weldon, *The Court and Character of King James,* (London, 1651).

9. C. H. Herford and Percy Simpson, eds., *Ben Jonson* (London: Oxford University Press, 1925), 1:197.

10. Jonson's truest dramatic heir in this vein might thus be William Wycherley, in whose *Country Wife* the brazen Horner puts into practice a scheme more thoroughgoing and more successful than what Volpone finds himself able to accomplish.

11. Lawrence Stone charts the legal instability of these two conceptions of marriage in *The Road to Divorce: England 1530–1987* (Oxford: Oxford University Press, 1990).

12. Donaldson, *The World Upside-Down: From Jonson to Fielding* (Oxford: Clarendon, 1970), 38–41.

13. Martin Ingram points out the similarities between the informal sanctions of the *charivari* and the formal ones of the ecclesiastical courts in "Ridings, Rough Music, and Mocking Rhymes in Early Modern England," *Past and Present* 105 (November 1984), 92, 111.

14. In *London Church Courts and Society on the Eve of the Reformation* (Cambridge, Mass.: Medieval Academy of America, 1981), 137–39, Richard Wunderli traces dissatisfaction with the enforcement capacity of London ecclesiastical courts back to the 1490s.

15. As is recognized by Anne Barton, who complains about *Epicoene*'s "scrupulously maintained distance between people," and the lack of "an honest, genuinely significant relationship with anyone else." *Ben Jonson: Dramatist* (New York: Cambridge University Press, 1984), 128.

16. P. K. Ayers, "Dreams of the City: The Urban and the Urbane in Jonson's *Epicoene*," *Philological Quarterly* 66 (1987): 75.

17. Comments on the "epicene" quality of the various male characters are endemic to the criticism of this play: "even these apparently normal men [the gallants] are somewhat ambiguous, sexually" writes Partridge in *The Broken Compass* (London: Chatto and Windus, 1958), 170. Barbara Millard in "An Acceptable Violence: Sexual Contest in Jonson's *Epicoene*," *Medieval and Renaissance Drama in English* 1 (1984): 153, likewise claims that "if the implied norms are valid, there is not a normal male in the play except Epicoene in his/her silent period."

18. Barbara Baines and Mary C. Williams, "The Contemporary and Classical Antifeminist Tradition in Jonson's *Epicoene*," *Renaissance Papers* 1977, 43–58; Karen Newman, "City Talk: Women and Commodification in Jonson's *Epicoene*," *ELH* 56 (1989): 503–41.

19. Judith Butler, *Gender Trouble* (New York: Routledge, 1990), viii.

20. The criticism of Jonson's Latinism is at least as old as the late seventeenth century. Herford and Simpson (1:358) quote William Wotten commenting on Jonson's *Grammar*: "for want of reflecting upon the grounds of a language which he understood as well as any man of his age, he drew it by violence to a dead language that was of a quite different make"

21. Jonson was apparently the first to use the word *epicoene* to refer to human gender. See Philip Mirabelli, "Silence, Wit, and Wisdom in *The Silent Woman*," *SEL* 29 (1989): 309–36, and Steve Brown, "The Boyhood of Shakespeare's Heroines: Notes on Gender Ambiguity in the Sixteenth Century," *SEL* 30 (1990): 243–63.

22. For the first option, see the influential discussion of *Epicoene* in C. H. Herford and Percy Simpson's edition of Ben Jonson's collected works, and Alan Dessen, *Jonson's Moral Comedy* (Evanston: Northwestern University Press, 1971), 107 ff. For the second, see Edward Partridge's introduction to *Epicoene* in the Yale edition: "That Jonson sees [the wits'] plots against Daw, La Foole, and Morose as at least partly judicial, does not mean that he places himself on their side" (19). John Enck, in *Ben Jonson and the Comic Truth* (Madison: University of Wisconsin Press, 1957), and Jonas Barish, *Ben Jonson and the Language of Prose Comedy* (Cambridge: Harvard University Press, 1960), believe Jonson cannot make up his mind about how to portray these characters.

23. See e.g. Harry Levin, "Jonson's Metempsychosis," *Philological Quarterly* 22 (1943): 231–39; Enck, *Ben Jonson and the Comic Truth;* Barish, "Feasting and Judgment in Jonsonian Comedy," *Renaissance Drama,* n.s., 5 (1972): 3–51; Katharine Eisaman Maus, *Ben Jonson and the Roman Frame of Mind* (Princeton: Princeton University Press, 1985), 126–34.

24. For general accounts of the erotic charge of the transvestite boy, see Lisa Jardine, " 'As boys and women are for the most part cattle of this colour': Female Roles and Elizabethan Eroticism," *Still Harping on Daughters: Women and Drama in the Age of Shakespeare* (Totowa, N.J.: Barnes and Noble, 1983); Stephen Greenblatt, "Fiction and Friction," *Shakespearean Negotia-*

tions (Berkeley: University of California Press, 1988), 66–93; Stephen Orgel, "Nobody's Perfect: Or, Why Did the English Stage Take Boys for Women," *South Atlantic Quarterly* 88 (1989); 7–29; Bruce R. Smith, *Homosexual Desire in Shakespeare's England* (Chicago: University of Chicago Press, 1991), 145–56; Marjorie Garber, *Vested Interests* (New York: Routledge, 1992), 165–85.

Examen of *The Silent Woman* (1667–1668)

JOHN DRYDEN

'Tis evident that the more the persons are, the greater will be the variety of the Plot. If then the parts are managed so regularly that the beauty of the whole be kept entire, and that the variety become not a perplexed and confused mass of accidents, you will find it infinitely pleasing to be led in a labyrinth of design, where you see some of your way before you, yet discern not the end till you arrive at it. And that all this is practicable, I can produce for examples many of our *English* Plays: as the *Maid's Tragedy,* the *Alchemist,* the *Silent Woman;* I was going to have named the *Fox,* but that the unity of design seems not exactly observed in it; for there appear two actions in the Play; the first naturally ending with the fourth Act; the second forced from it in the fifth: which yet is the less to be condemned in him, because the disguise of *Volpone,* though it suited not with his character as a crafty or covetous person, agreed well enough with that of a voluptuary: and by it the Poet gained the end at which he aimed, the punishment of Vice, and the reward of Virtue, both which that disguise produced. So that to judge equally of it, it was an excellent fifth Act, but not so naturally proceeding from the former.

As for Johnson, to whose Character I am now arrived, if we look upon him while he was himself, (for his last Plays were but his dotages) I think him the most learned and judicious Writer which any Theater ever had. He was a most severe Judge of himself as well as others. One cannot say he wanted wit, but rather that he was frugal of it. In his works you find little to retrench or alter. Wit and Language, and Humour also in some measure we had before him; but something of Art was wanting to the *Drama* till he came. He managed his strength to more advantage than any who preceded him. You seldom find him making Love in any of his Scenes, or endeavouring to move the Passions; his genius was too sullen and saturnine to do it gracefully, especially when he knew he came after those who had performed both to such an height. Humour was his proper Sphere, and in that he delighted most to represent Mechanic

From *Of Dramatic Poesie, An Essay* (1667–1668).

people. He was deeply conversant in the Ancients, both *Greek* and *Latin,* and he borrowed boldly from them: there is scarce a Poet or Historian among the Roman Authors of those times whom he has not translated in *Sejanus* and *Catiline.* But he has done his Robberies so openly, that one may see he fears not to be taxed by any Law. He invades Authors like a Monarch, and what would be theft in other Poets, is only victory in him. With the spoils of these Writers he so represents old *Rome* to us, in its Rites, Ceremonies and Customs, that if one of their Poets had written either of his Tragedies, we had seen less of it than in him. If there was any fault in his Language, 'twas that he weaved it too closely and laboriously, in his Comedies especially: perhaps too, he did a little too much Romanize our Tongue, leaving the words which he translated almost as much *Latin* as he found them: wherein though he learnedly followed their language, he did not enough comply with the Idiom of ours. If I would compare him with *Shakespeare,* I must acknowledge him the more correct Poet, but *Shakespeare* the greater wit. *Shakespeare* was the *Homer,* or Father of our Dramatic Poets; *Johnson* was the *Virgil,* the pattern of elaborate writing; I admire him, but I love Shakespeare. To conclude of him, as he has given us the most correct Plays, so in the precepts which he has laid down in his *Discoveries,* we have as many and profitable Rules for perfecting the Stage as any wherewith the French can furnish us.

Having thus spoken of the Author, I proceed to the examination of his Comedy, *The Silent Woman.*

Examen of the Silent Woman

To begin first with the length of the Action, it is so far from exceeding the compass of a Natural day, that it takes not up an Artificial one. 'Tis all included in the limits of three hours and an half, which is no more than is required for the presentment on the Stage. A beauty perhaps not much observed; if it had, we should not have looked on the *Spanish* translation of *Five Hours* with so much wonder. The Scene of it is laid in *London;* the latitude of place is almost as little as you can imagine: for it lies all within the compass of two Houses, and after the first Act, in one. The continuity of Scenes is observed more than in any of our Plays, except his own *Fox* and *Alchemist.* They are not broken above twice or thrice at most in the whole Comedy, and in the two best of *Corneille's* Plays, the *Cid* and *Cinna,* they are interrupted once. The action of the Play is entirely one; the end or aim of which is the settling *Morose's* Estate on *Dauphine.* The Intrigue of it is the greatest and most noble of any pure unmixed Comedy in any Language: you see in it many persons of various characters and humours, and all delightful: As first, *Morose,* or an old Man, to whom all noise but his own talking is offensive. Some who would be thought Critics, say this humour of his is forced: but to remove that objection, we may consider him first to be naturally of a delicate hearing, as many are to whom all sharp sounds are unpleasant; and secondly, we may attribute much of it to the peevishness of his Age, or the wayward authority of an old man in his own house, where he may make himself obeyed; and to this the Poet seems to allude in his name *Morose.* Beside this, I am assured from diverse persons, that *Ben Johnson* was actually acquainted with such a man, one altogether as ridiculous as he is here represented.

Besides *Morose,* there are at least 9 or 10 different Characters and humours in the *Silent Woman,* all which persons have several concernments of their own, yet are all used by the Poet, to the conducting of the main design to perfection. I shall not waste time in commending the writing of this Play, but I will give you my opinion, that there is more wit and acuteness of Fancy in it than in any of *Ben Johnson's.* Besides that, he has here described the conversation of Gentlemen in the persons of *True-Wit,* and his Friends, with more gaiety, air and freedom, than in the rest of his Comedies. For the contrivance of the Plot 'tis extreme elaborate, and yet withal easy; for the λύσις, or untying of it, 'tis so admirable, that when it is done, no one of the Audience would think the Poet could have missed it; and yet it was concealed so much before the last Scene, that any other way would sooner have entered into your thoughts. But I dare not take upon me to commend the Fabric of it, because it is altogether so full of Art, that I must unravel every Scene in it to commend it as I ought. And this excellent contrivance is still the more to be admired, because 'tis Comedy where the persons are only of common rank, and their business private, not elevated by passions or high concernments as in serious Plays. Here everyone is a proper Judge of all he sees; nothing is represented but that with which he daily converses: so that by consequence all faults lie open to discovery, and few are pardonable. 'Tis this which Horace has judiciously observed:

Creditur ex medio quia res arcessit habere
Sudoris minimum, sed habet Comedia tanto
Plus oneris, quanto veniæ minus.—

But our Poet, who was not ignorant of these difficulties, has made use of all advantages; as he who designs a large leap takes his rise from the highest ground. One of these advantages is that which *Corneille* has laid down as the greatest which can arrive to any Poem, and which he himself could never compass above thrice in all his Plays, viz. the making choice of some signal and long-expected day, whereon the action of the Play is to depend. This day was that designed by *Dauphine* for the settling of his Uncle's Estate upon him; which to compass he contrives to marry him: that the marriage had been plotted by him long beforehand is made evident by what he tells *True-Wit* in the second Act, that in one moment he had destroyed what he had been raising many months.

There is another artifice of the Poet, which I cannot here omit, because by the frequent practice of it in his Comedies, he has left it to us almost as a Rule; that is, when he has any Character or humour wherein he would show a *Coup de Maistre,* or his highest skill, he recommends it to your observation by a pleasant description of it before the person first appears. Thus, in *Bartholomew Fair* he gives you the Pictures of *Numps* and *Cokes,* and in this those of *Daw, Lafoole, Morose,* and the *Collegiate Ladies;* all which you hear described before you see them. So that before they come upon the Stage you have longing expectation of them, which prepares you to receive them favourably; and when they are there, even from their first appearance you are so far acquainted with them, that nothing of their humour is lost to you.

I will observe yet one thing further of this admirable Plot; the business of it rises in every Act. The second is greater than the first; the third than the second, and so forward to the fifth. There too you see, till the very last Scene, new difficulties arising to obstruct the action of the Play; and when the Audience is brought into despair that the business can naturally be effected, then, and not before, the discovery is made. But that the Poet might entertain you with more variety all this while, he reserves some new Characters to show you, which he opens not till the second and third Act. In the second, *Morose, Daw,* the *Barber* and *Otter;* in the third the *Collegiate Ladies:* All which he moves afterwards in by-walks, or under-Plots, as diversions to the main design, lest it should grow tedious, though they are still naturally joined with it, and somewhere or other subservient to it. Thus, like a skillful Chess-player, by little and little he draws out his men, and makes his pawns of use to his greater persons.

Every Man in His Humor: The Comedy of Non-Interaction

GABRIELE BERNHARD JACKSON

When Ben Jonson placed *Every Man in His Humor* at the head of his collected works and alluded to it in his dedication as his first-fruits, both position and allusion were symbolically appropriate, as he was no doubt fully aware. He had earlier dramatic writing to his credit, including at least one full-length comedy; but unlike what had come before, this springtime production held all the flavors of the mature harvest. All Jonson's characteristic concerns, values, turns of mind and phrase, dramatic techniques, structural designs—all are here, ready to be selected, developed, recombined. The very copiousness is, from the point of view of dramatic consistency, this play's disability: it offers too much simultaneously, sometimes contradictorily. It exceeds itself, and so displays its author better than almost any single later play. It is quintessential Jonson.

Jonsonian comedy is the comedy of non-interaction. In the characteristic Jonsonian plot, a group of personages in a state of chronic introspection is brought together by a central action which loosely unites them, or rather, brings them into proximity. Each character, though responsive in his own way to outside stimuli, acts essentially alone; he moves along the line of force directed by his nature, and comes into collision, when time or a manipulator decrees, with another character moving along an intersecting line. It follows that Jonsonian plot is not plot in the ordinary sense. It does not develop outward from a coherent center, but moves inward from widely separated points to an accidental, as opposed to essential, meeting point—accidental in terms of action, though at its best essential in significance. For this reason, the plot of a Jonson comedy is peculiarly hard to recall; we remember individual characters and confrontations, as though the story were a means to achieve certain juxtapositions. These moments of intersection constitute characteristic Jonsonian comedy; the design is not organic but geometric.

From G. B. Jackson, ed., *Every Man in His Humor* (New Haven: Yale University Press, 1969), 1–34. Reprinted by permission of Yale University Press.

A Jonsonian comic plot is a group of subplots collected in one place. How deeply this comedy of non-interaction differs from comedy of interaction is evident if we think of Shakespeare's comic plots: where subplot and main plot meet, they merge into one another, each clarifying the other: the moment of meeting is the moment of resolution—consider the confrontation of Portia and Shylock, the Duke and Malvolio, Oliver and Orlando, or Theseus joined in celebration with the midsummer-night's lovers and the workmen. The motto for Shakespeare's comedy could well be taken from this last play: "All the story of the night told over, / And all their minds transfigured so together, / . . . / . . . grows to something of great constancy." In Jonson there is no *together;* each mind is transfigured separately. If these separate transfigurations are simultaneous, their crisscrossing only exhibits more strikingly the need to avoid gullibility. They teach, perhaps, the source of transfiguration and the means of escaping it, but the condition itself contains nothing valuable. No mutual element of great constancy can de deduced from the interweaving of confusions. On the contrary, the moment when Jonson's subplots coincide is a moment of chaos; instead of merging, they rebound from one another; insteady of clarifying, they confound. The chaos is funny to the observer, who, aware of all the motivations which compose it, laughs at the disparities he, but not the characters, can perceive—for the audience, too, is detached. This comedy of non-interaction is what Theseus expressly rejects; when his master of ceremonies predicts that he will enjoy the workmen's botched play only if he "can find sport in their intents," he rebukes him: "Our sport shall be to take what they mistake." In Jonson the sport of those who play audience is all in the performers' intents; as Wellbred says when he has aroused Dame Kitely's jealousy, "This may make sport anon."

Furthermore, the coming together of plots in Shakespeare is a moment of resolution and merging because the plots are already organically connected by the relationships between their central figures. Oliver and Orlando are brothers; the Duke and the mid-summer lovers are court and courtiers, and besides the Duke's group includes Hermia's father; Olivia and Malvolio are two halves of a household; Portia defends her husband's best friend. When the plots make contact we experience relief and release, for what has been artificially fragmented is reassembled. It is what we have been waiting for. In Jonson, on the other hand, although families do exist, they occcupy the same subsection of plot to begin with, so that the meeting of two or more plot lines has no reason to bring a sense of fitting union. The separate subplots are not interconnected by previous personal relationships. Corvino and Corbaccio happen to be fellow citizens, and the Would-bes happen to be visiting their city; Drugger and Dapper and Sir Epicure Mammon happen to encounter Face at different times; Cokes (or Wasp) happens to choose John Littlewit to draw up a marriage license. Of course, in these great plays the characters are brought together by a far more subtle relationship than that of family ties: they have similar complexions of soul. The "something of great constancy" which transfigures their minds is a capacity for similar evil (or folly—which Jonson always sees as weak evil). But since the evil is invariably such as to cut them off from other men, what metaphorically unites them actually divides them.

Now I do not think that Jonson was yet aware, when he wrote *Every Man in His Humor,* that his great comic genius lay in documenting and exploring this division; nor could he possibly foresee that the triumphs of that genius would be reserved for a time when he would find dramatic correlatives for his ultimately metaphysical belief that, while pursuit of an absolute good leads to unity and a constructive ordering of society, pursuit of evil leads to fragmentation and absolute isolation. But in *Every Man In* he is already attempting to introduce such a dramatic correlative in the debate about poetry; he sees, though perhaps but hazily, the direction in which he will have to move. The debate about poetry frames the play, whether one begins with the dedication to Camden, with the Prologue, or with Knowell's opening speech. Its settlement at the end by Clement, whose word is in every sense law, immediately precedes the proper ordering of society metaphorically ("I will do more reverence to him [a true poet], when I see him, than I will to the Major") and in fact (in the arrangements for rewards and punishments). General unification follows: Clement exhorts each participant to put off his divisive humor, to enjoy the symbolically unifying banquet; and he insists on a final procession properly emblematic of unity: "every one, a fellow!" (The occasion, of course, is a wedding.) So the identification of a metaphysically valid ideal, poetry, is forced into linkage with constructive organization of society—forced, because the society has no more than the most tangential concern with poetry and seems unlikely either to be constructive or to remain, under pressure, organized. Clement has to push and shove to make them "put off all discontent": "You, Mr. Downright, your anger; you, Master Knowell, your cares; Master Kitely and his wife"—this is hard work. The picture of a society in the process of being constructively organized is always the weakest part to Jonson, and in his most satisfying plays he cuts it down to a minimum. In his least satisfying, *Catiline* and *Cynthia's Revels,* he makes it, alas, the major part of the proceedings. In these two plays and in *Poetaster* he tried again to use poetry as the ideal which could unite society, in all three works making eloquence a centrally important part of the plot, whereas in *Every Man In* it is very lightly dealt with in the action, though given disproportionate symbolic weight to bear. The relationship between the value of a society and the position of poetry within it was a theme dear to Jonson, but perhaps too indirectly dramatic to make a really great play, since poetry itself is still only a symbol for the moral and spiritual qualities it embodies.

That Jonson had not yet clearly perceived the drift of his own creativity is plain in his attempt to superimpose an organic unification on the arbitrary unification demanded by Justice Clement. The marriage between Edward and Bridget literally makes the "worthwhile" characters one big family. Even

Cob and Tib are worked in as household retainers, with their allotted place in the buttery. Clement, who might be considered an exception, has his special role above and outside of the action, sanctioning and repairing family ties and providing the family mansion and the family dinner. Only Matthew and Bobadill remain literally unrelated on either side of the family; their position is evidently intended to correspond to their moral state, for they are specifically excluded from humanitarian concern as unsalvageable ("these two have so little of man in 'em, they are not part of my care"). Since they do not share in the communion of humanity they get no organic dinner, either. But while this gesture toward a discriminating interactive comedy provides an agreeable and symbolically correct ending to the played-out action, it is utterly mechanical. The marriage, a most unconvincing piece of work patched up by Wellbred ("Hold, hold, be temperate," the fortunate bridegroom begs him), is as much of a contrivance as Clement's final procession. Clement dedicates "this night . . . to friendship, love, and laughter" as though he were articulating the elements of the action, three motivations joined to bring about the final success. But major laughter in *Every Man In,* when connected with these two emotions at all, is based—as laughter typically is in Jonson—on perversions or negations of love (Kitely's for his wife, Knowell's for his son, Matthew's courtship of Bridget) and friendship (Kitely's suspicions of Cash, Brainworm's deception of Knowell, Edward's baiting of Stephen, and Wellbred's of Bobadill and Matthew). Clement is asking for the simultaneous celebration of effects opposed at the very root. All Brainworm's laughter-making talents have been dedicated, as talents in Jonson always are, to the pleasant task of self-aggrandizement, which separates father from son, brother from sister, husband from wife (with the false message delivered to Kitely), master from servant (Formal from Clement as much as Brainworm from Knowell), for as long as the laughter is able to continue.

To be sure, there is not much separation needed; as in the great comedies, all that is wanted is judicious intensification of a spiritual state that already exists. And Clement's conjunction of friendship, love, and laughter is only unconvincing, not, as it might be, offensive, for Brainworm is not yet Mosca or Face, the non-understanding between Knowell and Edward is not yet the deadly opposition of Corbaccio to Bonario, Kitely's treatment of his Dame is not Corvino's treatment of Celia, Brainworm's deception of Knowell is not Mosca's betrayal of Volpone, and to counterfeit a London Justice's warrant is not to pervert the Venetian courts. But as folly is a weak evil, so *Every Man In* is an incipient *Volpone* or *Alchemist.* The situations are basic to Jonsonian humanity: bonds of relationship are always denied by separation of spirit.

Clement, thus circumscribed by human nature itself, can only create, as family relationships do, a tenuous physical pairing. The characters Jonson would like, in *Every Man In,* to present as "fellows" are incapable of fellowship. Can there be anywhere in literature a more tedious pair of friends than Edward and Wellbred? Their sterile interchange of witticisms is outgone only by the silence of the stony young lovers, who exchange not a single remark either before or after marriage. The place for emotional activity is in soliloquy; there old Knowell can protest his paternal affection, but confronted with his newly-married son he does not address a word to him, until the opportunity to mock Edward's poetic inclination unseals his lips. His one disagreeable sentence is the sum total of communication between them. Kitely, even more lavish of passion in soliloquy, dredges up four direct remarks to his wife (one is "How now? What?"), of which the last seems promising: "Kiss me, sweetheart"; but his final pronouncement, "When air rains horns, all may be sure of some," does not augur well for the harmony of his union. Indeed, the Quarto text, continuing to the very end Kitely's suspicious questions—intermixed with his assurances that he is cured of jealousy—makes explicit the rocky future of his marriage.

The natural conclusion of Jonsonian comedy is complete fragmentation, coupled with (since this is comedy and not tragedy) an arbitrary reconstitution of some kind of society—the ending of *The Alchemist, Volpone, Bartholomew Fair.* It is the conclusion of *Every Man In,* too, but here the fragments are unstably glued together in the hope that the traditional judgment, marriage, and banquet may retain their face value. Jonson continued to use them: marriage and banqueting (projected in the epilogue) conclude *The Alchemist;* judgment imposed from without, *Volpone;* a combination of the two, *Bartholomew Fair.* But in these, conventional comic form no longer compromises, but rather illuminates, the inner logic of Jonson's individual comic content: two of the three marriages are frankly utilitarian, the third emotionally insignificant (while the clear mandate for romance between Celia and Bonario is ignored); one banquet celebrates the success of manipulation ("laughter," but certainly not love or friendship), the other a recognition of general inability to amend—and in *The Silent Woman,* the banquet celebrates Morose's un-marriage. As for judgment, in *Volpone* it merely confirms the special isolation each character has selected for himself; in *Bartholomew Fair,* it is abandoned as unsuited to a society in which all human relationships turn out to be deceptive. The great Jonsonian ending is a parody of the traditional ending of interactive comedy: its symbols of unity become affirmations of fragmentation. On a large scale as on a small (Volpone's morning hymn, Face's catechism), Jonson is a master of revelation through ironic form.

Although in *Every Man In* Jonson composes not ironically but straightforwardly, as if he were writing comedy of temporary, not permanent, noninteraction, the special nature of his characters and plot already exhibits itself everywhere. From the moment Knowell strikes the keynote in his opening lines by making Brainworm the bearer of his own paternal authority, each major character conducts his important relationships through a go-between. Brainworm shuttles back and forth between Knowell and Edward; Edward's courtship is conducted by Wellbred; Kitely sends his reprimand to Wellbred through Downright, whom he also uses as a stand-in at the connubial breakfast table; Kitely makes Cash his informant about his wife—and Cash delegates the position to Cob; Bobadill attacks Downright through a law clerk, whom he approaches through Matthew, and serves the resulting warrant by intermediary; even Justice Clement deals at one remove with the petitioner standing before him:

> CLEMENT. Tell Oliver Cob he shall go to the jail, Formal.
>
> FORMAL. Oliver Cob: my master, Justice Clement, says you shall go to the jail.

Further, the most powerful fear of the characters is the development elsewhere of an unmediated relationship. All the primary action of the play springs from this anxiety. Knowell's trip to town is prompted by his dismay at the friendship of Edward and Wellbred; Wellbred, though with less animus, would like to pry Edward loose from his father: "change an old shirt for a whole smock with us. . . . Leave thy vigilant father alone to number over his green apricots." Kitely and Dame Kitely need no commentary. Brainworm, besides wishing to prevent a specific confrontation (between Knowell and Edward), is concerned to avoid confrontations in general (for example, between Downright and Stephen), since interaction is the natural enemy of manipulation. But the most striking exponent of non-interaction is kindly old Knowell, who first comes to town in vague hopes of somehow counteracting his son's friendship, then rushes to prevent his rendezvous, and finishes by exclaiming: "My son is not married, I hope!"

This intense recoil from any form of direct emotional contact appears more subtly in the later comedies, though Mosca's ingenuity in dividing families, Subtle's and Face's voluble resistance to their own "indenture tripartite," and Morose's obsessive self-insulation sufficiently show that it can still give direct impetus to plot developments. More typically it becomes a psychological quantity fused with and expressed by cruder forms of self-interest, but casts against the backdrop a shadow under which all action takes place. Structurally, it presents itself as that recoil in the action which I have before described as occurring when two or more plot lines meet. The shock of contact, instead of impelling the action in a new direction, brings it to a temporary or even permanent standstill. After the successful courtroom scene, as after the debacle of Volpone's attempt at seduction, Mosca and Volpone have to start the action going all over again; the accidental conjunction of all plots at the end of *The Alchemist* finishes Face's comic action; just as the appearance of half the cast at Cob's house in *Every Man In* leaves each person present powerless except to shift the responsibility for action to a magistrate. The need to interact is a challenge Jonson's characters cannot meet, and it is just this disability which really interests Jonson.

The successful pursuit of this interest raises formal problems of coherence in the play as artifact, which Jonson solves by the strictest economy and unity of structure. What he erects in the Prologue into a universal creed is really the intuitive perception by an individual artist of the form he needs. The formal Unities take over the role which in interactive comedy is played by motivation, while motivation performs the splintering which in interactive comedy can be accomplished by separation in time and space. The implications as to what is the essence and what the accident in human behavior are, of course, precisely opposite. The frequent presence of a manipulator like Brainworm serves exactly the same purpose. Not only does his puppeteer-like control of the disparate actions tie them into an artistic whole—his feverish sleight-of-hand, without which there would be no plot at all, emphasizes the artificiality of simultaneous motion.

The characters themselves cohere by contrast—not only the general, and therefore structurally loose, contrast between a Downright and a Matthew, but the detailed and therefore structurally unifying contrast between, say, Matthew and Stephen. Whether or not the characters have met is immaterial; what is important is that Jonson, through parallels in their situations, puts them conceptually side by side. They throw psychological and moral light on one another by means of this non-personal unification, which in interactive comedy may reinforce the personal unification of emotional relationship, but in Jonsonian comedy replaces it. Jonson's balanced pairing sets off against one another those who seem identical and links those who seem opposite. Only when we meet the town gull, aping the fashion just coming in (rapier dueling) and praising the configuration of a friend's leg in a boot, can we comprehend the full idiotic pathos of the country gull, aping the fashion just going out (hawking) and praising the configuration of his own leg in a woolen stocking. Only beside his carefree "double" Wellbred can Edward be clearly seen as his father's serious-minded son, urging upon his counterpart temperance, abstention from oaths, and the gravity of their situation; Edward's sexual purity—or indifference—which keeps him from ever making an indecent remark stands out against Wellbred's penchant for bawdry as the latter seizes every opportunity for playing a heavy-handed Mercutio to Edward's anemic Romeo.

More telling still, because they reveal not so much character as the ultimate significance of character, are those surprising juxtapositions of the apparently unconnected or antithetical which pinpoint a character's position in a universal pattern. In the great plays such unifying contrast is a major source of ironic illumination. Consider Corbaccio, the old man who obsessively pretends that he is young and vigorous, target of scorn for Volpone, the young man who obsessively pretends that he is old and impotent. Or Tribulation Wholesome, whom Subtle the Alchemist wittily baits for serving a false and self-seeking religion. Or Trouble-all and Quarlous, Bartholomew Fair's real and pretended madmen, of whom the real seeks a "warrant" for his every action and the pretended does whatever self-involvement directs. In *Every Man In,* Jonson is already intrigued with the structural balance to be obtained through such mirror images, but, as I have noted before, his sense of irony is not yet equal to his intuitive perception of ideal form. Whatever ironic insight could be provided by identification of Brainworm (the fake fake soldier) as a version of Bobadill (the real fake soldier) is denied by the straightforward view of Brainworm we are required to take; and Bobadill as a version of Brainworm is either obvious or untrue. What we do already get from this doubling is a forceful sense—forceful because of the surprise with which we recognize the likeness—that the play operates in a unified world, where the bases of unification lie in the realm of disguise and deception. The unexpected conjunction of Brainworm and Bobadill jolts us into the characteristic universe of Jonsonian comedy, though it is not yet, as by later conjunctions, brilliantly particularized.

Yet there are certain kinds of particularity and invitations to evaluate in this comedy which are in essence the same as the structural interplay of later work. These characters, while going about their unrelated business, parody one another's behavior in as effective, if not as far-reachingly significant, a way as they do in the great plays. Not only is Cob, in his jealousy, a burlesque of Kitely; both are travesties of the troubled, spying Knowell, distorted mirror images which come together in the grand superimposition before Cob's house. Further, Knowell's acquaintanceship with the eccentric and easygoing Clement, the worried father's only reassurance, is an exact replica of the source of his worries: Edward's acquaintanceship with Wellbred—which is in its turn caricatured by that of Matthew with Bobadill (for Edward "is almost grown the idolator / Of this young Wellbred"). The cautious and unimaginative will always attach themselves respectfully to Pharaoh's foot. And so Stephen, who is even more cautious and less imaginative than Matthew, joins the pattern by giving his allegiance to that gentleman, and via him to Bobadill—for which Edward very rightly scoffs at him; while Edward's father muses in disbelief over Wellbred's letter, "Is this the man / My son hath sung so for the happiest wit, / The choicest brain the times hath sent us forth?" Everything depends on where one stands.

Knowell himself, despite his name, does not stand in the position of final authority. Personally he is appealing: the archetypal fond parent ("but why does he pick such inferior friends?"), he gives careful thought to his son's upbringing, exercises restraint and psychological insight in his discipline, puts himself to a good deal of trouble to follow his paternal course; a kindly and humane master, he risks an obviously poor investment in the begging Fitzsword, then forgives him immediately when he turns out to be Brainworm making a laughing stock of his employer; he is human enough in his customary moralism to stretch a moral point ("This letter is directed to my son; / Yet I am Edward Knowell, too . . ."), human enough in his customary generosity to be stung by the imputation of pettiness ("Why should he think I tell my apricots?"), and generous enough to recognize spontaneously that he deserves tricking, "to punish my impertinent search—and justly." But when he is placed in perspective, now with regard to this piece of similar behavior, now with regard to that, his actions lose their individuality and their coherence; he becomes depersonalized. The effect is just the opposite of that in interactive comedy, where the more links a character forms with others, the more personal qualities he displays. Knowell is instead subjected again and again to partial re-evaluation through people he has never met. His kinship with Kitely and Cob forces his reasoned solicitude to fall under the shadows of irrationality and possessiveness; his benign incomprehension of Brainworm's character must take its overall place beside Kitely's malign incomprehension of Cash's; his understandable outburst at Stephen's idiocy, "'fore heaven, I am ashamed / Thou hast a kinsman's interest in me," is qualified by Downright's excessive outburst over Wellbred's pranks: "I am grieved it should be said he is my brother, and take these courses"—an unpleasantly similar refusal of indulgence on the grounds of personal dignity. Indeed, though Knowell has never set eyes on any member of Kitely's household, what he thinks he is doing is constantly compromised by what we know they are doing. How can we retain faith in his admirable theory of discipline when we hear it parroted by futile Kitely to incompetent Downright? Here is Knowell's original: "I am resolved I will not . . . / . . . practice any violent mean to stay / The unbridled course of youth in him; . . . / . . . / There is a way of winning more by love / And urging of the modesty, than fear: / . . . / [he will] By softness and example, get a habit." And an act later, here is Kitely: "But, brother, let your reprehension, then, / Run in an easy current, not o'er-high / Carried . . . / But rather use the soft persuading way, / Whose powers will work more gently, and compose / Th'imperfect thoughts you labor to reclaim: / More winning, than enforcing the consent." We know how to value Downright's "Aye, aye, let me alone for that, I warrant you"; and Knowell's psychological validities are integrated into a pattern of useless educational theory. These implied equivalences between Knowell and others—particularly his major counterpart, Kitely—produce an interesting complication of value judgment. We are forced to look at a piece of behavior first in isolation and then all over again in juxtaposition. The positive values projected by a Knowell seen as complete in himself are as true as, but no truer than, the negative values acquired by a Knowell divided into spiritual parts with matching doubles. Who would not live in kindly, generous, softhearted Knowell's household? And yet all over London men like him are misunderstanding their servants, denying their relatives, failing their juniors, and beating their wives.

This dramatic guilt by association is not yet the glittering web of corruption woven by characters in the great plays, but it displays the identical complex of personalities, totally disparate in type, unconnected by emotional relationship, yet held together by a single spiritual disorder. But whereas *Volpone, The Alchemist,* and *The Silent Woman* are tightly constructed, each around one central spiritual disease, *Every Man In* resembles *Bartholomew Fair* in its multiplicity of aberrations, without a connecting character like the latter's Trouble-All to raise one overreaching question with his refrain, "Have you a warrant?" Instead, Jonson here strings the characters together like beads, on thematic threads which hold a few at a time. So the central question of use and misuse of poetry is touched upon by everyone except Wellbred and Brainworm; Stephen, Matthew, Kitely, Edward, and Cob are, each in his own way, ineffectual lovers; Stephen, Matthew, and Cob are foolishly concerned with lineage, on which Knowell has the deciding say; Stephen, Kitely, and Matthew all affect melancholy; and book-learning is honored and dishonored by Knowell, Cob (who likes to bring Roger Bacon and King Cophetua into the conversation), Edward, Matthew, and Stephen—each of the three last being, in his special sense, "at his book." Jonson, who dedicated this first product of his own muse to Camden, the paragon of true learning, must have enjoyed writing the mischievous counterpoint in Scene I: "*Knowell.* Myself was once . . . / Dreaming on naught but idle poetry, / . . . / But since, time and the truth have waked my judgement, (*Enter Stephen.*) / And reason taught me better to distinguish / The vain from th'useful learnings.—Cousin Stephen!"—as gratifying in its way as "the heaven's breath / Smells wooingly here: . . . / . . . / The air is delicate. (*Enter Lady Macbeth.*)"

Distortion of education, of poetry, of love, of social status—Johnson's favorite issues are all here; like the pairing of characters and the unities of time and place, they tie together the action in a delimited realm where the same problems come up over and over again. Taken together, they amount to an enumeration of abuses similar to that formed by the aggregate of Juvenal's satires, or, contemporaneously, Marston's. Jonson, who drew liberally on Juvenal in *Every Man In,* had in mind a similar anatomizing of a diseased society, though here the disease is so mild as to be merely the common cold. As Juvenal devotes one satire to dramatizing one vice, and Marston follows suit with one central representative character in each such satire, Jonson here assembles a sub-group of his characters around each separate folly and connects the groups into a play. The sum of all the parts is Society, or, more correctly, Humanity in a specific microcosm, built up out of a multitude of local references until the existence of the characters in time and place becomes indisputable.

This definition of an ethical whole by adducing all possible parts is the characteristic additive technique of Jonson's comedy. In *Every Man In* he still makes some use of the iterative technique favored by interactive comedy, in which a subplot repeats the situation of the main plot, but in the mature comedies he abandons it. Even here the iteration (Cob's and Kitely's jealousy, Edward's and Wellbred's images in their elders' eyes) is subordinate to the introduction of more and more individual examples of varied human folly. Characteristically, instead of a proliferation from one original source—of absurd passions, say, as in *A Midsummer Night's Dream,* or of hopeless adorations as in *Twelfth Night,* or of rulers and usurpers as in *The Tempest*—Jonson gives us one fox, one fruit-fly, one vulture, one crow, one raven, one parrot-turtle, and adds them together into a definitive summation of human animal life. The play's significance grows inductively, not deductively.

In *Every Man In* this typical profusion of unlike examples coheres structurally but not essentially. The absence of that pervasive symbolic imagery (e.g. of gold, of alchemy) so integral to the great plays is indicative of the absence of a pervasive metaphysical concern; the play lacks an ethical center. The attempt to make this center a loose, and moreover a practical, concept, society, is not artistically satisfying. Venice, Bartholomew Fair, an alchemical workshop—these set certain symbolic limits on the meaning of "society"; they postulate a select *kind* of society. The appearance in these settings of an apparently random sample of personages ceases to have sociological significance and instead becomes interpretable much as an emblem with separate constituents is interpretable. "Society" becomes a warped construct of warped spirits, and the accepted temporal values are so many clues to the eternal, world-controlling values which have been flouted. But London is a neutral setting in which society means merely a collocation of varied types; it cannot offer a hard ethical core. The constant insistence upon the locale, by providing a conceptual center, goes some way toward disguising the lack of an evaluative center, but it is no substitute.

In addition to this more or less artificial centralization, Jonson provides a tentative ethical norm in Justice Clement, which with sufficiently ingenious acting might prove palatable in performance. In theory Jonson is proposing a synthesis between excessive devotion to imagination (Brainworm, Wellbred, Kitely) and excessive devotion to practical concerns (Knowell, Downright) as the ordering principle in society. Clement, the orderer, is himself an older man of practical understanding, successful in the world of affairs, who recognizes the desirability of becoming "a staid man" but also sympathizes with youthful energy and excess (thus joining the two generations divided in the rest of the play), and both values and exhibits "mirth," eccentricity, and nimble wit—not to mention the nominal spiritual criterion of the play, poetry. He is the man of judgment as well as imagination. But Clement is only abstractly a satisfying character. His merry tricks are not among Jonson's happiest strokes. It is hard to be much tickled by his donning armor to meet Bobadill or by his natty scatological quatrain. His treatment of supplicant Cob borders on mild sadism ("I but fear the knave"), and his mechanical invocations of a drink of sack (four times), to signify that jollity has yet again conquered all, have the quality of slightly dipsomaniac reflex. As always, the supposedly constructive norm is by far the weakest part of Jonson's play.

The inadequacy of Justice Clement is typical of Jonson's drama because at bottom his plays are neither satire nor normative comedy, though they utilize some of the devices of each and Jonson believed them to be both. Satire, and especially social satire, constantly invokes the desirable norm whose violation it portrays. When Pope, for example, presents us with full-dress portraits of Atticus, Bufo, and Sporus in the "Epistle to Arbuthnot," he not only does it in order to advance our progressive comprehension of his own antithetical, normative self-portrait, but does it by means of allusion to ever-present and ever-recognizable norms of emotional and ethical behavior. "Damn with . . . praise," "civil leer," "timorous foe" are all phrases of crucial, deliberate paradox, which irresistibly invite the mind to contemplate their rationally and ethically coherent opposites. The pervasive technique is inversion of an established conjunction or an established standard: "Words we teach alone," "Placed at the door of Learning . . . / We never suffer it to stand too wide"—so in the *Dunciad* IV anti-education is defined by implicit appeal to the normally expected. The brilliance consists partly in the choice of just those principles which can be inverted to best effect, partly in inventing a totally unexpected form of inversion, and partly in matching the linguistic inversion to the conceptual. Jonson was very familiar with this technique, to be sure; he used it often for local effect. One thinks of the condemnation of youth in *The New Inn:* "Instead of backing the brave steed, o' mornings, / To mount the chambermaid," or of Knowell's indictment of upbringing: "only feared / His palate should degenerate, not his manners," "Can it call 'whore'? cry, 'bastard'? Oh, then kiss it," or, for a compressed paradoxical phrase, "grey gluttony." But these fine examples of concise sarcasm are, in Jonson, set pieces, not illustrations of the basic principle of design. Jonson's great successes are not posited on the functioning of antithesis, but on the inherent fascination of the thing itself. Bufo's collection of poetic busts contains what might well be taken as an emblem of satirical antithesis: "a true *Pindar* . . . without a head." A headless bust is funny because the concept of a bust depends upon the head. But upon what conceptual norm does the funniness of Bobadill, or even of Stephen, depend? Only upon the broad assumption that human beings behave with a degree of moderation, rationality, and adherence to fact. Even Jonson's powerfully irradiated metaphysical norms operate only as beacons from which to measure the distance to a character's actual location. They illuminate grandly but generally. So Volpone's religious invocation to his gold and Subtle's catechism of Face impart to these characters' actions the thrill of blasphemy, but make them infinitely culpable without instilling any corresponding sense of the desirability of conventional worship or, indeed, of any particular mode of behavior except the avoidance of what we see. Jonson's success, in such moments, is the combination of shudder and laugh.

Just as Jonson's greatest strokes are independent of the support of any precisely defined norm, so it is impossible to deduce a specific norm from them by contrast, as one can deduce Pope from the negation of Atticus, Bufo, and Sporus. This definition of a norm by contrast is a technique satire shares with normative comedy. From *Twelfth Night*'s Duke and Olivia we can deduce the ideal of Viola; from the midsummer-night's lovers, Theseus; from the couples in the Forest of Arden, Rosalind. But Celia and Bonario are not delineated by their opposition to the other characters except insofar as good is the opposite of bad—rather too broad a contrast to serve for integrated dramatic structure. It is not just that Celia and Bonario are unsuccessfully characterized, as Justice Clement is unsuccessfully characterized. True, they are bores, and Justice Clement is a bore, and Crites in *Cynthia's Revels* is a bore—but so, at times, is Milton's God, without invalidating his normative function. What is peculiar about Jonson's normative characters is that they are extraneous to the real dramatic activity of the play. They are not engaged in the same type of action as the others in a more desirable way (like Viola, Theseus, and Rosalind)—they are simply not engaged in the same type of action. The nature of Jonson's comedy precludes the integrated normative character. Justice Clement is a try at it, but he, too, remains dramatically irrelevant, though his eccentricity is certainly an attempt to show him behaving like the others in a more desirable way. He is intractably extraneous to Stephen and Matthew, if not to Brainworm and Wellbred, and, what is much worse, hopelessly extraneous to the chief ornaments of the play, Kitely and Bobadill. Jonson's attempt to proffer him symbolically as a normative version of Bobadill by making him dress up as a soldier is only embarrassing.

The truth is that Jonson's greatness is not the greatness of satire at all, except in the supremely general sense in which all great comedy is satire because it exposes neglected truths about human behavior. Nor is it the greatness of normative vision. Jonson, in his numerous manifesto-like utterances, has himself been the most diligent obfuscator of his creation. Evidently he regarded himself, and wished to regard himself, as a writer of corrective comedy and satire. Indeed, his compelling moral and ethical bias caused him to punish all his highly imaginative characters for deviation from spiritual and social equipoise—perhaps a form of self-flagellation for his own zest in portraying their feats. But no amount of beating or imprisonment can convince us that Bobadill is less worthwhile than Justice Clement, or that Bonario should have been a model for Volpone. Jonson's devotion to the ideals of correction and satire pulls in a direction contrary to his bent for pure comedy, and creates an unevenness in the progress of his work. His social satire is by turns brilliant, dull, and incandescent: brilliant when it constitutes a beautifully composed aria; dull when it affords merely "an image of the times" (Cob on fasting days); incandescent when it plays into Jonson's comedy of solipsism by giving his characters recognizable objects of obsession. When it is incandescent it is not at all corrective. To lampoon the affectations of fencing or the popularity of tobacco is no more the real point of Bobadill than to decry the disproportionate concentration of wealth among the aristocracy is the point of *Volpone.* The road of normality from which Bobadill and Volpone have diverged is lost to view, and well lost, behind the picturesque landscape of the territory in which they have arrived.

On the grounds of successful presentation of a comic norm, we would have to give the palm to *Poetaster,* since Horace, if not lovable, is at least deducible. But this evaluation is manifest nonsense. It is evident that Jonson is writing a different sort of comedy: non-normative comedy. Jonson's success is invariably to be gauged by the strength of the anti-norm. His greatest plays succeed not by enforcing a concept of balance but by impressing upon us the overwhelming force of imbalance. So *Every Man In* succeeds not insofar as Justice Clement succeeds but insofar as Bobadill and Kitely succeed. For Jonson is not writing about common agreement on the outside world at all. He is writing about diverse and unmergeable inner worlds, about the impossibility of common agreement, about the psychological artificiality of a commonly defined outer world, even when it is a moral necessity. We recognize him as a writer of genius when he exchanges the mandatory optimism of satire for the deep pessimism of comedy.

Jonson's comedy is of the type afforded by a really thoroughgoing marital quarrel or a United Nations debate. It is the comedy of minds which never touch, of confinement within an insurmountable point of view. Jonson's so-called humor characters and his later elaborations upon them are human beings whose minds have become (or have been from the beginning) rigid in a certain position—a phenomenon by no means uncommon. In fact it is the frustrating familiarity of the immovable mind in ordinary life that makes its objectification on the stage so welcome. Anyone who has been much concerned with logical demonstration—anyone who has taught—has bowed to the inert strength of Stephen's type of mind, as pliable and as resilient as rubber. Give him your best twenty-five lines on the social, moral, and logical impossibility of standing upon gentility, and he will yield you the following harvest: "Nay, we do'not stand much on our gentility, friend; yet you are welcome, and I assure you, mine uncle here is a man of a thousand a year, Middlesex land; he has but one son in all the world, I am his next heir (at the common law), Master Stephen, as simple as I stand here . . . though I do not stand upon my gentility neither in't."

But it is not only specific types of fixity that we recognize in Jonson. It is the inherent capacity of every mind to retreat, as it does in extreme joy or extreme pain, deep into itself, and there to relate every event to its own pleasure or suffering. It is the impulse which upheld for thousands of years the natural assumption that the sun revolves around the earth. It is the impulse which convinces us that the automobile turning at the same corner with us contains guests for the party to which we are going. When Knowell before Cob's house absurdly mis-sees Kitely ("Soft, who is this? 'tis not my son, disguised?")—when, unregenerately solipsistic in the very utterance which proclaims his supposed comprehension, he nods wisely, "I do taste this as a trick, put on me / To punish my impertinent search—and justly; / And half forgive my son for the device"—he is the exact comic equivalent of Lear on the heath mis-seeing Edgar: "Didst thou give all to thy two daughters? And art thou come to this? . . . Nothing could have subdu'd nature to such a lowness, but his unkind daughters. . . . Judicious punishment!" They are both upholding a sense of personal significance and mental control in the face of a universe suddenly incomprehensible. Since both have chosen to define themselves by their relationships to their children, if they are to see themselves as centrally important they must see outer events as similarly defined. Lear responds to Kent's "He hath no daughters, sir," with "Death, traitor!" while Knowell reacts to Clement's "Your son is old enough to govern himself" with total deafness. Who can bear to be tangential?

Jonsonian comedy constantly plays upon its participants the cosmic joke of encouraging each to think himself central, while its author knows that they are every one tangential. This is exactly the joke Wellbred and Edward play upon Matthew and Stephen, Volpone and Subtle upon their visitors, Mosca and Face upon Volpone and Subtle, and Jonson upon Mosca and Face. Furthermore, since the characters, being non-interactive, are all tangential to one another, the action is a continual revelation that centrality is delusion. *Volpone* and *The Alchemist* play out the joke most perfectly, for here Jonson produces with inexhaustible copiousness another and yet another variation on the deluded figure of The Chosen, within a situation itself dependent upon the concept. Each of Volpone's dupes believes that "Only you / Of all the rest, are he commands his love," just as Volpone believes this in regard to Mosca; each dupe believes that the inheritance "is yours without a rival, / Decreed by destiny," just as Mosca believes this for himself. Each of Subtle's gulls believes not only that Subtle is an initiate, but also that he himself is uniquely selected to share in supernatural benefits, as long as he does not "cause the blessing leave you." The paradigm case is certainly Dapper, persuaded that "a rare star / Reign'd at your birth" and made him nephew and favorite of the Queen of Fairies; the really important action crowds him into the privy, to drop utterly out of memory for an act and a half. The audience itself becomes an accomplice in the existential joke; we forget him, his gag, his blindfold, his hopes, his illusions—and his sudden return into our consciousness, sick to his stomach, totally irrelevant, unwaveringly committed to his long-obsolete centrality, makes his *cri de coeur,* "For God's sake, when will her Grace be at leisure?" one of the great triumphs of comedy.

The essence of Dapper is already incarnated in *Every Man In:* in Stephen, "a wight that (hitherto) his every step hath left the stamp of a great foot behind him, . . . the true, rare, and accomplished monster—or miracle—of nature"; in Matthew, exemplar of "some peculiar and choice spirits to whom I am extraordinarily engaged"; in Bobadill, singled out for persecution by the multitude "Because I am excellent, and for no other vile reason on the earth"; all bear willingly the burden of unique importance. And the tangential privy is present, too, in the form of the buttery and courtyard to which these indispensable spirits are consigned—Matthew and Bobadill fasting, like Dapper, and urged to "pray there that we may be so merry within as to forgive or forget you."

Jonson's unwillingness or unreadiness to see his own implications in *Every Man In* makes him conceal the necessary ending of his joke behind the comforting charade of mutual centrality arranged by Justice Clement for the "worthy" characters; but though he is not yet prepared to admit that Clement himself, in a non-interactive universe, must be tangential in his attempt to impose order (an admission finally made in Justice Overdo of *Bartholomew Fair*), he is already drawing characters of stature whose claim to dignity is the degree of their delusion. For to accept tangentiality can only be a source of stature when the inner self is so strong and spiritually resourceful that it can afford to secede from what it has come to recognize as centrality, and to rely wholly on itself, or itself in combination with its few spiritual allies. It declares the central principles of the universe tangential to something of greater value which it possesses in itself. This is the condition of Lear in his final address to Cordelia, in which he welcomes their prison as a reflection of the tangentiality he desires. Jonson's "humor" characters counterfeit this condition of spiritual independence by ignoring the central principles of the universe and erecting whatever psychological principle is most crucial to their own inner lives into an objective truth or criterion of value. Having eschewed any painful confrontation with reality, they are subject to have their scheme of values destroyed by its intrusion, as Lear no longer is. Reality, in the very act of destroying what is dearest to Lear, can only confirm its importance. In destroying the humor character's psychological treasure, however, reality would simultaneously wipe out its significance. Consequently there is almost no limit to the amount of delusion Jonsonian characters are willing to accept or invent for themselves to fend off what would be—and in the end often is—psychological annihilation.

This clinging to a subjective construct is much closer to what most men do in real life than the behavior of Lear. Very few of us are willing to die and be born again; we would rather live with all our imperfections on our heads—preferably regarded as special versions of perfection. Who has not marveled at the extraordinary inner jugglings and compromises that human beings prefer to what an observer, with the smugness of detachment, can call "facing the facts"? Such self-delusion is the instinct of self-preservation dictating to the mind; despite all self-righteous superiority, we must recognize survival as victory—and especially survival with *panache.* Who could do other than applaud Bobadill's virtuoso recovery from the brutality of fact: "*Matthew.* . . . But what can they say of your beating? *Bobadill.* A rude part, a touch with soft wood, a kind of gross battery used, laid on strongly, borne most patiently: and that's all"—or refuse to admire that gallant vision of an ideal world especially constructed for him: "*Matthew.* Aye, but would any man have offered it in Venice—as you say? *Bobadill.* Tut, I assure you, no: you shall have there your *nobilis,* your *gentilezza,* come in bravely upon your reverse, stand you close, stand you firm, stand you fair, save your *retricato* with his left leg, come to the *assalto* with the right, thrust with brave steel, defy your base wood! But wherefore do I awake this remembrance?" *Nessun maggior dolore che ricordarsi del tempo felice nella miseria*—as they say in Venice.

This saving imbalance which invents its self-centralized Utopia ("*Knowell.* When I was young, he lived not in the stews, / Durst have conceived a scorn, and uttered it, / On a gray head; age was authority / Against a buffon"; "*Kitely.* See, what a drove of horns fly in the air, / . . . / Watch 'em, suspicious eyes, watch where they fall. / See, see! On heads that think th'have none at all!")—this imbalance was fitly imaged by contemporary medicine as physical incompatibility with the elements of the universe. The universe being, to the Elizabethan view, a balanced composition of the four elements—earth, air, fire, and water—the little world of man formed a corresponding amalgam of the four "humors," earth appearing as bile or melancholy (cold and dry), air as blood (hot and moist), fire as choler (hot and dry), and water as phlegm (cold and moist). Predominance of one element produced physical and thus psychological unbalance—the condition of a humor character. It is easy to see how this well-known medical theory would be symbolically suggestive for Jonson, interested as he was in the predominance of one element of the inner self and the ensuing lack of correspondence between the makeup of an individual and the makeup of his surroundings. It is equally easy to see how the simplistic concept of four humors would rapidly become inadequate for dramatic representation of mental convolutions in a character engaged in preserving his psychological existence. So even in *Every Man In* only Kitely is a true humor character, suffering from a recognizable medical condition of head-melancholy, while in the others "melancholy" is already a metaphor for a spiritual stance, and "humor" shorthand for "identifying aspect of self."

Jonson's cosmic joke is the disparity between the psychological need of human beings for this kind of significant identification and the inexorable demands of the universe or society. Refusing reduction of their unique selves to a balanced component of the impersonal universe; refusing the moral equivalent, a Christian self-abnegation for the common salvation; refusing the psychological analogue, yielding up a portion of the self to relationship with another human being—Jonson's comic characters revel in their delusion of freedom. Their solipsistic conviction of centrality renders them infinitely gullible and creates Jonson's special comedy of mutual deception. Sundered from the outside world by urgent attention to an inner clamor, these characters meet in a congenial setting (which fosters their illusions of a reality constructed around their needs) to assume the roles of dupe and manipulator-dupe. For the manipulators are merely solipsists with talent. Perceiving in their superior intelligence that other human beings render themselves cosmically ridiculous by a rigidity calculated as monumentality, they seek their escape into significance by way of volatility. Instead of one mask of self the manipulator assumes many, as though this were a difference in kind. But his varied masks prove to be only alternative ways of making a single statement about himself, for disguises in Jonson's mature plays are always as ironically revelatory of hidden springs of motivation as are the self-presentations of the dupes. The manipulator, though gifted with more consciousness of his surroundings than the people he manipulates, is still rigid in acting out his conviction that he defines the universe, that only the creations of his intellect are really real, and that events are arrangeable for his exclusive benefit. In the end his line of force, too, crosses another, and the collision overthrows him; he discovers that the action to which he is central is itself tangential to another which he did not comprehend. This is the fate of Brainworm. His disguises as manipulator, like the other typically Jonsonian elements in the play, are not ironically exploited, but they are already ironic in their deceptive offer of freedom. Not only is Brainworm entrapped by his disguise into the final accounting, but he has himself had to recognize at the outset—when he was less self-enamored—that disguise is a ruse by which the tangential character renders himself apparently central: "now I, . . . to insinuate with my young master (for so must we that are . . . men of hope and service, do . . .) have got me afore in this disguise." Whether he be nominally dupe or nominally manipulator, the Jonsonian character is ultimately confronted with the fact that every man's action involves him in, and subordinates him to, the action of others—whereupon Jonsonian man ceases to function.

This active and passive solipsism produces those moments of collision which, together with the inspired portrayal of self-delimited character, are the glory of Jonsonian comedy. Seen from without, a moment of collision is a point at which two (or more) consciousnesses, like billiard balls of different colors, touch surfaces with a perceptible click and part. One might take as its type this interchange between Mosca and Volpone:

MOSCA. You loathe the widow's or the orphan's tears
Should wash your pavements, or their piteous cries
Ring in your roofs, and beat the air for vengeance—
VOLPONE. Right, Mosca, I do loathe it.

The pleasures of Volpone's reply are manifold. One is simply the neatness of the collision itself, like a well-executed shot at billiards. Beyond this lies the sudden perception that what appears to be communication is only self-propulsion. Beyond this still, the intellectual pleasure of recognizing, in one sharp instant, the source of the collision, the gap between the ruthless, bored aristocracy of Volpone the Magnifico and the essentially conventional, bourgeois orientation of social-climbing Mosca. And just as the points at which moving objects collide with a stationary one define the outer limits of the latter, so this collision defines the outer limits of Volpone's human comprehension.

The defining collision is already one of the aural satisfactions of *Every Man In:*

BRAINWORM. [disguised as a soldier]. I assure you, the blade may become the side or thigh of the best prince in Europe.
EDWARD. Aye, with a velvet scabbard, I think.
STEPHEN. Nay, and't be mine, it shall have a velvet scabbard, cos, that's flat . . .

Here are fewer overtones, no doubt—less resonance; but that is in the nature of the body struck. Kitely gives off a deeper sound:

KITELY. if thou should'st
Reveal it, but—
CASH. How? I reveal it?
KITELY. Nay,
I do not think thou would'st; but if thou should'st:
'Twere a great weakness.
CASH. A great treachery.
Give it no other name.
KITELY. Thou wilt not do't, then?
CASH. Sir, if I do, mankind disclaim me ever.
KITELY. [*Aside.*] He will not swear, he has some reservation.

Here the *non sequitur* bears more clearly the identifying marks of such a moment of collision. Seen from within, it is a point at which one human being (often, though not here, himself the fantasy hero in his own world) enters the delusion of another in a supporting role—a moment when the nearness of outer reality, in the shape of an independent presence, only lights up the cavernous reaches of the deluded self.

It is Jonson's special gift to embody this illumination in an instant, in a single clash of phrase against phrase. But the mental process, which in Jonson always remains implicit, may be clearer if we look at a more expansive treatment. Novelistically seen, the bitter comedy of non-interaction unrolls as follows:

> "Remember, we are looking forward to a better sort of happiness even than this . . . Come, dear, tell me how soon you can be altogether mine."
>
> There was a serious pleading in Lydgate's tone . . . Rosamond became serious too, and slightly meditative; in fact, she was going through many intricacies of lace-edging and hosiery and petticoat-tucking, in order to give an answer that would at least be approximative.

> . . . "There would be the house-linen and the furniture to be prepared. Still, mamma could see to those while we were away."
> "Yes, to be sure. We must be away a week or so."
> "Oh, more than that!" said Rosamond, earnestly. She was thinking of her evening dresses for the visit to Sir Godwin Lydgate's, which she had long been secretly hoping for as a delightful employment of at least one quarter of the honeymoon . . . She looked at her lover with some wondering remonstrance as she spoke, and he readily understood that she might wish to lengthen the sweet time of double solitude.
>
> (*Middlemarch,* Bk. IV, Ch. xxxvi)

Here is the impenetrability of mind to mind upon which relationship thrives. If Rosamond and Lydgate understood one another, they would instantly part; just so Volpone and Mosca. But each would have to give up a crucial character in his personal drama, or even the drama itself as plotted by the self-creating sensibility. Anything rather than that; so, in the Jonsonian world, fuller than Middlemarch of comedy and hopelessness, incomprehension becomes the only basis of relationship. All important relationships in the plays could be seen as collisions drawn out into the semblance of interaction.

The converse is also true: a moment of collision occurring within what passes itself off, to either or both of the participants, as a relationship reveals its essence, and heralds the inevitable disintegration of its bonds. But it is a failed revelation. It is the moment we remember in retrospect and understand when acrid experience has confirmed it. Jonson's entirely external representation of it shifts the burden of comprehension from actor to observer: as audience, we pre-experience what the speaker may never come to feel. Kitely, who fears nothing so much as pseudo-relationship, is revealed in this moment as doomed to its creation; in his mental deflection from contact with Cash we can foresee the whole unraveling, from "He is a jewel, brother . . . in his place so full of faith that I durst trust my life into his hands" to "Oh, that villain dors me. . . . She's gone a'purpose, now, to cuckold me / With that lewd rascal, who, to win her favor, / Hath told her all." We can foresee it because, as in Volpone's reply, we have heard Kitely fix the limits of his comprehension. "Full of faith" can have no practical meaning for a man himself constitutionally incapable of faith, just as "sweet . . . solitude" can have no meaning for a woman who derives all sense of personal value from contact with others. Clement dimly perceives Kitely's plight when he offers his truism: "Horns in the mind are worse than on the head"; but Kitely never understands his disability at all, and so preserves his inner construct against the assault of Clement's good sense. Similarly, Stephen remains as impervious to Edward's indirect as to Clement's direct sarcasm, and to the implications of his final allotted place (with Cob and Tib in the buttery) for his gentlemanly pretensions. All his connections are laid open as false; but to Stephen the revelation does not signify for he is equally happy with relationship or pseudo-relationship—a position self-sufficient in its irony, and typically Jonsonian. Self-absorption is the source of all vital energy; relationship must crumble before it.

The crudest dramatic version of this statement—the leave-taking between Mosca and deaf Corbaccio—serves best as symbolic pattern for these unnoticed collisions which prefigure disruption:

MOSCA. You are he
For whom I labor here.
CORBACCIO. Ay, do, do, do.
I'll straight about it.
MOSCA. Rook go with you, raven.
CORBACCIO. I know thee honest.
MOSCA. You do lie, sir—
CORBACCIO. And—
MOSCA. Your knowledge is no better than your ears, sir.
CORBACCIO. I do not doubt to be a father to thee.

The closeness necessary to collision often masquerades as a high point of psychological intimacy. Deafness, of course, is essential, but then it is never lacking.

> Rosamond thought no one could be more in love than she was; and Lydgate . . . felt as if already breathed upon by exquisite wedded affection . . . by an accomplished creature who venerated his high musings . . . marriage would not be an obstruction but a furtherance.

These are the moments at which relationship becomes evidently hopeless.

Such collisions are undoubtedly the most ironic; yet there is another group of collisions which shares all their basic principles and is even more purely comic—those between people utterly unrelated to one another. Here the disparity between apparent intimate connection and actual indifference is absolute. Here the sole justification for a belief in connection is the construct of the individual mind. So intense is the craving for personal centrality that perception simply gulps down whole anyone who walks into range. One thinks of jealous Lady Wouldbe "unmasking" Peregrine as a harlot, or of pugnacious Kastril, interrupted in a deliberate breach of the peace—his attempt to start a fight with Surly—when Ananias brings Subtle the news of the Puritan capitulation to alchemy: "*Ananias.* Peace to the household. . . . Casting of dollars is concluded lawful. *Kastril.* Is he the constable?" Here the hopelessness of relationship is not grounded in personal difference; it appears rather as a category of experience. Out of the chaotic happenstance of ordinary life the mind constructs an orderly set of relationships—painful perhaps, but also full of meaning. By the end of this latter scene, the accidental convergence of a number of unrelated customers upon the Alchemist's house has been satisfactorily arranged into significant pattern in the mind of each—in each mind, a different significant pattern.

In these collisions the hopelessness of relationship and the mind's circumvention of it are represented dramatically in the sudden encounter between disparate actions. The great example in *Every Man In* is the scene before Cob's house, the play's climax. The fantasy of interaction can go no further than the mutual "recognition" of Kitely and Knowell, begun when Knowell identifies Dame Kitely ("Oh, this is the female copesmate of my son! / Now I shall meet him straight"), continuing with Knowell's assimilation of Kitely into his private world as Edward, and culminating in the moment of actual collision, as Kitely literally turns around and assimilates Knowell: "This hoary-headed lecher, this old goat, / . . . / O, old incontinent, dost not thou shame, / When all thy powers' inchastity is spent, / To have a mind so hot?" This is the very parody of Aristotle's "discovery and peripeteia," the conjunction by which tragic action becomes meaningful to its protagonist. If action has no inherent meaning, but is only a product of individual bent or of manipulation, then pattern in events is the product of the mind's illusion. And under the circumstances coexisting before Cob's house, the logic of delusion is at least as persuasive as the real explanation. We have a choice, momentarily, only between the crazy conclusion of Kitely ("*Knowell.* What lunacy is this, that haunts this man?") and the obsessive insistence of Knowell ("*Tib.* The constable? The man is mad, I think"), wherein either derangement is aesthetically far more satisfying, in its imaginative unity, than the truth. Is it not wholly natural to prefer the organically meaningful, internally consistent plot of either of these imaginary actions to the forced, meaningless machinations of Brainworm? and to prefer to see oneself as the hub of the one rather than a cog in the other? The moment is uniquely Jonsonian in inducting us into the satisfactions of imaginative delusion. The characters have successfully escaped epiphany. Like chaotic *Bartholomew Fair*'s Trouble-All, also haunted by lunacy and also calling for the official representative of law and order, they preserve faith in the "warrant" behind action by retreat into the self. The moment of collision, with its proffer of reality, is a dangerous invitation refused.

The ultimate importance of collision, then, is that it provides the occasion upon which the self is enabled to confirm its refashioning of reality. At these moments the deluded mind ties together events in the outside world, and ties itself to the world by the illusion of human relationship. Since neither connection really exists, commitment to them means further and further progress into fantasy—the typical mode by which action in Jonsonian comedy advances.

Though Jonson professed himself to be writing in the spirit of the ancients, and cited Greek authority for his belief that "The parts of a Comedy are the same with a Tragedy, and the end is partly the same" (*Discoveries* 2625–26), the premises of his comedy are directly anti-Aristotelian. Aristotle recommends the choice of incidents which have "an appearance of design as it were in them; as for instance the statue of Mitys at Argos killed the author of Mitys' death by falling down on him . . .; for incidents like that we think to be not without meaning. A Plot, therefore, of this sort is necessarily finer than others" (*Poetics,* 1452a). But this sort of fine plot is limited to the imaginations of Jonson's characters. In Jonson's own plot coherence is formal and symbolic, but never personally meaningful. If final coherence is established, it is imposed from without in the name of ethically necessary order—a process not inherently different from manipulation, or from the imposition of psychologically necessary order, but aimed away from, rather than toward, individual freedom. The need for bondage is also very strong. Jonson's comic action appeals to the aspiration for significance; his moral endings, to the conviction of mediocrity—the belief that real strength is social strength, that real meaning is the meaning of the group, the company, the university, the church. Without these saving structures we would live, in a Jonsonian universe, in the midst of the comedy of non-interaction forever. With them, we can join in composing a harmonious balance of which each element is equally unimportant.

Committed to both its comic action and its ending, *Every Man In* provides conflicting answers to that most basic Jonsonian question: is non-interaction the cause or the effect of the characters' delusions? Jonson the critic and satirist would like us to deduce that it is effect: that a beneficent universe is distorted by, then rescued from, abnormality. But Jonson the comic genius deduces for us, rather, from the premises of an indifferent universe, splendid abnormalities of the protesting imagination.

From "Upon the report of the printing of the Dramaticall Poems of Master *John Fletcher*" (1647)

William Cartwright

Johnson hath writ things lasting, and divine,
Yet his Love-Scenes, Fletcher, compared to thine,
Are cold and frosty, and expressed love so,
As heat with Ice, or warm fires mixed with Snow. . . .

This passage is from a lengthy commendation in the front matter of Francis Beaumont and John Fletcher's 1647 *Comedies and Tragedies.*

From the Preface to *The Humorists* (1671)

THOMAS SHADWELL

Mr. *Jonson,* I believe, was very unjustly taxed for personating particular men, but it will ever be the fate of them, that write the humors of the *Town,* especially in a foolish, and vicious Age.

I cannot be of their opinion who think he wanted wit, I am sure, if he did, he was so far from being the most faultless, that he was the most faulty Poet of his time, but, it may be answered, that his Writings were correct, though he wanted fire; but I think flat and dull things are as incorrect, and show as little Judgment in the Author, nay less than sprightly and mettled Nonsense does. But I think he had more true Wit than any of his Contemporaries; that other men had sometimes things that seemed more fiery than his, was because they were placed with so many sordid and mean things about them, that they made a greater show.

These prefatory remarks first appear in the 1671 version of Shadwell's 1670 play.

Epilogue to *The Humorists* (1691)

THOMAS SHADWELL

The Mighty Prince of Poets, learned *BEN,*
Who alone dived into the Minds of Men:
Saw all their wandrings, all their follies knew,
And all their vain fantastic Passions drew,
In Images so lively and so true;
That there each Humorist himself might view,
Yet only lashed the Errors of the Times,
And ne'er exposed the Persons, but the Crimes:
And never cared for private frowns, when he
Did but chastise public iniquity,
He feared no Pimp, no Pickpocket, or Drab;
He feared no *Bravo,* nor no Ruffian's Stab.
'Twas he alone true Humors understood,
And with great Wit and Judgment made them good.
A Humor is the Bias of the Mind,
By which with violence 'tis one way inclined:
It makes our Actions lean on one side still,
And in all Changes that way bends the Will.
This—
He only knew and represented right.
Thus none but Mighty *Jonson* e'er could write.
Expect not then, since that most flourishing Age,
Of *BEN* to see true Humor on the Stage.
All that have since been writ, if they be scanned,
Are but faint Copies from that Master's Hand.
Our Poet now, amongst those petty things,
Alas, his too weak trifling humors brings.
As much beneath the worst in Jonson's Plays,
As his great Merit is above our praise.

This epilogue, part of the original play in 1670, is quoted here from the 1691 edition.

For could he imitate that great Author right,
He would with ease all Poets else out-write.
But to out-go all other men, would be
O Noble *BEN!* less than to follow thee.
Gallants you see how hard it is to write,
Forgive all faults the Poet made tonight:
Since if he sinned, 'twas meant for your delight.
Pray let this find—
As good success, though it be very bad,
As any damned successful Play e'er had.
Yet if you hiss, he knows not where the harm is,
He'll not defend his Nonsense *Vi & Armis.*
But this poor Play has been so torn before,
That all your Cruelty can't wound it more.

From *Letters upon Several Occasions* (1696)

WILLIAM CONGREVE

The Character of *Cob* in *Every Man In his Humour,* and most of the under Characters in *Bartholomew Fair,* discover only a Singularity of Manners, appropriated to the several Educations and Professions of the Persons represented. They are not Humours but Habits contracted by Custom. Under this Head may be ranged all Country Clowns, Sailors, Tradesmen, Jockeys, Gamesters and such like, who make use of *Cants* or peculiar *Dialects* in their several Arts and Vocations. One may almost give a Receipt for the Composition of such a Character: For the Poet has nothing to do, but to collect a few proper phrases and terms of Art, and to make the Person apply them by ridiculous Metaphors in his Conversation, with Characters of different natures. Some late Characters of this kind have been very successful; but in my mind they may be painted without much Art or Labour; since they require little more, than a good Memory and Superficial Observation. But true *Humour* cannot be shown, without a Dissection of Nature, and a Narrow Search to discover the first Seeds, from whence it has its Root and growth.

From a letter to John Dennis, July 10, 1695, p. 90.

From *Dramatic Miscellanies* (1783–1784)

THOMAS DAVIES

Every Man In his Humour is founded on such follies and passions as are perpetually incident to, and connected with, man's nature; such as do not depend upon local custom or change of fashion; and, for that reason, will bid fair to last as long as many of our old comedies. The language of Jonson is very peculiar; in perspicuity and elegance he is inferior to Beaumont and Fletcher, and very unlike the masculine dialogue of Massinger. It is almost needless to observe that he comes far short of the variety, strength, and natural flow, of Shakespeare. To avoid the common idiom, he plunges into stiff, quaint, and harsh, phraseology: he has borrowed more words, from the Latin tongue, than all the authors of his time. However, the style of this play, as well as that of the *Alchemist* and *Silent Woman,* is more disentangled and free from foreign auxiliaries than the greatest part of his works. Most of the characters are truly dramatic: Kitely, though not equal to Ford in *The Merry Wives of Windsor,* who can plead a more justifiable cause of jealousy, is yet well conceived, and is placed so artfully in situation, as to draw forth a considerable share of comic distress.

Bobadil is an original. The coward, assuming the dignity of calm courage, was, I believe, new to our stage; at least, I can remember nothing like him. From Bobadil, Congreve formed his Noll Bluff; a part most admirably acted by Ben Jonson the comedian. Master Stephen is an honester object of ridicule than master Slender. One is nature's oaf, consequently rather an object of compassion than of scorn. The other is a fop of fashion, and the gulled imitator of the follies which he admires in his companions. Clement and Downright are strongly marked with humour, especially the first; and Brainworm is a fellow of merry and arch contrivance. In drawing this character, I believe the author had Terence, or rather, Plautus, of whom he was acknowledged to be an imitator, in his eye. Wellbred and young Knowell are distinguished by no particularities. Old Knowell is something like the anxious Simo of Terence.

This passage appears in chapter 13 of Davies' study.

Old Ben's *New Inn*

ROBERT N. WATSON

I

Ben Jonson's comedies are acts of theatrical imperialism. Dryden's famous praise of Jonson's adaptations—"He invades Authours like a Monarch; and what would be theft in other Poets is onely victory in him"—aptly describes these campaigns for artistic Lebensraum.[1] Jonson's thefts are not furtive: they are tactics in a proud campaign for sovereignty in the drama. He systematically subsumes the more conventional plays of his rivals, forcing them to work for his exaltation, like the Asian kings who lift Tamburlaine into greater glory by their very subjugation. Instead of placing ridiculous versions of those rival plays on his stage, as an ordinary parodist would, Jonson places them implicitly in the minds of his foolish characters. He then shows those characters trying to live out their melodramatic fantasies within the more realistic environment of Jacobean city-comedy, an environment that is as hostile to naive fantasies as Jonson was to the works of his naive fellow-playwrights. Allowing a Jonsonian satirist to exploit and defeat all these pretenders and pretensions implies Jonson's sovereignty over his conventional competitors.

The project Jonson undertakes in the realm of drama resembles the project Cervantes undertook in the realm of fiction during the same period, using self-dramatizing characters primarily to belittle unhealthy literary forms. Jonson establishes his own generic space by creating truly Quixotic characters, characters who in various ways suppose themselves central figures in a conventional plot suited to their humors. For example, Wasp, the Knowells, and the Penniboys anticipate a prodigal-son story; Drugger hopes for a citizen-comedy; Celia and Bonario await a sentimental melodrama; Kitely, Corvino, and Fitzdotterel fear a cuckolding fabliau; Deliro essays a Petrarchan courtship; Dapper believes in a fairy tale; Overdo constructs a disguised-magistrate plot; Volpone mimics a legacy-hunting fable; Kastril trains for a roaring-boy interlude; Pug attempts a morality play; Truewit stages

From Robert N. Watson, *Ben Jonson's Parodic Strategy: Literary Imperialism in the Comedies* (Cambridge: Harvard University Press, 1987), and adapted by the author for this volume. Reprinted by permission of Harvard University Press.

an antimasque; Subtle and Meercraft foresee a coney-catching tale; Brainworm and Mosca undertake a classical New Comedy; and so on. As if in a Pirandello play, each character fights with the others for the privilege of staging the story in which each imagines himself (or herself) as the hero.

Those who complacently await the fulfillment of their fantasies are surprised by satire. They fall into the hands of a playwright-figure who (as Jonson's surrogate) encourages the conventional and egoistical expectations to collide with each other, creating his own mordant and triumphant plot out of their collision. The audience's conventional expectations of plot, meanwhile, have been similarly aroused, exploited, and overruled by Jonson himself. He recognized, in the dynamics of reader response, an opportunity to ambush not only a variety of hackneyed traditions, but also the intellectual complacency that sustained those traditions. His victory is truly a coup de théâtre, a subversive seizure of territory within the dramatic genre.

Metadrama, which serves to blur the distinction between art and life in so many Renaissance plays, serves in Jonsonian comedy to insist on that distinction. If we allow ourselves to be lured into mistaking the characters' melodramatic self-conceptions for Jonson's signals of his own generic intentions, we leave ourselves vulnerable to a humiliating reminder that, like the characters onstage, we have been perceiving only residual images of our previous experiences at the theater rather than the more immediate reality confronting us. Only by casting away the stale melodramatic expectations we brought to the theater and approving instead Jonson's new approach, can we identify ourselves with the triumphant wits instead of with the fools who pay dearly for an unrealistic and unrewarding fantasy. The subliminal plays-within-the-play are the things wherein Jonson catches our literary consciences.

In the *New Organon,* Francis Bacon calls one crucial set of obstacles to scientific progress "Idols of the Theater." The theater was his metaphor for the human tendency to subjugate what we see to what we have read, to perceive according to received authoritative schemes (such as those of Aristotle) instead of applying our own rational judgment to the information provided by our own senses. Jonson endorses Bacon's warning in his critical *Discoveries,*[2] and in his comedies he literalizes the metaphor in order to warn against an obstacle to progress in the drama: the gulls in these plays are usually idolators of the theater. What to us are conventions of a genre, to these characters are delusions, usually of grandeur. Like the disillusioned Caesar in *Poetaster,* Jonson sharply and persistently asks his characters "[N]ot what you play? But, what you are?" (4.6.25).[3]

Jonson portrays the triumph of realism over grandiose fantasy in a way that allows the theory and the practice to legitimize each other. What are generally considered his weaker plays are the ones where the two projects are most distinguishable—where the story lacks any essential critical thrust and where the critical argument (in the form of a prologue or a chorus) takes place almost entirely apart from the story. The action of the stronger plays represents, in the form of a sequential plot, the gesture of superiority Jonson achieves by writing such a plot. His surrogates often triumph simply because Jonson puts them at the center stage rather than on the periphery, and ends the play when they happen to be ahead. It is largely a question of framing: if Brueghel chooses to diminish his story to a pair of bare legs in the corner of the canvas, Icarus becomes a bit player. Decentering a conventional motif is the artist's way of asserting control and independence. In this sense, the fate of Jonson's gulls frequently resembles the fate of Milton's Satan, whose proud display of classical heroism is transumed by the Christian superstructure of *Paradise Lost.* Jonson is, in Harold Bloom's terms, a strong poet, because his echoes of his literary rivals function less as servile imitations than as strategic reductions, making the works of those rivals appear as merely incomplete parts of his own complete work.

The confusing multiplicity that critics have often condemned in Jonson's plots thus becomes an artful bricolage: this is parody by pastiche. Jonson's innovation in comedy occurs at what Alastair Fowler calls a tertiary stage, where the generic conventions are exploited as symbols in their own right.[4] The wealth of allusions to earlier forms (Old and New Comedy, Estates Moralities, etc.) that Jonson's critics have dutifully listed are less a deferential gesture toward earlier writers than an ironic and didactic subsuming of those writers. What have been enumerated as Jonson's literary sources are in many cases merely the sources from which his characters have apparently derived their doomed heroic poses and social tactics.

To understand these allusions is to recognize that Jonson's attacks on his rivals are considerably more extensive than has commonly been acknowledged: beyond the famous poetomachia and the explicit parodies in *Bartholomew Fair* and *The Devil Is an Ass* are countless moments when the appetites and affectations of Jonson's comic characters take on a derivative literary coloring. Alvin Kernan has observed that great satire tends to exploit characters who "create grand inflated images of themselves and pompously attempt to reconstruct the world";[5] Jonson exploits characters whose grandiose self-images oblige them to reconstruct the Globe. The idea of the *theatrum mundi,* which pervades medieval and Renaissance literature (and takes a provocative form in the name and motto of the Globe theater), hovers in Jonson's comedies somewhere between an allusive tactic and an existential principle: in satirizing other playwrights, Jonson is also satirizing the self-dramatizing instinct by which people seek to give their lives scope and order. Jonson's world as well as his plays must have been full of people striking half-conscious poses as unrequited lovers, court intriguers, family revengers, underpromoted malcontents, and underappreciated poetic geniuses.

Indeed, Jonson's relentless attacks on this tendency may reflect a life-long struggle against his own impulses to replace reality with literary poses. In describing how he killed a man during his service in the Low Countries,

Jonson's rhetoric suggests that he was essentially "acting out things he had read."[6] His love lyrics repeatedly portray his frustrated hopes to replace the unromantic realities of his body with his poetic inventions. His critical commonplace-book suggests that "our whole life is like a Play: Wherein every man forgetfull of himselfe, is in travaile with expression of another. Nay, wee so insist in imitating others, as wee cannot (when it is necessary) returne to our selves; like Children, that imitate the vices of Stammerers so long, till at last they become such; and make the habit to another nature, as it is never forgotten."[7] Characters who understand this susceptibility (as do figures such as Clement, Macilente, Face, Dauphine, and Mosca) can both mock and manipulate those who do not; the playwright who recognizes his fellow-playwrights' naive conventionality can achieve a similar and simultaneous conquest. Within the plays, to adapt a Socratic precept, the unexamined role is not worth playing; Jonson thereby implies that plays lacking his sophisticated self-consciousness about the conventions of the genre were not worth writing.

Jonson's dramatic structures thus become devices for carrying on the War of the Theaters by other and subtler means, and some Renaissance equivalents of Walter Mitty are his secret agents in that war, eventually immolating themselves behind enemy lines and taking much of the enemy arsenal with them. The peculiar shape of Jonsonian comedy can be explained as the result of what might be termed generic engineering. The parodic strategy gives these plays many of the complexities and capabilities that the great theorist Mikhail Bakhtin attributes only to the novel, which "parodies other genres (precisely in their role as genres); it exposes the conventionality of their forms and their language; it squeezes out some genres and incorporates others into its own peculiar structure, re-formulating and re-accentuating them."[8] Beneath the surface action of the plays is the ruthless and resourceful struggle of a new kind of drama—satiric city-comedy—for a place in the Renaissance constellation of genres.

A Jacobean audience would have been far better prepared to recognize Jonson's parodic barbs than a modern audience would be in an outwardly similar situation. The world of London's playwrights and theatergoers was a cozy one, and inside jokes about rival companies and their plays were the rule rather than the exception. The famous War of the Theaters that occupied London's stages in the first years of the seventeenth century was merely a well-publicized eruption of a battle royal that drew in many Jacobean playwrights. Even Shakespeare, though he put himself further above the battle than most, could not resist parodying Marlowe's popular *Tamburlaine* in *2 Henry IV* (2.4.163–67), devastating crude melodrama in the mechanicals' performance in *Midsummer Night's Dream* (5.1.108–362) and complaining in *Hamlet* (2.2.338–61) about the popularity of the rival children's companies, with their incongruous, stylized performances of grand tragedies and sex farces. Beaumont and Fletcher, in *The Knight of the Burning Pestle,* and Marston, in *The Malcontent* and *Antonio and Mellida,* display a similarly ironic self-consciousness about dramatic conventions and make similarly sophisticated use of them. Chapman and Webster made occasional gestures to show that they were far from naive about the conventions in which they worked. Only Jonson, however, used parody systematically throughout his career to exalt himself over his rivals.

In the humors plays, Jonson simply herds his rivals onto the stage to be humiliated; this gives the plays as much entertainment value, and as little integrity of plot, as a massive street brawl. They are satires, but they express some initial reservations about the suitability of the bitter satiric spirit to the comic stage, which Jonson understood as a place of pleasure and positive social morality. In "comical satyres," such as *Cynthia's Revels* and *Poetaster,* the attacks become so overt, and so often against the playwright rather than his plays, that the parodic strategy fades into irrelevance. The great middle comedies, from *Volpone* to *The Devil Is an Ass,* succeed in subordinating both the rivalrous and the satiric impulses to unitary plots. Jonson invents settings and stories that perfectly coordinate the humiliation of his literary rivals with the humiliation of his self-dramatizing characters. Lovewit's house and Bartholomew Fair serve as metaphors both for the actual stages of London and for the metaphorical great stage of the world—places to which people naturally bring their fantasies and their money, and then are finally compelled to surrender them both to Jonson's superior wit. But just as Jonson's onstage surrogates such as Volpone and Face seem constitutionally unable to stop creating complications and simply enjoy their profits, so Jonson himself seems unable to switch off the parodic mechanism and rest on his satiric laurels. Instead, he turns his punitive dramatic weaponry against punitive figures, and his plays become steadily more forgiving toward both human nature and popular drama. This progression leads predictably to the sentimentality that has provoked critics from Dryden onward to dismiss the late plays as "dotages"; but perhaps the problem is less sentiment than structure. In *The Staple of News* and *The Magnetic Lady,* the vigorous synthesis of the middle comedies begins to fade, and the arguments about the right course for drama often become isolated in choral figures rather than generated by the plots themselves.

The epilogue to *Every Man Out of His Humor* concludes with the hope that a reformed audience "may, in time, make lean Macilente as fat as Sir John Falstaff." It was a rash wish. Jonson may have become quite fat, but he also became increasingly poor and neglected, and whereas Falstaff is still loved for his faults, Jonson is increasingly disliked for his virtues. A devoted and systematic reformer of literary modes is generally no more popular than a similar reformer of social mores. Jonson's great kinsman, in this regard, is Milton; the comparison can be at least as instructive as the facile conventional comparison with Shakespeare. Given the undeniable appeal of traditional heroes and traditional literary flourishes, how could either poet successfully challenge simultaneously the moral and the generic complacencies of Renaissance literature? What, finally, is the appeal of a play that proceeds by rejecting all the plots the audience has learned to appreciate, leaving only a critical attitude to fill the narrative void? Jonson's victories over his literary rivals are always in danger of becoming Pyrrhic victories. The triumphs of Jonson's satirists, like those of Milton's God, have been widely criticized for being too punitive, too easy, too unemotional. Jonson's dismissal of the melodramatic missions of his gulls as irrelevant resembles Milton's creation of the magnificent battle in heaven, which he similarly dismisses: in both cases the slow-witted portion of the audience is likely to feel simply disappointed, and the quicker-witted may feel deliberately misled and affronted. Jonson's program was not without its risks, and it is no wonder that he felt compelled to employ such a variety of tricks, threats, and rewards to draw the audience from the romantic to the satiric side. He is not simply playing inside jokes on his fellow-dramatists; he is a revolutionary trapped in a highly conservative medium, struggling in an ingenious way to win the recruits he needs for artistic survival.

II

The disastrous unpopularity of *The New Inn* (1629) must rank among the cruelest ironies of English literary history because the play represents a profound and ceremonious concession to the popular tastes Jonson had resisted for so long. For the audience as well as the characters, this new inn is a place where their long-cherished fantasies are miraculously fulfilled. That the inn is located in a distant London suburb may reflect the plays position halfway between the satiric world of city-comedy and the romantic world of pastoral. L. A. Beaurline suggests that the reputation of suburban inns would have kept the audience wondering "whether the inn can be merry without being debauched";[9] I believe Jonson is raising the same question about the institution of comedy. He may well have believed he had found a way to please a general audience without rendering himself vulnerable to the sort of intellectual scorn he had formerly visited on his popular rivals, but he failed on both counts. Jonson's indignant "Ode to Himselfe" and his peevish complaints about the actors and the audience suggest not only that this rejection infuriated him even more than the failure of *Catiline,* but also that, this time, he was not sure whom or what to blame first. In his "Dedication to the Reader" Jonson says that he prefers to entrust the play "rather to thy rustic candour than all the pomp of [the original audience's] pride and solemn ignorance" (lines 14–16); he now resents the ostentatiously sophisticated theatergoers of Caroline London at least as much as he mistrusts the unsophisticated sort of audience against whose nostalgic desires the earlier plays had positioned themselves. Jonson is not willing to forget all about satiric comedy, but he does the next best thing. He locks it down in the basement of *The New Inn,* where all the low-life characters pass their time much as the similar swindlers, gulls, and profligates did in the earlier comedies: crudely indulging their greed, lust, anger, and appetite, and toying in very Jonsonian ways with their names and their roles.[10] If, as detractors of the play maintain, these are rather boring versions of Jonson's satiric dramatis personae, it may be because Jonson himself was becoming bored with them. The epilogue points out that Jonson

> could have haled in
> The drunkards and the noises of the inn
> In his last act; if he had thought it fit
> To vent you vapours in the place of wit:
> But better 'twas that they should sleep or spew
> Than in the scene to offend or him or you.
> (lines 13–18)

Because this playwright "meant to please you" (epilogue, line 5) he would not allow the characters of satiric city-comedy to taint the romantic solutions achieved in the exalted world upstairs, let alone exploit those solutions as they surely would have in the early comedies. Where formerly the romantic fantasies would have been marginalized in favor of these below-stairs puns and schemes and brawls, in *The New Inn* the wily servants are gradually forgotten while the play focuses on fulfilling the romantic expectations of the dreamy aristocrats and the credulous members of the audience. Jonson feints at leaving these romantic stories similarly unfulfilled—both Lovel and the host Goodstock complain about the unsatisfying way their little plays have apparently ended (4.4.247–53, 5.1.24–33)—but then relents. Even such self-indulgent characters as Beaufort and Lady Frampul are finally led to the wedding altar of comedy rather than to the whipping post of satire. Jonson follows his usual pattern by propelling his audience from romantic expectation to satiric disillusionment, but in this case he then invites us back into the pleasures of romantic illusion. Jonson is not completely retracting his criticisms of the unrealistic oversights and reunions of romance plots; like Shakespeare in *The Winter's Tale,* he insists repeatedly that we recognize the story as a literary fantasy. But he seems to be acknowledging that such things have a place in the theater because they can evoke real feelings by corresponding to the real desires of the human heart. This may be one reason critics have been so radically divided on whether *The New Inn* is a romantic indulgence or a dismissive burlesque of romance.[11] It is the work of a man who could neither submit completely to dramatic illusions nor resist completely their seductive appeal. Jonson plays the literary conventions and improbabilities to their height, but he never suggests, either within the play or in his subsequent defenses of it, that he wants the play to be taken ironically. Indeed, the fact that his "Dedication to the Reader" places so much blame for its failure on the way it was "negligently play'd" argues against the ironic reading, since awkward performances would damage a delicate romantic fantasy far more than they would a broad burlesque of such fantasies.

By emphasizing the literary-conventional quality of the play without denying the profit and pleasure such a story could bring to its audience as well as its characters, Jonson invites the contradictory responses that have characterized criticism of *The New Inn.* The contradictions can be partly resolved by recognizing that the play offers a running commentary on the struggle between satiric distance and romantic absorption involved in its own composition. The play comprises Jonson's genial reevaluation of his approach to moral drama, and at its center is a reevaluation of his parodic strategy. The irony is that the critical spirit Jonson had nurtured for so long, a spirit whose natural prey is conventional romantic melodrama, escaped from the cellar of the new inn into the audience at the first performance, and (like Frankenstein's monster) attacked its maker. Jonson found himself trapped in a bitter role-reversal, chastised by his audience for his own apparent excursion into melodramatic conventionality; this may explain why Jonson's next (and last) full play, *The Magnetic Lady,* is a kind of disheartened, mechanical revival of his parodic strategy.

In *The Devil Is an Ass* Jonson violated his parodic principles by allowing Mrs. Fitzdotterel to discover her true self through theater, a self which would otherwise have remained submerged. *The New Inn* expands that moment into an entire play. Jonson still realizes that theatricalism can be self-deception: he invites to the new inn, for the purpose of chasing them out, Nick and Pinnacia Stuff, who use costumes and role-playing to deceive themselves about their own and each other's true identities. But the play indulges, and shares with the audience, the more enlightened kind of role-playing that allows Lady Frampul and Lovel to discover and develop their mutual romantic interest, and allows Prudence to discover and develop the nobility of her inner nature. So long as the characters know that they are playing, and so long as the audience is kept similarly aware that this is only a play, Jonson will permit such indulgences. By acting out their roles in the play-within-the-play, the characters can become what they have long yearned to be. At the same time, by remembering that the play is merely a fiction, Jonson frees himself to fulfill the audience's posited yearning for the sort of romantic conclusion he had formerly refused to tolerate.

The new inn, like Lovewit's house in *The Alchemist* and the bedchamber in *Volpone,* is a metaphorical theater. The comparison is established in the first lines of the prologue: "You are welcome, welcome all, to the new inn; / Though the old house"—apparently the Blackfriars Theater—where "the same cook / Still, and the fat," will concoct them a play. Still aware that the line between players and real people can be shaky, Jonson no longer assumes it is ethically imperative. When Prudence fears that Lady Frampul will be dishonored if some of her clothing ends up adorning actors, the Lady replies that "all are players, and but serve the scene, Pru" (2.1.39)—a platitude, but here also a truth. Is the *theatrum mundi* commonplace ironized, or is it vindicated, when it is expressed by a character whose world is indeed a play? The tendency of life to imitate art, which Jonson had earlier used in a penetrating critique of both human behavior and dramatic convention, here becomes mostly a subject of whimsically detached observation. Lovel questions Goodstock's decision to run an inn, "It being i'your free-will (as 'twas) to choose / What parts you would sustain" (1.3.108–9), and Goodstock responds that the inn allows him to

> imagine all the world's a play;
> The state and men's affairs all passages
> Of life, to spring new scenes, come in, go out,
> And shift, and vanish; and if I have got
> A seat to sit at ease here i' mine inn,
> To see the comedy; and laugh, and chuck
> At the variety and throng of humours
> And dispositions that come jostling in
> And out still, as they one drove hence another:
> Why, will you envy me my happiness?
> (1.3.128–37)

In his late plays Jonson seems increasingly content to observe the variety of the world's humors and steer them toward a standard happy ending.

Like the disguised Lord Frampul, Jonson is the host of this new inn, and both men are determined to make the Light Heart suit its name. Jonson's tenacious dignity in poetry, earthy realism in drama, and general scorn for humors all melt away in the person of the host:

> HOST: "Be merry, and drink sherry"; that's my posy!
> For I shall never joy i' my light heart
> So long as I conceive a sullen guest,
> Or any thing that's earthy!
> LOVEL: Humorous host.
> HOST: I care not if I be.
> (1.2.29–33)

To emphasize that the host is a version of the jovial playwright, the play brings in the otherwise superfluous information that, before assuming his disguise as this innkeeper, Lord Frampul had worked for some time as a "puppet-master" for "Young Goose, the motion-man" (1.5.61–62). When he finally reveals his true identity at 5.5.91–100, his speech "reads almost like [Jonson's] autobiography, personal and literary."[12] The disguise-plots from which Jonson generates his happy ending are also "[s]uppositious fruits of a host's brain" (5.5.41).

Prudence is another version of the playwright, assigned as "sovereign / Of the day's sports devised i'the inn" (1.6.43–44). She shares with Jonson the responsibility (as efficient cause and first cause, respectively) for introducing the peculiarities for which *The New Inn* has been condemned: the somewhat forced shift into romance, and Lovel's long presentations on love and valor that slow the action. Pru rescues the inn, as Jonson does the theater, from a melancholic, alienated, anatomical spirit—the spirit of satire—and converts it to a joyous spirit of union and reunion—the spirit of romantic comedy. Her main decree compels Lovel (who, we learn at 1.1.24–33, has been conducting scientific anatomies in the new inn) to play the advocate of love for two hours (the standard duration of an Elizabethan play) to Lady Frampul, in her role as a disdainer of such tender sentiments. Since that is precisely what Lovel had long wished he could do, theater becomes a way of achieving authenticity rather than of compromising it. The characters in Pru's little drama, like those in Jonson's larger one, become more real, more true to themselves, in their roles than they were before they started playing. She herself is able to display her true nobility only because she is given the role of Queen of the Revels, and the result is her transformation into a true noblewoman by marriage to Lord Latimer.[13]

As Lovel's discourse begins to move her heart, Lady Frampul acknowledges the transformation in terms that remind us of the false transformations in *The Alchemist.* Her speech about Lovel could very easily be spoken about Subtle by any of the gulls in that play:

> How am I changed! By what alchemy
> Of love or language am I thus translated!
> His tongue is tipped with the philosophers' stone,
> And that hath touched me thorough every vein!
> I feel that transmutation o' my blood
> As I were quite become another creature,
> And all he speaks it is projection!
> Pru: Well feigned, my lady: now her parts begin!
> Latimer: And she will act 'em subtly.
>
> (3.2.169–77)

We are likely to share the mistaken assumption of Pru and Latimer that this is merely another theatrical illusion, but the new inn is a place where such transformations can actually take place, under the guise and even the guidance of theater. Thirty lines later, Prudence again praises as a theatrical performance Lady Frampul's affectionate commendation of Lovel: "Excellent actor! How she hits this passion!" But reality is rapidly catching up to the fiction, as the jealous Latimer senses: "But do you think she plays?"

The answer is, of course, yes and no. Both the context and the content of this courtship are literary, but the literature liberates and reflects genuine sentiments; life engages in a dialogue with art, instead of merely imitating it. Lovel's bookish speech about love generates real love from Lady Frampul, and then, conversely, his real act of valor generates a call from Lady Frampul for a bookish speech about valor. Lovel's speeches and Lady Frampul's reactions display the sort of derivative literary flavoring that in earlier plays would have invited humiliation and augured defeat for a character's desires. Lady Frampul praises Lovel's discourse on love as

> the marrow of all lovers' tenets!
> Who hath read Plato, Heliodore, or Tatius,
> Sidney, D'Urfe, or all Love's fathers, like him?
> He is there the master of sentences,
> Their school, their commentary, text, and gloss,
> And breathes the true divinity of Love!
>
> (3.2.202–7)

Evidently Lovel's reading of Sidney did not include the first sonnet in the "Astrophil and Stella" sequence, which warns against the futility of trying to express one's own passion by imitating the high-poetical expressions of earlier lovers. Jonson's earlier plays would surely have admonished an anthologist such as Lovel in much the same way that Sidney's Astrophil is admonished: " 'Fool,' said my Muse to me, 'Look in thy heart and write.' " But *The New Inn* provides Lovel with a more receptive audience in Lady Frampul, who replies by offering to "say some hundred penitential verses, / There, out of Chaucer's 'Troilus and Criseyde' " to atone for her earlier impieties toward love (3.2.217–18). After Lovel scatters the ruffians, she praises him in terms that (as the closing parenthetical remark makes clear) are better suited to an encomium from classical drama than to ordinary conversation:

> I ne'er saw
> A lightning shoot so, as my servant did,
> His rapier was a meteor, and he waved it
> Over 'em like a comet! As they fled him!
> I marked his manhood! Every stoop he made
> Was like an eagle's at a flight of cranes!
> (As I have read somewhere.)
>
> BEAUFORT: Bravely expressed:
>
> LATIMER: And like a lover!
>
> (4.3.11–18)

Is it necessarily wrong to indulge in the brave poetical expressions that love inspires? Lady Frampul's approach to praising is a little absurd, but Lovel's action was essentially heroic, and her reaction comes from her heart as well as from her reading.

As those who interpret the play ironically have stressed, speeches throughout *The New Inn* have this sort of derivative literary flavor, which renders them vulnerable to mockery. That only makes it more striking, however, that Jonson does not mock them, either by offering the commentary of a witty author-surrogate or by leaving the yearnings they express notably unfulfilled. Self-dramatizing poses are punished so systematically in Jonson's earlier comedies that some critics virtually hallucinate such punishments in *The New Inn,*[14] but Jonson no longer seems determined to challenge the validity of literature as a mediator for human experience. Lovel begins his presentation on love by swearing on a copy of Ovid's *De Arte Amandi* (3.2.40) and his presentation on honor by similarly swearing on a copy of Thomas Usk's *Testament of Love;* but because Lovel truly adores Lady Frampul and truly rescues Pinnacia Stuff, Jonson is not inclined to prosecute him for experimenting with literary fantasies about his own passions and virtues. What is wrong with lovers being dreamers and role-players, if those dreams and roles are ways of expressing and promoting authentic sentiments?

The chief danger to a romance that has been, in effect, jump-started by drama is that the participants themselves may assume that the romance must cease when the play does. After Lady Frampul gives Lovel his second kiss, Lovel pleads for more, but Prudence forbids it:

> PRU: The Court's dissolved, removed, and the play ended.
> No sound, or air of Love more, I decree it.
> LOVEL: From what a happiness hath that one word
> Thrown me into the gulf of misery?
> To'what a bottomless despair? How like
> A court removing or an ended play
> Shows my abrupt precipitate estate.
>
> (4.4.247–53)

These actors temporarily assume that they cannot carry the reality they have discovered within their theatrical roles back into their lives. This, of course, is virtually the opposite of the errors mocked by Jonson's earlier comedies, in which the only successful characters were those who knew and respected the moment when playing yielded to an entirely different reality. Lady Frampul is quite prepared to remove the "visor" or "mask" of her role as a scorner of love and allow Lovel to continue his wooing in a more direct manner. She cannot modestly suggest it herself, however, and Pru, the playwright-figure with the "authority" to compel it, fails to "read" that desire in Lady Frampul's "character" (4.4.283–401). Pru has not realized the potential of theater to shape a better reality, and she therefore deserves to sink from her costumed role as Queen of the Revels back to her original identity as a servant:

> PRU: I thought you had dissembled, madam,
> And doubt you do so yet.
> LADY FRAMPUL: Dull, stupid wench!
> Stay i'thy state of ignorance still, be damned,
> An idiot chambermaid! Hath all my care,
> My breeding thee in fashion, thy rich clothes,
> Honours and titles wrought no brighter effects
> On thy dark soul than thus?
> (4.4.310–16)

The failure to integrate drama and life properly, to read and write them into each other, is now as serious an error as the failure to separate them properly was in the earlier plays.

By the same token, the specific lesson of *Epicoene* about the dangers of mistaking theatrical truth for actual truth is reversed in Laetitia's cross-dressing. In *Epicoene,* Jonson plays on the theatrical assumptions of a Jacobean audience to hide the fact that the bride is really—that is, within the reality of the play's world—a boy. Because the audience would have adjusted its perceptions to the fact that girls' parts were conventionally played by boys, it would not have recognized what might otherwise have been an obvious truth, and that failure generated not only a surprise ending but also a rebuff to the audience's conventional thinking. In *The New Inn* the audience can hardly be expected to penetrate Laetitia's long-standing disguise as the boy Frank, because the actor is in fact a boy, and when she is cast and costumed as "Laetitia," she may indeed look more like a transvestite than like a revealed woman. Our hardwired theatrical reflexes, our willing surrender to dramatic conventions, make us as susceptible as Morose to Epicoene's disguise. But the lesson of Jonson's satiric comedies—to think skeptically about such dramatic illusions—now renders us less perceptive than the shallow Lord Beaufort, who takes Laetitia's "costume" for a reality, more of a reality than her everyday self as "Frank."

The audience might well have expected that "Laetitia" would turn out to be a boy, as the actor playing the role was actually a boy; Ferret has compared Frank to a skillful "play-boy" (1.3.5), and act five, scene three seems like an outtake from *Epicoene.* This time, however, to the surprise of the clever characters onstage as well as of the audience, the confusion finally resolves into romantic fulfillment rather than into a satiric attack on romantic illusions. Beaufort's marriage turns out to be not a farce, like Morose's, but a real and happy conclusion. Like a naive spectator at the theater, Beaufort assumes that the body dressed up as a girl is really a girl, that her costume is a reality that will allow him to fulfill his romantic dreams, and instead of being punished for those assumptions, he is rewarded. What appears to be Laetitia—the name means "joy"—turns out to be Laetitia and joy after all, not merely an alluring fraud set out to entice dreamers into the frank world of satire. The theatrical view, so often humiliated on stage in the earlier plays, here triumphs over what we had assumed was our more realistic perspective. We are forced to suppress our cynical awareness that the actor is nonetheless a boy—in larger terms, that the play is finally just an illusion—if we want to share in the pleasures of a happy ending. Like Busy at the puppet show in *Bartholomew Fair,* we are induced to surrender our censorious attitude and (like Goodstock watching over his own "new inn") become happily passive beholders with the rest.

When the disguised Laetitia is assigned to "play" a girl, Lady Frampul quite accidentally gives her her real name. This suggests another area in which *The New Inn* inverts the parodic strategy of the earlier plays. The problem now is not that characters, in search of melodramatic vindications, pursue their names too avidly; on the contrary, the problem is often that characters are slow to recognize the melodramatic truths their names reveal. As Harriett Hawkins points out, Frances Frampul speaks more truly than she is aware when she tells young "Frank" that her name is "the same as yours"; they in fact share a last name, just as they appear to share a first.[15] The host's assumed name, Goodstock, is a clue to his noble blood, and also to the fact that "Frank" is actually his lost child: his wife (disguised as the nurse) describes the boy as "descended of a right good stock, sir" (2.2.23, 2.6.23). When the host of the new inn asks Lovel, "But is your name Love-ill, sir, or Love-well?" he simply replies, "I do not know't myself, / Whether it is. But it is love hath been / The hereditary passion of our house" (1.6.95–98). In earlier plays a character named Lovel would probably have complacently pursued his name into erotic humiliation. Now, however, both Jonson's play and Pru's pursue the question on Lovel's behalf, compelling him to show that he loves well, and then making him well in love.

Some characters in *The New Inn* do let themselves be bullied by simplistic readings of their own names, and mock the names of others in equally reductive ways. But this narrowing and degrading reading of names, which Jonson imposed on complacent characters throughout the earlier comedies, is now confined to the below-stairs group, whose relentless literal-minded quibbling has often been adduced as evidence of Jonson's dotage.[16] It may be so, but the enlightening exploration of names upstairs suggests that Jonson is deliberately establishing a contrast between the limiting ironies of his former satiric practice and the satisfactions of this new play that permits self-discovery through theatricality.

Jonson establishes a similarly sharp contrast within *The New Inn* between the healthy role-playing that propels the play into the realm of romance and the self-dramatizing disease that invites satire. Sir Glorious Tipto is a less attractive version of Bobadill from *Every Man in His Humor;* because his martial role directly contradicts his true cowardly nature, Jonson explodes Tipto's pretenses early in the fourth act and banishes him from the stage and the story thereafter. The tailor Nick Stuff is a similarly degraded version of Puntarvolo from *Every Man Out of His Humor,* who woos his wife each day in the guise of a visiting knight-errant. Pinnacia Stuff explains,

> When he makes any fine garment will fit me,
> Or any rich thing that he thinks of price,
> Then must I put it on and be his countess,
> Before he carry it home unto the owners.
> A coach is hired and four horse, he runs
> In his velvet jacket thus to Rumford, Croydon,
> Hounslow, or Barnet, the next bawdy road:
> And takes me out, carries me up, and throws me
> Upon a bed.
>
> (4.3.66–75)

Stuff's error lies, not in role-playing itself, but in playing roles derived from pornography rather than some higher literary form, and in using those roles to efface true selves and feelings rather than to evoke them. This falsehood produces not just silliness, but a form of sexual-political false consciousness that allows fetishistic domination to compensate Stuff for class subordination. Beaufort calls this "A fine species / Of fornicating with a man's own wife," not merely because it emphasizes concupiscence, but because it involves a standard fantasy of sexual violation, a fantasy in which his wife's personal identity is obliterated by the role her costume implies. Indeed, when Pru finally receives the dress Pinnacia was wearing (which was supposed to be Pru's costume as Queen of the Revels), Lady Frampul assures her that the tailor will ravish her too if she

> com'st unto him
> In forma pauperis to crave the aid
> Of his knight errant valor, to the rescue
> Of thy distressed robes! Name but thy gown,
> And he will rise to that!
>
> PRU: I'll fire the charm first,
> I had rather die in a ditch with Mistress Shore,
> Without a smock, as the pitiful matter has it,
> Than owe my wit to clothes, or ha' it beholden.
>
> HOST: Still spirit of Pru!
>
> (5.2.19–27)

Like Mistress Shore, Pru is toying with a royal identity, but she will not permit the role implied by her costume to override her own desires or erase her own identifying qualities.

A few scenes earlier Pru had similarly threatened to abandon her makeshift costume as Queen of the Revels, to preclude further insults from Lady Frampul. What is interesting about the precedent is that Pru was insulted for failing to understand the way roles can play into reality. She had failed to extrapolate from her own happy transformation that Lady Frampul might want to carry Lovel's courtship from its theatrical context into her real life (4.4.283–316). Lady Frampul therefore compared her to Pinnacia Stuff:

LADY FRAMPUL: Were not the tailor's wife to be demolished,
Ruined, uncased, thou shouldst be she, I vow.
PRU: Why, take your spangled properties, your gown
And scarfs.
LADY FRAMPUL: Pru, Pru, what dost thou mean?
PRU: I will not buy this play-boy's bravery,
At such a price, to be upbraided for it,
Thus, every minute.

(4.4.317–23)

A play-boy's bravery is exactly what it is; a boy is playing a chambermaid who is playing a queen. But within the context of a theater it is also the costume of a queen, and the new inn is a place of theatrical truth. By the fifth act, Pru has recovered her rightful costume, and resumed her royal role so ably that Lord Latimer will insist on making her a noblewoman in real life. Her grace in these grand garments is now ostentatiously contrasted with Pinnacia's ungainliness:

LADY FRAMPUL: Sweet Pru, aye, now thou art a queen indeed!
These robes do royally! And thou becom'st 'em!
So they do thee! Rich garments only fit
The parties they are made for! They shame others.
How did they show on goody tailor's back!
Like a caparison for a sow, God save us!

(5.2.1–6)

Costume and body complement each other here, as role and reality do so often in *The New Inn.* Theatricalism becomes a ritual of discovery rather than an instrument of deception.

Jonson characteristically ends his fourth acts with a *catastasis* that represents the defeat of a predictable ending in favor of a more satiric ending that exalts Jonsonian wit. It seems for a while that Goodstock's hopes for a light comic resolution, in which Lovel would win Lady Frampul, will similarly fall victim to the false ending of *The New Inn.* He expresses the defeated bewilderment experienced by so many gulls in the earlier comedies who waited overconfidently for a conventional happy ending:

> I had thought to ha' sacrificed
> To merriment tonight, i' my Light Heart, Fly,
> And like a noble poet to have had
> My last act best: but all fails i' the plot.
> Lovel is gone to bed; the Lady Frampul
> And sovereign Pru fallen out: Tipto and his regiment
> Of mine-men all drunk dumb. . . .
> No project to rear laughter on but this,
> The marriage of Lord Beaufort with Laetitia.
> (5.1.24–33)

Goodstock is disappointed that the romantic comedy he envisioned has degenerated into a sex farce, and he will be surprised again (as I think Jonson expected his audience to be surprised) when the romantic comedy triumphs after all. But Goodstock will appreciate that triumph when it comes, and will find that he is part of it himself, rescued from the alienation he had hidden for so long under his merry disguise as a comic humorist. The host finally bequeaths the inn to Fly before departing, which offers a highly suggestive contrast with Shakespeare's farewell in which Prospero sets the Ariel of his imagination free before returning to the grim realistic business of governing the mortal flaws in himself and his city. Eighteen years later, in badly failing health, Jonson's surrogate authorizes a familiar spirit of satire (a nominal kinsman of Mosca) to carry on the admonitory business of city-comedy in his theater, but he himself escapes into the fulfillment of an airy romantic dream.

At the end of his hours of theatrical courtship, Lovel goes to bed to "sleep, / And dream away the vapour of Love" (4.4.280–81), but he awakens in the final scene to the news that his play-love Lady Frampul will indeed be his wife, and he asks his host,

> Is this a dream now, after my first sleep?
> Or are these fantasies made i'the Light Heart?
> And sold i'the new inn?
> HOST: Best go to bed,
> And dream it over all.
> (5.5.120–23)

The allegory now rests lightly on the happy reality of the play-world; Jonson acknowledges, without criticizing, the pleasant fantasy he has sold to his London audience and perhaps to his own often melancholic heart. The Host's reply takes us beyond the ending of *Bartholomew Fair,* which invites us to "have the rest of the play at home," toward something like the ending of Shakespeare's *A Midsummer Night's Dream,* which enchantingly blurs all boundaries separating fantasy from reality. Real life melts into theater as wakefulness melts into sleep, and in that sleep of fantasy the dreams that come are not costly delusions, but instead pleasant fulfillments that at moments can bring a little of their fantastic happiness across the now unguarded border into the lives of the audience.

III

The mixed tone that made *The New Inn* so unpopular at its initial performance, and so unsettling to critics ever since, allows Jonson to acknowledge a retreat from the harshness that his parodic strategy had created in his plays, without conceding any loss in his powers of discernment. The many unfulfilled hints of parody in the play's grandiose and derivative speeches are Jonson's way of calling his critical strictures before the bar for reexamination.

The combination has not proved a great success; it demands far too much alertness from the audience to the history and the implications of Jonson's parodic strategy. But it is certainly interesting for what it attempts. Though Jonson may have surrendered some of his most powerful satiric weapons on his way to *The New Inn,* he was fully conscious of the genial choice he was making, so conscious that he explains it metaphorically in the course of the play. He was too sharp a satirist not to perceive the trite and sentimental qualities of this late play, but his benevolence seems all the more touching if we understand that he was fully aware of its costs. *The New Inn* is an act of generosity toward its characters, who seem to appreciate that fact, and toward its audience, who evidently did not. It is an act of generosity toward the natural desires of the human heart, and toward theater itself, which Jonson now concedes can sometimes help fulfill those desires without generating either naive self-dramatization or manipulative cynicism.

Lovel is reluctant to play the role of Lady Frampul's wooer in Pru's play because he fears that the joy of those two hours will only accentuate his exclusion from that role in all the other hours of his life. The Host urges him to participate nonetheless: "take your hours and kisses, they are a fortune" (2.6.197). Jonson seems to be encouraging the audience to accept the two hours of romantic indulgence represented by *The New Inn* in much the same way. Jonson's theater is no longer simply a mirror of manners, as he so often said it should be; it is now an escape from the harsh disappointments of life.

At the time he wrote the play Jonson would have been feeling sharply all the sufferings Lovel enumerates as the most fearful: "poverty, restraint, captivity, / Banishment, loss of children, long disease" (4.4.106–7).[17] After struggling from a working-class background and a series of prison terms into power and glory as the leading poet of the royal court, Jonson found himself crippled and permanently confined to his room by a stroke, banished from royal favor, pleading repeatedly for a more adequate pension, and forever deprived of the children—his daughter Mary and his son Benjamin—for whom he mourns so affectingly in his epitaphs. *The New Inn* is a poignant document in Jonson's personal biography precisely because it is such a distinct palinode in his literary career. It is both striking and suggestive that, after a career devoted to separating the grim truths of life from the pleasant fantasies of popular theater, and extirpating romantic melodrama from that theater, Jonson could propose so seductively that life can be like theater after all, that he could dismiss realism in favor of a conventional happy ending which brings lost children miraculously back to life and a melancholic old intellectual back into the flow of life. The romantic plot of *The New Inn* may have been for him, as it was for Lovel, a fantasy so badly needed that it overrode the guiding principles of a lifetime.

Notes

1. John Dryden, *Essay of Dramatic Poesie,* in his *Works* (Berkeley: University of California Press, 1971), 17:57. Cf. Jonson's own *Discoveries,* in his *Works,* ed. C. H. Herford and Percy and Evelyn Simpson (London: Oxford University Press, Clarendon Press, 1947), 8:567, 627, and 638–39.

2. Herford and Simpson, *Works,* 8:627; Jonson is here responding to *The Advancement of Learning* rather than to the *New Organon,* but the point is the same.

3. This and all subsequent references to Jonson's plays are based on *The Complete Plays of Ben Jonson* (Oxford: Oxford University Press, 1981–82), a modern-spelling adaptation of Herford and Simpson.

4. Alastair Fowler, *Kinds of Literature* (Cambridge: Harvard University Press, 1982), 156, 162–64.

5. Alvin Kernan, *The Plot of Satire* (New Haven: Yale University Press, 1965), 36.

6. Anne Barton, *Ben Jonson, Dramatist* (New York: Cambridge University Press, 1984), 2.

7. Herford and Simpson, *Works,* 8:597.

8. Mikhail Bakhtin, "Epic and Novel," in *The Dialogic Imagination,* ed. Michael Holquist, trans. Caryl Emerson and Michael Holquist (Austin: University of Texas Press, 1981), 4–5.

9. L. A. Beaurline, *Jonson and Elizabethan Comedy* (San Marino, Calif.: Huntington Library, 1978), 260.

10. That this is less a class distinction than a distinction between types of drama is clear from the banishment of the miles gloriosus, Sir Glorious Tipto, to the cellar, and the promotion up the stairs of the virtuous servant Pru. C. G. Thayer, *Ben Jonson* (Norman: University of Oklahoma Press, 1963), 210–23, argues that the below-stairs world represents satiric Old

Comedy, whereas the upstairs world is occupied with the business of New Comedy. Anne Barton argues in *Ben Jonson* that the "underworld of characters below stairs . . . exists primarily to express the chaos of society when it does not admit the ordering influences of true valour or true love" (272). I would add only that one could say precisely the same thing about the world of Jonson's satiric city-comedy.

11. Herford and Simpson, in *Works,* II, 194, reflect the early twentieth-century consensus that *The New Inn* is Jonson's ungainly but sincere attempt to write romance. More recently, some critics have perceived quality as well as sincerity: see Beaurline, *Jonson and Elizabethan Comedy,* 257–74, and Barton, *Ben Jonson,* 258–84. Richard Levin, in "The New *New Inn* and the Proliferation of Good Bad Drama," *Essays in Criticism* 22 (1972): 41–47, argues that the play is simply bad romance and that efforts to rescue it by viewing it as ironic are misguided. Several critics, however, assert quite forcefully that Jonson is writing at least passable burlesque rather than execrably bad romance: see Larry Champion, *Ben Jonson's "Dotages"* (Lexington: University of Kentucky Press, 1967), 76–103; Edward Partridge, *The Broken Compass* (New York: Columbia University Press, 1958), 189–205; and Robert Knoll, *Ben Jonson's Plays* (Lincoln: University of Nebraska Press, 1964), 181–90. Alexander Leggatt, in *Ben Jonson* (London: Methuen, 1981), comes closest to my own position in arguing for "some sort of a balance between a delight in the creative fantasy and a satire on its absurdity" (43–44).

12. Thayer, *Ben Jonson,* 230.

13. Barton observes that Pru, by acting "the part of a great lady, mistress of the day's entertainment, as Gonzaga's Duchess had been at Urbino, in Castiglione, comes into triumphant possession of aspects of her real self formerly stifled and hidden by her inferior social position" (*Ben Jonson,* 270).

14. Partridge concludes his analysis of the play by claiming that the role of clothing in shaping the reality of characters in *The New Inn* "is characteristic of Jonson's method. . . . The folly detested by Jonson becomes the virtue cherished by the characters he creates [who] are turned loose in a world of their own making and create their own hell, usually unaware of the hell of it" (*Broken Compass,* 205). It is hard to see why characters joyously united in long-sought marriages and joyously reunited with long-sought kinspeople should deduce that they are being punished in hell. Knoll sees evidence in the play that Jonson "is too old to think us able to attain our aspirations" (*Ben Jonson's Plays,* 188). Although it is true that Lovel cannot perfectly embody the principles of love and valor he advocates, the play as a whole culminates in the miraculous attainment of aspirations considerably greater than any the younger Jonson was willing to endorse.

15. Harriet Hawkins, "The Idea of a Theatre in Jonson's *The New Inn,*" *Renaissance Drama* 9 (1966): 214 n.

16. This began as early as Owen Feltham's "Ode Against Ben Jonson" and has been reaffirmed by Coleridge and many other critics. Barton comments insightfully on the peculiarities of naming in this play and on the contrast in the ways names are used below and above stairs (*Ben Jonson,* 273–76).

17. Barton points out the autobiographical overtones of this list (269).

Ode to Himselfe (1629)

Ben Jonson

I

Come leave the loathed Stage,
And the more loathsome Age,
Where pride and impudence in faction knit,
Usurp the Chair of wit:
Indicting and arraigning every day,
Something they call a Play.
Let their fastidious vain
Commission of the brain,
Run on, and rage, sweat, censure, and condemn,
They were not made for thee, less thou for them.

II

Say that thou pour'st 'em wheat,
And they would Acorns eat:
'Twere simple fury, still thyself to waste
On such as have no taste:
To offer them a surfeit of pure bread,
Whose appetites are dead:
No give them Grains their fill,
Husks, Draff to drink, and swill:
If they love Lees, and leave the lusty Wine,
Envy them not, their palate's with the Swine.

This poem, presumably written shortly after the failure of *The New Inn* in 1629, was first published in 1640.

III

No doubt a mouldy Tale,
Like Pericles, and Stale
As the Shrives crusts, and nasty as his Fish,
Scraps out of every Dish,
Thrown forth and raked into the common Tub,
May keep up the play Club.
Brooms sweepings do as well
There, as his Master's meal:
For who the relish of these guests will fit,
Needs set them but the Alms-basket of wit.

IV

And much good do't ye then,
Brave Plush and Velvet men
Can feed on Orts, and safe in your scene clothes,
Dare quit upon your Oaths
The Stagers, and the stage wrights too; your Peers,
Of stuffing your large ears
With rage of Comic socks,
Wrought upon twenty Blocks;
Which if they're torn, and foul, and patched enough,
The Gamesters share your guilt, and you their stuff.

V

Leave things so prostitute,
And take th' Alcaîke Lute;
Or thine own Horace, or Anacreon's Lyre;
Warm thee by Pindar's fire:
And though thy Nerves be shrunk, and blood be cold,
Ere years have made thee old,
Strike that disdainful heat
Throughout, to their defeat:
As curious fools, and envious of thy strain,
May blushing swear, no Palsy's in thy brain.

VI

But when they hear thee sing
The glories of thy King;
His zeal to God, and his just awe of men,
They may be blood-shaken, then
Feel such a flesh-quake to possess their powers,
That no tuned Harp like ours,
In sound of Peace or Wars,
Shall truly hit the Stars:
When they shall read the Acts of Charles his Reign,
And see his Chariot triumph 'bove his Wain.

The Cuntrys Censure on Ben Jonsons New Inn (1631)

ANONYMOUS

Listen (decaying Ben) and Counsel hear,
wits have their date and strength of brains may wear;
Age, steeped In sack, hath quenched thy Enthean fire,
we pity now, whom once we did Admire.
Surrender then thy right to th' stage; forbear
to dare to write what others Loathe to hear,
and justly, since thy Crazy Muse doth now
To quit her Spartan province faintly know.
Swear not by God 'tis good, for if you do,
The world will tax your zeal, and Judgement too.
for In a Poet, if that's last regarded,
New Inn's discretion hath thee quite discarded;
from Aganippe's pale and placed thee Among
Not the giddy headed, but the *Unbrowed* Throng.
Rail not at the Actors; do not them Abuse,
Action to dullness Cannot Life Infuse;
for *Velvet, Scarlet, Plush,* do tell you true,
t'was not their Clothes, but they did blush for you
to see; and was not that, Just cause of rage?
Weakness and Impudence possessed the stage,
Injured the strength of Wit, now cloyed and dry.
Goodestocke, Prue, Frampole, Huffell, Burst, Typ, Fly,
And their Comrades, whose Language but to hear
Might strike a surfeit Into A gentle ear.
But let me tell thee this, Ben, by the way,
Thy Argument's as tedious as thy play;
Thou sayest no Palsy doth thy Brain pan vex,
I pray thee tell me what? an Apoplex?

This anonymous attack, probably written in 1631, is a modernized version of the text provided by D. H. Craig, *Ben Jonson: The Critical Heritage 1599–1798* (London: Routledge, 1990), 155–56, which draws on the Bodleian Library MS Ashmole 38.

Thy Pegasus can stir, yet thy best Care
Makes her but shuffle like the parson's mare
who from his own side wit says thus by me:
he hath bequeathed his belly unto thee
To hold that little Learning, which is fled
Into thy Guts from out thy Empty head.
Yet thou art Confident, & darest still swear,
the fault's not In thy Brain, but In their ear.
What dismal fate is this, thus on thee ceaseth?
Thy worth doth fail; thy Arrogance Increaseth;
Pride and presumption hath dethroned thy wit,
And set up *Philauty* In place of it,
Thy Innbred Darling, whose strong self Conceit,
forestalling praise, did thy Just praise defeat.
Worth being self praised, doth fall; he is the best Poet
Can justly merit Praise, & yet scarce know it.
But 'tis *New Inn*'s disaster, not to know
What or thyself, or others can Allow.
We wrong thee not, for take thy enraged Appeal,
'twill rather fester thy Mad wound than heal.
For know, what Justly doth despise,
doth prove A greater scandal to our eyes;
And sure that censure must Impartial be
where readers and spectators both agree:
Yet, if pure need Enforce thee to this shame,
we proner are to Advise thee, than to blame.
Since Wits do fail, thou wert best, poor Cracked brain elf,
To turn mine host, and keep new Inn thyself:
But Change thy sign if thou'lt be ruled by me,
No more Light Hart, but Light Brain let it be.
        Thy Hostler *Peck* Abused thus the Jade
        of this fat-bellied Parson, who this made.

To Ben Jonson. Upon occasion of his Ode of defiance annext to his Play of the new Inne (1640)

THOMAS CAREW

'Tis true (dear Ben) thy just chastising hand
Hath fixt upon the sotted Age a brand
To their swoln pride, and empty scribbling due,
It can nor judge, nor write, and yet 'tis true
Thy comic Muse from the exalted line
Toucht by thy Alchymist, doth since decline
From that her Zenith, and foretells a red
And blushing evening, when she goes to bed,
Yet such, as shall out-shine the glimmering light
With which all stars shall guild the following night.
Nor think it much (since all thy Eaglets may
Endure the Sunny trial) if we say
This hath the stronger wing, or that doth shine
Tricked up in fairer plumes, since all are thine;
Who hath his flock of cackling Geese compared
With thy tun'd quire of Swans? or else who dared
To call thy births deformed? but if thou bind
By City-custom, or by Gavel-kind,
In equal shares thy love on all thy race,
We may distinguish of their sex, and place;
Though one hand form them, & though one brain strike
Souls into all, they are not all alike.
Why should the follies then of this dull age
Draw from thy Pen such an immodest rage
As seems to blast thy (else-immortal) Bays,
When thine own tongue proclaims thy itch of praise?

Thomas Carew, *Poems* (1640), 108–10.

Such thirst will argue drouth. No, let be hurled
Upon thy works, by the detracting world,
What malice can suggest; let the Rout say,
The running sands, that (ere thou make a play)
Count the slow minutes, might a Goodwin frame
To swallow when th'hast done thy ship-wrackt name.
Let them the dear expence of oil upbraid
Sucked by thy watchful Lamp, that hath betray'd
To theft the blood of martyr'd Authors, spilt
Into thy ink, whilst thou growest pale with guilt.
Repine not at the Taper's thrifty waste,
That sleeks thy terser Poems, nor is haste
Praise, but excuse; and if thou overcome
A knotty writer, bring the booty home;
Nor think it theft, if the rich spoils so torn
From conquered Authors, be as Trophies worn.
Let others glut on the extorted praise
Of vulgar breath, trust thou to after days:
Thy labour'd works shall live, when Time devours
Th' abortive off-spring of their hasty hours.
Thou art not of their rank, the quarrel lies
Within thine own Virge, then let this suffice,
The wiser world doth greater Thee confess
Then all men else, then Thy self only less.

From "A Sessions of the Poets" (1646)

Sir John Suckling

The first that broke silence was good old *Ben,*
Prepared before with Canary wine,
And he told them plainly he deserved the Bays,
For his were called Works, where others were but Plays.
And
Bid them remember how he had purged the Stage
Of errors, that had lasted many an age;
And he hoped they did not think the *Silent Woman,*
The *Fox,* and the *Alchemist* outdone by no man.

Apollo stopped him there, and bid him not go on,
'Twas merit, he said and not presumption
Must carry't; at which *Ben* turned about,
And in great choler offerd to go out:
But
Those that were there thought it not fit
To discontent so ancient a wit;
And therefore *Apollo* called him back again,
And made him mine host of his own new Inn.

John Suckling, *Fragmenta Aurea* (1648 edition), St. 3, 4.

To Benjaminum Jonsonium (1601)

CHARLES FITZGEOFFREY

Jonson, I call thee, come thou forth to justice,
I'm here to drag thee to the bar of Phœbus,
Guilty of stealing and of wicked thieving,
All the nine Muses sitting by in circle.
Know then that certain plays of wondrous beauty,
Which in the shade of an Elysian rose-bed,
Plautus most merry of the choir of poets
Lately composed, and to the gods recited
On starry seats, all sitting round to listen,
Moving to peals of laughter the Eternals,
And drawing smiles from Jupiter's grim visage.
Each pole of heaven thundering with applauses.
  These plays, I say then—plays so wondrous clever,
Thou stolest basely while the gods were busy,
And now proceedest as thine own to vend them:
Jonson, to justice come thou forth—I call thee!
  Lo, to defend thee, king and father Phœbus
Rises at once, O Jonson, and before all
Bears solemn witness that indeed thine own were
These famous plays, and that thou didst compose them,
Himself being privy to them and assisting.
Whence then, I pray, did Plautus having got them,
Read them aloud to Jove and the Eternals?
Lo, Maia's son and Atlas' clever grandson,
Wings on his swift feet, on his fingers birdlime,
Mercury, sharp boy, and a very rascal,
Aught to conceal with merry theft and laughter;
As once before, when love of his own torches
He deftly stripped, and robbed him of his quiver,

"*Ad Benjamin Jonsonium,*" in *The Poems of the Rev. Charles Fitzgeoffrey,* ed. and trans. Alexander Grosart (1881).

So, lately (since he often is accustomed
With thee to play, and clap his hands, and crack jokes),
From thee he stole these scattered sheets of paper,
And bade them mount up with him to the Heavenlies.
Now, put to shame, I'm silent, thou dost conquer,
O Jonson, Phœbus being thy judge and patron!

Prologue to *The Sad Shepherd* (1640–1641)

BEN JONSON

He that hath feasted you these forty years,
And fitted Fables, for your finer ears,
Although at first, he scarce could hit the bore;
Yet you, with patience harkning more and more,
At length have grown up to him, and made known,
The Working of his Pen is now your own:
He prays you would vouchsafe, for your own sake,
To hear him this once more, but, sit awake.
And though he now present you with such wool,
As from mere English Flocks his Muse can pull,
He hopes when it is made up into Cloath,
Not the most curious head here will be loath
To wear a Hood of it; it being a Fleece,
To match, or those of Sicily, or Greece.
His Scene is Sherwood: And his Play a Tale
Of Robin-Hood's inviting from the Vale
Of Be'voir, all the Shepherds to a Feast:
Where, by the casual absence of one Guest,
The Mirth is troubled much, and in one Man
As much of sadness shown, as Passion can.
The sad young Shepherd, whom we here present,
Like his woes Figure, dark and discontent,
For his lost Love; who in the Trent is said,
To have miscarried; 'las! what knows the head
Of a calm River, whom the feet have drowned?
Hear what his sorrows are; and, if they wound
Your gentle breasts, so that the End crown all,
Which in the Scope of one day's chance may fall:
Old Trent will send you more such Tales as these,
And shall grow young again, as one doth please.

From the 1640–1641 Folio of Jonson's *Works*, vol. 2.

But here's an Heresy of late let fall;
That Mirth by no means fits a Pastoral;
Such say so, who can make none, he presumes:
Else, there's no Scene, more properly assumes
The Sock. For whence can sport in kind arise,
But from the Rural Routs and Families?
Safe on this ground then, we not fear today,
To tempt your laughter by our rustic Play.
Wherein if we distaste, or be cried down,
We think we therefore shall not leave the Town;
Nor that the Fore-wits, that would draw the rest
Unto their liking, always like the best.
The wise, and knowing Critic will not say,
This worst, or better is, before he weigh,
Where every piece be perfect in the kind:
And then, though in themselves he difference find,
Yet if the place require it where they stood,
The equal fitting makes them equal good.
You shall have Love and Hate, and Jealousy,
As well as Mirth, and Rage, and Melancholy:
Or whatsoever else may either move,
Or stir affections, and your likings prove.
But that no style for Pastoral should go
Current, but what is stamped with Ah, and O;
Who judgeth so, may singularly err;
As if all Poesy had one Character:
In which what were not written, were not right,
Or that the man who made such one poor flight,
In his whole life, had with his wingéd skill
Advanced him upmost on the Muse's hill.
When he like Poet yet remains, as those
Are Painters who can only make a Rose.
From such your wits redeem you, or your chance,
Lest to a greater height you do advance
Of Folly, to contemn those that are known
Artificers, and trust such as are none.

The False Ending in *Volpone*

STEPHEN J. GREENBLATT

This essay aims at exploring Jonson's use in *Volpone* of a characteristic formal device of Elizabethan and Jacobean drama, and of his own plays in particular, the false ending.[1] At the close of Act IV, Volpone has completely triumphed: Celia and Bonario have been led off to await sentencing as adulterers and slanderers; the gulls believe more than ever that Volpone is dying; even the law court—sole seat of authority and justice within the world of the play—has been duped. If we yet feel that the innocent cannot be left to suffer, it is in this play only a vague and conventional sentiment.

The force of this "ending" should not be underestimated in reading the drama, as indeed it cannot be in performance. For *Volpone* up to this point has been an enormously *busy* play. The stage has been filled with frenetic activity: endless plotting, self-transformations, narrow escapes, hucksterism, sadistic jokes, attempted rape. Like the mountebank's patter, there have been almost no pauses: one monstrous manifestation of greed and low cunning is no sooner out the door than another pushes in to Volpone's chamber. And the language of the play fully reinforces this busyness and profusion. In keeping with the characters' obsession with wealth, there is an extraordinarily detailed "thingness" in their speech: pills of butter, Romagnia and rich Candian wines, Lombard's vinegar, nativity pie, furs and footcloths, bright chequins, plate, pearls, musk-melons, pome-citrons, Colchester oysters, Selsey cockles, sheep's gall, roasted bitch's marrow, sod earwigs, pounded caterpillars, capon's grease, fasting spittle, flayed apes, brains of peacocks, and so on, and so on. This is a play of lists, recipes, and catalogues; even Volpone's attempted seduction of Celia has the ring of an exotic inventory:

> Thy bathes shall be the iuyce of iuly-flowres,
> Spirit of roses, and of violets,
> The milke of vnicornes, and panthers breath
> Gather'd in bagges, and mixt with *cretan* wines.

From *The Journal of English and Germanic Philology,* 75 (1976): 90–104. Reprinted by permission of the University of Illinois Press.

Our drinke shall be prepared gold, and amber;
Which we will take, vntill my roofe whirle round
With the *vertigo:* and my dwarfe shall dance,
My eunuch sing, my foole make vp the antique.
Whil'st, we, in changed shapes, act OVIDS tales,
Thou, like EVROPA now, and I like IOVE,
Then I like MARS, and thou like ERYCINE,
So, of the rest, till we haue quite run through
And weary'd all the fables of the gods. (III.vii.213–25)

Profusion in Shakespeare creates, in Yeats's expressive phrase, "the emotion of multitude," the sense that the whole cosmos is involved in the action of the play.[2] In *Volpone,* instead of the emotion of multitude we have precisely the avoidance of depth in a vertiginous swirl of words. Volpone's speech, like the actions he generates, must flow on without pause, for in silence lurks the hidden meaning of his words, the anxiety of "run through" and "weary'd." And we, in the audience, participate in this flow, for we do not want Volpone to stop, any more than the crowd at a circus wants the tightrope walker to fall, though its enjoyment is predicated on that possibility.

Volpone's act culminates in the first trial scene. The latter half of Act IV has the feeling of a finale: up to now, great care has been taken to keep the gulls apart; at last they have all gathered together in the courtroom. We are reminded of the close of *Every Man in His Humour:* the isolated monads, locked in their own egotism and scheming, are brought together before the seat of judgment. This sense of an ending is compounded by the movement from darkness to light; Volpone is forced to perform the part of an invalid not in the convenient obscurity of his bedroom but in the glare of the Scrutineo. Jonson himself in the *Discoveries* provides the perfect description of the situation: "*Truth* and *Goodnesse* are plaine and open: but, *Imposture* is ever asham'd of the light. A Puppet-play must be shadow'd, and seene in the darke; for draw the Curtaine, *Et sordet gesticulatio.*"[3] The play metaphor here serves to remind us that what is at stake in the trial scene is not simply Volpone's con-game but the principle of theatrical illusion on which it is based. As all of our enjoyment has been derived from that illusion, we may dread its exposure before the judges, but we deem that exposure an inflexible rule of the moral universe: "*Imposture* is ever asham'd of the light." But in Act IV of *Volpone,* imposture unexpectedly triumphs: judgment fails, the innocent are condemned, and the fox is set free.

What is the effect of this "finale"? For a moment, Jonson offers the audience a resolution precisely the reverse of the one he will finally provide. It is as if he were testing the spectators, forcing them to re-examine their own sympathies: "You have identified with Volpone, enjoyed his machinations, taken his part against his victims, even the virtuous but vapid Celia and Bonario. All right, I give you Volpone's triumph." The audience must ask itself, "What would a world be like in which Volpone has triumphed?" In reply, it wills

Volpone's ultimate downfall. The spectators do not know exactly why they insist that the play continue—they scarcely have time to analyze their responses—but they do not applaud and they do not move for the exits. The victory they longed for has the taste of ashes.

Jonson's source for this brilliant device is probably Marlowe's *Jew of Malta,* in which we find a similar, if cruder, situation.[4] Thrown over the walls "To be a prey for vultures and wild beasts" (V.i.59), Barabas lies for a moment as if dead and then pops up like a toy that rights itself no matter how often it is floored. With the aid of the Turks who conveniently arrive at that precise moment, the Jew unexpectedly triumphs over his enemies. As the Christians are led away in chains, the audience is given a momentary vision of an ending diametrically opposed to the one they finally see: Barabas' "I now am Governor of Malta."

In both Marlowe's play and Jonson's, then, there is the same structural pattern: a near defeat (anticipating the true finale) and a false triumph. But there is an important difference. In *Volpone,* as we shall see, there is a highly significant pause before the plot resumes; Marlowe's hero scarcely pauses for breath. Barabas' declaration of triumph does not even fill out the line. The last syllable—"true"—marks the decisive turn toward those events that will finally destroy him:

> I now am Governor of Malta; true,
> But Malta hates me, and in hating me
> My life's in danger, and what boots it thee
> Poor Barabas, to be the Governor,
> When as thy life shall be at their command?
> No, Barabas, this must be looked into;
> And since by wrong thou got'st authority,
> Maintain it bravely by firm policy,
> At least unprofitably lose it not. (V.ii.30–38)

Whatever reasons Barabas may offer here for doing so, the audience *expects* him immediately to divest himself of the governorship; the space that he has carved out for himself to bustle in is defined precisely by his isolation. Thus when he rises from the dead, his first words reveal the essential condition of his existence: "What, all alone?" (V.i.61). Significantly, it is in the moments just prior to this resurrection, rather than in the moments following his victory, that the audience is given time to ask itself questions: not, "what would a world be like in which Barabas has triumphed?" but "what would a world be like without Barabas?" In *The Jew of Malta,* the audience wills not the hero's downfall, but his return to life.

In Jonson's play, the crucial pause occurs *after* Volpone's triumph. As Dryden noted, "there appear two actions in the play; the first naturally ending with the fourth act; the second forced from it in the fifth."[5] At the close of Act IV, the stage clears and must for a moment at least be completely bare, until Volpone enters, now safely back in his house. Where Barabas' speech after his triumph had slurred over the similar structural break, Volpone's calls attention to it: "Well, I am here; and all this brunt is past" (V.i.1). What is striking about this monosyllabic line—and about the entire opening of Act V—is its *deadness.* Volpone throughout has been a master of the alchemy of language, transforming vulgar wealth into precious wonders, but suddenly his powers fail him. This must be one of the rare instances in the history of the drama in which the author's genius is manifested in the collapse of his verse. The deadness has all along been lurking just beneath the glittering surface of Volpone's existence, and now in the pause after the Fox's triumph, it is revealed. We suddenly glimpse that dark thing which lay hidden behind all of the frenetic activity—not criminality or satanic evil but something subtler and more insidious: emptiness, boredom, the void.

In the flatness of these scenes—the flatness which prompts Mosca's superficially solicitous but deeply ironic "You are not taken with it, enough, me thinkes?"—we fully understand for the first time the meaning of Volpone's extraordinary energy, as we glimpse the void which that energy has been struggling to fill. What we perceive, I suggest, are those vast spaces that opened up on both a physical and psychological plane in the Renaissance.[6] Heirs of nineteenth-century liberalism, we think of this expansion as a triumph of the human spirit, a breakthrough into the light, an awakening:

> Man [in the Middle Ages] was conscious of himself only as member of a race, people, party, family, or corporation—only through some general category. In Italy this veil first melted into air; an *objective* treatment and consideration of the State and of all the things of this world became possible. The *subjective* side at the same time asserted itself with corresponding emphasis; man became a spiritual *individual,* and recognized himself as such.[7]

"This veil first melted into air"—how optimistic Burckhardt sounds And indeed Volpone seems to strive heroically to bear out this optimism. He is pre-eminently a man no longer "conscious of himself only as member of a race, people, party, family, or corporation":

> What should I doe,
> But cocker vp my *genius,* and liue free
> To all delights, my fortune calls me to?
> I haue no wife, no parent, child, allie,
> To giue my substance to; but whom I make,
> Must be my heire: and this makes men obserue me.
> (I.i.70–75)

Volpone speaks about himself and to himself here with that odd combination of engagement and detachment that characterizes most Western self-consciousness from precisely this period to the present time. He achieves the jaunty self-regard exuded by that virtual slogan of Renaissance confidence, "cocker vp my *genius,* and liue free," by regarding himself from the outside, by looking through the eyes of those who observe him. Because we ourselves live in just this way, because we are, ironically enough, Volpone's heirs, we are not fully conscious of the remarkable process occurring in these lines, though it determines the shape and meaning of the whole play: Volpone transforms himself into a theater in which he is both actor and audience. Of course, he plays for others as well, for the whole flock of gulls, but he would not be able to function at all had he not first performed the act of theatrical self-consciousness manifested here. He hears what he sounds like, sees what he looks like to others; and he can do so only because he has taken the others into himself. Moreover, he has separated himself off from himself, so that he can perform operations upon his own being. "Our bodies are our gardens, to the which our wills are gardeners": the speaker is Iago, but the principle is Volpone's as well.

For ourselves, as I have suggested, this kind of self-consciousness is all but automatic, so much so that we are lured into a belief that its development is "natural," that we inevitably grow into our peculiar way of regarding and manipulating our identities. Indeed, an influential modern social psychologist like George Herbert Mead assures us that only by forming within ourselves a "generalized other"—a kind of permanent, non-paying theater audience that judges all our thoughts and actions—do we develop a "complete self."[8] But in *Volpone,* the fashioning of this theatrical self, at once detached and committed, has the air of something original and willed, just as Volpone seems deliberately to will that adoration of gold which comes "naturally" to most men. Part of the contemporary fascination of Jonson's play is precisely that we feel ourselves present at the very fountainhead of modern consciousness, present just as the decisive, formative steps in the direction of our own minds are being taken. And we see that these steps are not natural or inevitable; we are invited rather to view them with mingled attraction and repulsion.

Volpone is consummately a man who has created his own identity, fashioned parts for himself which he proceeds to play with all the technical skill of a fine actor. Liberated from any hierarchy in the universe which would impose limits on his being, dependent only upon his own powerful imagination, he seems freer than anyone in his world. Indeed, with his ready disguises, he is liberated even from himself, uncommitted to a single, fixed role. He has the energy of Proteus.[9] Yet in the lull following the false ending, we perceive the converse, as it were, of this splendid energy, a yawning emptiness which at once permits its flowering and swallows it up. "We are all hollow and empty," wrote Montaigne: "It is not with wind and sound that we have to fill ourselves; we need more solid substance to repair us."[10]

The essential action of *Volpone*—thrown into relief by its momentary collapse at the start of Act V—is the hero's attempt to "fill himself." It is thus that he embarks on his endless accumulations of things, the items inventoried in such loving detail by Mosca as the gulls frantically question him about his master's will: Turkey carpets, nine; two suits of bedding, tissue; of cloth of gold, two more; of several vellets, eight; eight chests of linen; six chests of diaper, four of damask; down-beds, and bolsters; ten suits of hangings; two cabinets, one of ebony, the other, mother of pearl; one salt of agate, a perfumed box made of onyx, and so forth. There is something heroic about this relentless acquisitiveness. But no matter how many things he may amass, the space is never filled; its outer boundaries keep receding into the darkness.

If Volpone has no limiting relationships, by the same token he has no authentic relationships. He is alone. His condition epitomizes that isolation which obsesses the great seventeenth-century writers, the sense that man has lost any immediate relationship to the order of the world, the feeling that he is no longer enclosed in a web of sympathetic intercommunication linking all created things. "I haue no wife, no parent, child, allie, / To giue my substance to"—he is cut off from the past (parent), the present (wife), the future (child), and the society of men. And what of his "substance"? The succeeding lines make clear that Volpone intends by this word his wealth, all of the gold and jewels he has been amassing. But "substance" has an odd animation, an effect like that we find so often in Dickens: Volpone's wealth is intermingled with his name, his identity, that whole complex being one would share with others. Volpone's substance is his alone; this is the very condition and principle of his freedom. And if this autonomy transforms time into a theater in which he can act, it also means that for Volpone time does not offer the assurance of continuity. He is vouchsafed only a vision of a temporal void still more vast than the spatial:

> Sunnes, that set, may rise againe:
> But if, once, we lose this light,
> 'Tis with vs perpetuall night. (III.vii.171–73)

Catallus to the contrary, sexual pleasure does not relieve Volpone's solitude; indeed there is a distinctly hollow note in his professions of desire, marked by his lapse into literary parody:

> But angry CVPID, bolting from her eyes,
> Hath shot himselfe into me, like a flame;
> Where, now, he flings about his burning heat,
> As in a fornace, an ambitious fire,
> Whose vent is stopt. (II.iv. 3–7)

The deliberate grossness of the final words mocks the poetic convention, but expresses no more genuine passion than "My liuer melts" a few lines further on. It is not simply in order to deceive the judges that Volpone is brought into court "as impotent"; this has been a buried suggestion throughout the play.

When Lady Would-be appears instead of Celia, Volpone fears "that my loathing this / Will quite expell my appetite to the other" (III.iii.28–29). And even his great seduction speech, with its vision of endless self-metamorphoses in the service of erotic excitement, suggests sexual anxiety, the fear already noted in those disturbing words "run through" and "weary'd."

The succession of masks Volpone offers Celia are an attempt to stave off the boredom that follows hard on a voluptuary's pleasure.[11] They aim at a continual arousal, so as to prevent any dull pause between moments of satiety. In other words, like the plate, jewels, and bright chequins, they are an attempt to fill a void, here not a physical space but the dark gap between discontinuous experiences. The "changed shapes" Volpone lovingly describes—

> some sprightly dame of *France,*
> Braue *Tuscan* lady, or proud *Spanish* beauty;
> Sometimes vnto the *Persian Sophies* wife;
> Or the grand-*Signiors* mistresse; and, for change,
> To one of our most art-full courtizans,
> Or some quick *Negro,* or cold *Russian* (III.vii.227–32)

—are in a sense, more important than sexual gratification itself, since that gratification is always succeeded by a pause. It is as if Volpone has displaced his sexual energy from its usual instinctual object onto masquerading. Indeed in the lull after the courtroom triumph, he openly acknowledges his preference:

> MOSCA. You are not taken with it, enough, me thinkes?
> VOLPONE. O, more, then if I had enjoy'd the wench:
> The pleasure of all woman-kind's not like it. (V.ii.9–11)

But if, as I have suggested, the erotic masks are calculated to fill the gaps between points of time and thus to achieve a kind of timelessness, they are doomed to failure. For beneath the masquerade, time is secretly at work, bearing men toward old age and oblivion. The destructive effects of time are vividly manifested in the horrible old miser, Corbaccio, on whom Volpone muses:

> So many cares, so many maladies,
> So many feares attending on old age,
> Yea, death so often call'd on, as no wish
> Can be more frequent with 'hem, their limbs faint,
> Their senses dull, their seeing, hearing, going,
> All dead before them; yea, their very teeth,
> Their instruments of eating, fayling them:
> Yet this is reckon'd life! Nay, here was one,
> Is now gone home, that wishes to liue longer!

> Feeles not his gout, nor palsie, faines himselfe
> Yonger, by scores of yeeres, flatters his age,
> With confident belying it, hopes he may
> With charmes, like AESON, haue his youth restor'd:
> And with these thoughts so battens, as if fate
> Would be as easily cheated on, as he, *Another knocks.*
> And all turnes aire! (I.iv.144–59)

This is a strange and revealing moment: we expect derision, but the tone of the speech is more complex, mingling scorn, wonder, and a deep fear. The knock on the door—merely another gull presenting himself—has an eerie effect, like the sound of a string snapping, slowly and sadly dying away, in *The Cherry Orchard. All turnes air!*—for a brief moment we glimpse that void which is perceived again more powerfully at the false ending, that sense of emptiness against which Volpone struggles. Once again, he attempts to cheat or at least to mock this vision through disguise, the disguise which enacts every one of the horrors of age on which he had brooded. "An old, decrepit wretch," Corvino describes Volpone, as Volpone had described Corbaccio,

> That ha's no sense, no sinew; takes his meate
> With others fingers; onely knowes to gape,
> When you doe scald his gummes; a voice; a shadow.
> (III.vii.42–45)

By pretending to be old, sick, and dying, Volpone transforms time into a mere fiction of time. But to the extent to which he succeeds, he commits himself to living in a fiction, a "waking dreame" (I.i.18).[12]

Volpone's relationships with the other characters are tinged with the same unreality. To be sure, he appears unmasked with Mosca and indeed speaks with an affection that borders on love: "My beloued MOSCA"; "Excellent MOSCA! / Come hither, let me kisse thee"; "I cannot hold; good rascall, let me kisse thee"; "Let me embrace thee. O, that I could now / Transforme thee to a VENVS." But in their dialogues Jonson brilliantly suggests Volpone's fundamental incomprehension of the existence of a consciousness other than his own:

> VOLPONE. Dispatch, dispatch: I long to haue possession
> Of my new present.
> MOSCA. That, and thousands more,
> I hope, to see you lord of.
> VOLPONE. Thankes, kind MOSCA.
> MOSCA. And that, when I am lost in blended dust,
> And hundred such, as I am, in succession—

VOLPONE. Nay, that were too much, MOSCA.
MOSCA. You shall liue,
Still, to delude these *harpyies.*
VOLPONE. Louing MOSCA. (I.ii.116–22)

Mosca's bitter self-consciousness is more than matched by Volpone's anaesthetized egotism.[13]

If Volpone, in his theatrical self-consciousness, has absorbed the other characters into himself, he has, through that very process, "unrealized" them and created them anew, as a playwright creates his characters. There is something at once spurious and pathetic in Volpone's observation of his victims' reaction to his "death":

Now, they begin to flutter:
They neuer thinke of me. Looke, see, see, see!
(V.iii.16–17)

He has after all fashioned all of the conditions of their response. Of course we delight in the cheating of the scavengers who hover about what they think is a dying man; we share in the sadistic pleasure Volpone so frankly offers:

Letting the cherry knock against their lips,
And, draw it, by their mouths, and back againe. (Ii.89–90)

But here again the false ending serves to focus our latent perception of the limitations of such pleasure. Volpone's sadism has no power to sustain itself, to build anything lasting; the moment the gulling ceases, the pleasure utterly vanishes.

In committing himself to a fictive existence, a life of masks and pseudo-relationships, Volpone cuts himself off from the experience of duration. He must renew himself each moment—as Mosca renews his patron's make-up—lest the whole performance simply cease and vanish. Saint Augustine had written, in a phrase on which Renaissance thinkers meditated, that if God "were to withdraw what we may call his 'constructive power' from existing things, they would cease to exist, just as they did not exist before they were made."[14] Jonson's play is, as it were, a demonic imitation of such a universe, with Volpone replacing God as the agent of continual creation. Should his energy lapse for an instant, his world would collapse and he would fall into nothingness. Such a collapse is precisely what is threatened—in theatrical rather than philosophical terms—in the aftermath of the courtroom triumph. For a moment, we are allowed to feel, within the play itself, the emptiness of the stage after the performance is over. And even when the stage is reanimated by the presence of Mosca and Volpone, their dialogue is the backstage chatter of actors after the play is done:

MOSCA. 'T seem'd to mee, you sweat, sir.
VOLPONE. In troth, I did a little. (V.ii.37–38)

At the start of Act V, then, Volpone is in the surrealistic situation of a character who has somehow survived his play. He has no plot to sustain him, no external guarantees of duration. For an instant during the trial, he recalls nervously, he thought he had lost the very essence of his theatrical existence—his mimetic power:

'Fore god, my left legge 'gan to haue the crampe;
And I apprehended, straight, some power had strooke me
With a dead palsey. (V.i.5–7)

There is nothing in the play to make us believe that the "power" Volpone suddenly fears is anything but an illusion, a superstitious projection. The threat here is not the supernatural but the physical: the fear of real paralysis in place of feigned. The "dead palsey" is the radical antithesis of that transcendence of the body which an exultant Mosca celebrates as the highest achievement of a successful parasite like himself:

But your fine, elegant rascall, that can rise,
And stoope (almost together) like an arrow;
Shoot through the aire, as nimbly as a starre;
Turne short, as doth a swallow; and be here,
And there, and here, and yonder, all at once;
Present to any humour, all occasion;
And change a visor, swifter, then a thought!
This is the creature, had the art borne with him.
(III.i.23–30)

The creature who can perform these feats has literally to be nothing, a bodiless fiction. Hence the terror lurking in a mere cramp: a sign that the body resists the will and thus that the fiction is collapsing. For Volpone, to sense the body's resistance is to sense death.

On regaining his lair at the start of Act V, Volpone's first response is to call for "a boule of lustie wine" to chase away the cold deadness at his center: "This heate is life," he declares after drinking. But wine is obviously not enough. As he himself suggests, he will continue to exist only if he can somehow regenerate the plot:

Any deuice, now, of rare, ingenious knauery,
That would possesse me with a violent laughter,
Would make me vp, againe! (V.i.14–16)

In Volpone's world—the world of continual creation—to stand still is to vanish. It is thus that Mosca, employing the simplest negative psychology, pushes his patron towards his fatal misstep:

> We must, here, be fixt;
> Here, we must rest; this is our master-peece:
> We cannot thinke, to goe beyond this. (V.ii.12–14)

Of course, Volpone's great fear is to be fixed, to be struck, as it were, with a dead palsey. He must think "to goe beyond this"; otherwise he and the play simply end.

The device he chooses to make himself up again is to give out that he is dead. This is, in a sense, the supreme triumph of Volpone's art for his strategy is to turn what he fears into fiction, and what he fears most of all is death. But at this point, Mosca intervenes, in an attempt to trap Volpone in this ultimate masquerade and establish himself permanently in his own new part, that of Volpone's heir. And with this attempt to freeze the roles, the whole elaborate charade collapses.

Significantly, at the true end of the play, Mosca and Volpone are both condemned to be "fixed," the former as a perpetual prisoner in the galleys and the latter still more tightly:

> since the most was gotten by imposture,
> By faining lame, gout, palsey, and such diseases,
> Thou art to lie in prison, crampt with irons,
> Till thou bee'st sicke, and lame indeed. (V.xii.121–24)

"Crampt with irons"—like Proteus, Volpone will be held fast until all metamorphoses cease. Or rather he will be permitted one last, bitter metamorphosis, until his being finally and irrevocably assumes the shape of his mask.

The assault on metamorphosis strikes not only at Volpone as a character but at the whole world which he has brought into being in the opening moments of the play. As one may say that Lear symbolically kills Cordelia in the first scene and spends the rest of the play enduring the consequences of his action, so as the curtain rises Volpone performs the determining action of the play: he ritually displaces God from the center of the universe. From this primal displacement flow all of the subsequent transformations; from it too derive those vast spaces, in both the world and the self, which the transformations strive vainly to fill.

Perhaps this has too orthodox a ring. There is at least a suggestion, I believe, that the seeds of Volpone's downfall lie not in his displacement of God but in the play-world itself, in a universe with no guarantees of continuity. From this perspective, it does not matter whether the agent of creation is God, or gold, or the artist; the scheme of things itself is wrong. After all, the finale of Volpone does not attempt to replace God in the central position; indeed the corruption of the judges undermines even the more modest conclusion that Justice has triumphed. What the fettering of Volpone and Mosca does accomplish is to end the play, to destroy that principle whereby not only these characters but any dramatic characters exist. If at the false ending Jonson keeps the audience in their seats and thus proves that Volpone's triumph is empty, so at the true ending, he makes part of the meaning of the work the audience's exit from the playhouse. He directs the audience, as it were, to reject the theatrical principles of displacement, mask, and metamorphosis.

That this rejection cut very deep for Jonson himself is suggested, above all, in the scene in which Volpone masquerades as Scoto of Mantua. The real Scoto was a professional actor, leader of a company licensed by the Duke of Mantua, and Volpone's Scoto is also a kind of playwright-actor, mounting his bank to perform for the rabble. In his astonishing verbal facility, his bombastic defensiveness, his proud boast that he has "past the craggie pathes of studie, and come to the flowrie plaines of honour, and reputation" (II.ii.169–70), and even in the incidental details of his career, Volpone's Scoto seems to be a striking parody of Jonson himself. Alvin Kernan, who has noted the many parallels, suggests that Jonson is working to distinguish false art from true: "Just as Volpone's opening speech on gold calls our attention to those vital natural and social forces which have been perverted by the substitution of a gold coin for the sun, so here our attention is focused on the nature of true medicine, *and true playing,* by the distortion of both those arts wrought by greed and lust, the moving powers behind Scoto-Volpone's performance."[15] But if my reading of the close of the play is correct, Jonson's vision is far more radical. We reject not the abuse of playing but playing itself.

Indeed Scoto's pitch for his worthless snake oil seems to me a brilliant and bitter parody of the central Renaissance defense of the stage. The mountebank tells us that his product is a sovereign cure for all ailments: "the *mal-caduco,* crampes, conuulsions, paralysies, epilepsies, *tremor-cordia,* retyred-nerues, ill vapours of the spleene, stoppings of the liuer, the stone, the strangury, *hernia ventosa, iliaca passio,*" and on and on. We know that the claims are nonsense, but we listen out of sheer delight in the performance itself. The mountebank knows that we know that it is nonsense, but he will never let on, for that would spoil the game and drive away business.

Is this not derisive laughter at those sixteenth- and seventeenth-century apologists for the drama who never tire of telling us that our tuppenny admission is the best investment we could ever make, that plays cure all our moral hernias? Is this not the disturbing self-mockery of the man who in the Dedicatory Epistle to *Volpone*—an epistle addressed to those greatest of gulls, the universities of Oxford and Cambridge—wrote with a straight face of the "impossibility of any mans being the good Poet, without first being a good man"? And the Epistle does not even stop at that extravagant claim for the poet:

> He that is said to be able to informe yong-men to all good disciplines, inflame growne-men to all great vertues, keepe old-men in their best and supreme state, or as they decline to child-hood, recouer them to their first strength; that comes forth the interpreter, and arbiter of nature, a teacher of things diuine, no lesse then humane, a master in manners; and can alone (or with a few) effect the businesse of man-kind: this, I take him, is no subject for pride, and ignorance to exercise their rayling rhetorique vpon.

Now it is clear that Jonson was strongly drawn to these claims, that throughout his career he wanted very much to believe in them. But as a man with a remarkably acute ear for cant and hucksterism, he understood quite well how closely they resembled a mountebank's patter.

If there is a convincing defense of the stage in *Volpone,* it is not the pretensions of the humanists but the comically medical promise of the prologue:

> All gall, and coppresse, from his inke, he drayneth,
> Onely, a little salt remayneth;
> Wherewith, he'll rub your cheeks til (red with laughter)
> They shall looke fresh, a weeke after.

The promise of amusement is recalled at the very close of the play by Volpone himself, who steps forward and speaks directly to the audience:

> The seasoning of a play is the applause.
> Now, though the FOX be punish'd by the lawes,
> He, yet, doth hope there is no suffring due,
> For any fact, which he hath done 'gainst you;
> If there be, censure him: here he, doubtfull, stands.
> If not, fare iouially, and clap your hands.

If earlier Volpone seemed like a character who had somehow survived his play, here for a moment he is literally that. And as such he can call attention to the drama as entertainment, hearty fare for which the "seasoning" is applause. A gap is deliberately opened between the play's moral structure—by which Volpone must be punished—and its power to delight. In *The Alchemist* and *Bartholomew Fair,* this gap is exploited to effect a new (if qualified) acceptance of theatricality. But in *Volpone* Jonson has incorporated not only the audience's applause but, as I have suggested, its departure. The exit may be irksome, as Volpone's histrionics are enormously vital and attractive, but as this play bitterly insists, you cannot stay in the theater forever.

Notes

1. All citations to *Volpone* are from *Ben Jonson*, ed. C. H. Herford and Percy and Evelyn Simpson (Oxford, 1925–50), v.

For a useful discussion of Jonson's recurring structural "formula which provided a tentative solution in Act IV and a reversal in Act V," see Edgar Knowlton, "The Plots of Ben Jonson," *MLN*, 44 (1929), 77–86. The most explicit example of this formula is at the end of Act IV of *The Magnetic Lady*. Much of the recent critical discussion of Volpone's structure has focused on its subplot. There has not, to my knowledge, been any extended treatment of the false ending itself, though there has been considerable debate about the justice of the finale and its relations to the rest of the play. Cf. Ralph Nash, "The Comic Intent of *Volpone*," *SP*, 44 (1947), 26–40; John S. Weld, "Christian Comedy: *Volpone*," *SP*, 51 (1954), 172–93; E. B. Partridge, *The Broken Compass* (London, 1958), p. 103; P. H. Davison, "*Volpone* and the Old Comedy," *MLQ*, 24 (1963), 151–57; S. L. Goldberg, "Folly into Crime: The Catastrophe of *Volpone*," *MLQ*, 20 (1959), 233–42; Alexander Leggatt, "The Suicide of Volpone," *University of Toronto Quarterly*, 39 (1969), 19–32; Alan C. Dessen, *Jonson's Moral Comedy* (Evanston, 1971), pp. 74–104.

2. W. B. Yeats, "Emotion of Multitude," in *Essays and Introductions* (London, 1961), pp. 215–16. For a fine discussion of the "swirling profusion" of Jonson's plays, see Alvin B. Kernan, "Alchemy and Acting: The Major Plays of Ben Jonson," *Studies in the Literary Imagination*, 6 (1973), 1–3.

3. *Timber, or Discoveries*, ll. 238–41, in Herford and Simpson, VIII, 570.

4. All citations to *The Jew of Malta* are to the New Mermaids edition, ed. T. W. Craig (New York, 1966).

5. John Dryden, *Of Dramatic Poesy and Other Critical Essays*, ed. George Watson (London, 1962), i, 61.

6. See, esp., Georges Poulet, *The Metamorphoses of the Circle*, trans. Carley Dawson and Elliott Coleman (Baltimore, 1966), pp. 15–16. In his introduction to the Yale edition of *Volpone*, Alvin Kernan suggests that the play's "gold-centered world is . . . a grotesque image of the materialistic culture of the Renaissance" (p. 4).

7. Jacob Burckhardt, *The Civilization of the Renaissance in Italy*, trans. S. G. C. Middlemore (New York, 1958), 1, 143.

8. "The organized community or social group which gives to the individual his unity of self can be called 'the generalized other.' . . . Only insofar as he takes the attitudes of the organized social group . . . does he develop a complete self or possess the sort of complete self he has developed"; George Herbert Mead, *On Social Psychology*, ed. Anselm Strauss (Chicago, 1956), pp. 218–19.

9. See Thomas M. Greene, "Ben Jonson and the Centered Self," *SEL*, 10 (1970), 337–38, and Kernan's introduction to the Yale edition, pp. 13–15. For a general discussion of the histrionic sensibility, see my *Sir Walter Ralegh: The Renaissance Man and His Roles* (New Haven, 1973), pp. 22–56.

10. "Of Glory," in *The Complete Essays of Montaigne*, trans. Donald M. Frame (Stanford, 1958), p. 468.

11. See Alexander Leggatt, "The Suicide of Volpone": "the endless disguises which form the major part of his sexual fantasy suggest that ordinary copulation has become boring through excessive repetition, and that it has to be dressed up exotically before he can savour it" (p. 21).

12. The sense of unreality reaches its height in Mosca's dizzying reply to Volpone's question, "Were they gull'd / With a beliefe, that I was SCOTO?—"Sir, / SCOTO himselfe could hardly haue distinguish'd!" (II.iv.34–36).

13. Empson quotes this passage and speaks of the "golden glow of this poetry" which "depends here upon a moral sympathy, even if a mixed and fleeting one, from the audience to

the comic hero" ("Volpone," *Hudson Review,* 21 [1968], 657). I think such sympathy is felt elsewhere, but certainly not here.

14. St. Augustine, *The City of God,* trans. Henry Bettenson (London, 1972). II, xii. 26, p. 506. See, for example, Sir Walter Ralegh, *The History of the World* (London, 1614), I. i, 10, p. 11: "For as it is Gods infinite power, and eueriewhere-presence (compassing, embracing, and piercing all things) that giueth to the Sunne power to draw vp vapours, to vapours to be made cloudes, cloudes to containe raine, and raine to fall: so all second and instrumental causes, together with Nature it selfe, without that operatiue faculty which God gaue them, would become altogether silent, vertulesse, and dead." See also Georges Poulet, *Studies in Human Time,* trans. Elliott Coleman (Baltimore, 1956), p. 19.

15. Kernan, Yale Edition, p. 215.

From *Letters upon Several Occasions* (1696)

John Dennis

I

I have now read over the Fox, in which though I admire the strength of *Ben Jonson's* Judgment, yet I did not find it so accurate as I expected. For first the very thing upon which the whole Plot turns, and that is the Discovery which *Mosca* makes to *Bonario;* seems to me, to be very unreasonable. For *I* can see no Reason, why he should make that Discovery which introduces *Bonario* into his Master's House. For the Reason which the Poet makes *Mosca* give in the Ninth Scene of the third Act, appears to be a very Absurd one. Secondly, *Corbaccio* the Father of *Bonario* is exposed for his Deafness, a Personal defect; which is contrary to the end of Comedy Instruction. For Personal Defects cannot be amended; and the exposing such, can never divert any but half-witted Men. It cannot fail to bring a thinking Man to reflect upon the Misery of Human Nature; and into what he may fall himself without any Fault of his own. Thirdly, the play has two Characters, which have nothing to do with the design of it, which are to be looked upon as Excrescences. Lastly, the Character of *Volpone* is inconsistent with itself. *Volpone* is like *Catiline, alieni appetens, sui profusus,* but that is only a double in his Nature, and not an Inconsistency. The Inconsistency of the Character appears in this, that *Volpone* in the fifth Act behaves himself like a Giddy Coxcomb, in the Conduct of that very Affair which he managed so Craftily in the first four. In which the Poet offends first against that Famed rule which *Horace* gives for the Characters.

> Servetur ad imum,
> Qualis ab incepto processerit, et sibi constet.

This and the following selection are from letters to William Congreve, in *Letters upon Several Occasions,* (1696), 73–79.

And Secondly, against Nature, upon which, all the rules are grounded. For so strange an Alteration, in so little time, is not in Nature, unless it happens by the Accident of some violent passion; which is not the case here. *Volpone* on the sudden behaves himself without common Discretion, in the Conduct of that very Affair which he had managed with so much Dexterity, for the space of three Years together. For why does he disguise himself? Or why does he repose the last Confidence in *Mosca?* Why does he cause it to be given out that he's dead? Why, only to Plague his Bubbles. To Plague them, for what? Why only for having been his Bubbles. So that here is the greatest alteration in the World, in the space of twenty-four hours, without any apparent cause. The design of *Volpone* is to Cheat, he has carried on a Cheat for three years together, with Cunning and with Success. And yet he on a sudden in cold blood does a thing, which he cannot but know must Endanger the ruining all.

II

I will not augment the Trouble which I give you by making an Apology for not giving it you sooner. Though I am heartily sorry that I kept such a trifle as the enclosed, and a trifle writ Extempore, long enough to make you expect a laboured Letter. But because in the enclosed, I have spoken particularly of *Ben Jonson's Fox,* I desire to say three or four words of some of his Plays more generally. The Plots of the Fox, the silent Woman, the Alchemist, are all of them very Artful. But the Intrigues of the Fox, and the Alchemist, seem to me to be more dexterously perplexed, than to be happily disentangled. But the Gordian knot in the Silent Woman is untied with so much Felicity, that that alone, may Suffice to show *Ben Jonson* no ordinary Hero. But, then perhaps, the Silent Woman may want the very Foundation of a good Comedy, which the other two cannot be said to want. For it seems to me, to be without a Moral. Upon which Absurdity, *Ben Jonson* was driven by the Singularity of *Morose's* Character, which is too extravagant for Instruction, and fit, in my opinion, only for Farce. For this seems to me, to Constitute the most Essential Difference, betwixt Farce and Comedy, that the Follies which are exposed in Farce are Singular; and those are particular, which are exposed in Comedy. These last are those, with which some part of an Audience may be supposed Infected, and to which all may be supposed Obnoxious. But the first are so very odd, that by Reason of their Monstrous Extravagance, they cannot be thought to concern an Audience; and cannot be supposed to instruct them. For the rest of the Characters in these Plays, they are for the most part true, and Most of the Humorous Characters Masterpieces. For *Ben Jonson's* Fools, seem to show his Wit a great deal more than his Men of Sense. I Admire his Fops, and but barely Esteem his Gentlemen. *Ben* seems to draw Deformity more to the Life than Beauty. He is often so eager to pursue Folly, that he forgets to take Wit along with him. For the Dialogue, it seems to want very often that Spirit, that Grace, and that Noble Raillery, which are to be found in more Modern Plays, and which are Virtues that ought to be Inseparable from a finished Comedy. But there seems to be one thing more wanting than all the rest, and that is Passion. I mean that fine and that delicate Passion, by which the Soul shows its Politeness, even in the midst of its trouble.

From *The Tatler* (1709)

RICHARD STEELE

This Night was acted the Comedy called, *The Fox;* but I wonder the Modern Writers do not use their Interest in the House to suppress such Representations. A Man that has been at this, will hardly like any other Play during the Season: Therefore I humbly move, That the Writings, as well as Dresses, of the last Age, should give way to the present Fashion. We are come into a good Method enough (if we were not interrupted in our Mirth by such an Apparition as a Play of *Jonson's*) to be entertained at more Ease, both to the Spectator and the Writer, than in the Days of Old. It is no Difficulty to get Hats, and Swords and Wigs, and Shoes, and everything else, from the Shops in Town, and make a Man show himself by his Habit, without more ado, to be a Counselor, a Fop, a Courtier, or a Citizen, without being obliged to make those Characters talk in different Dialects to be distinguished from each other. This is certainly the surest and best Way of Writing: But such a Play as this makes a Man for a Month after overrun with Criticism, and enquire, What every man on the Stage said? What had such a one to do to meddle with such a Thing? How came t'other, who was bred after such a Manner, to speak so like a Man conversant among a different People? These Questions rob us of all our pleasure; for at this Rate, no one Sentence in a Play should be spoken by any one Character, which could possibly enter into the Head of any other Man represented in it; but every Sentiment should be peculiar to him only who utters it.

Laborious *Ben's* Works will bear this Sort of Inquisition, but if the present Writers were thus examined, and the Offences against this Rule cut out, few Plays would be long enough for the whole Evening's Entertainment. But I don't know how they did in those old Times: This same *Ben Jonson* has made everyone's Passion in this Play be towards Money, and yet not one of them expresses that Desire, or goes about obtaining it, in any Way but what is peculiar to him only: One sacrifices his Wife, another his Profession, another his Posterity, from the same motive; but their Characters are kept so skillfully apart, that it seems prodigious, their Discourses should rise from the Invention of the same Author.

From *The Tatler* 21 (May 1709): 26–28.

The Jonsonian Corpulence, or The Poet as Mouthpiece

JOSEPH LOEWENSTEIN

All those given to silence are dyspeptic.

—Nietzche, *Ecce Homo*

One enters a fine, if young, tradition of Jonson scholarship to take up that poet's "Inviting a Friend to Supper" (*Epigrams,* 101). Central themes in Jonson's career may be discovered there—the ethical calibration, or moderation, of pleasure and the nature of civil, even bourgeois, festivity.[1] With such centralities of theme, and perhaps because of them, goes a centrality of poetic achievement: if it is permissible to speak of such matters in such terms, then this poem may be called a triumph of the plain style.[2] With the couplets firmly placed, the verse is possessed of both closure and continuance. Jonson has found an even more craftsmanlike solution than Wyatt's to the problematics of an English epistolary verse: his couplets figure the constant achievement of a poise that is nonetheless capable of procession, whereas Wyatt's sinuous *terza rima* can only yearn toward poise, can achieve only its own agility, can aspire only to an ethics and a prosody, not English, but (and I use the term as a Tudor might) Italian.[3]

Criticism has said as much, at least obliquely. The fundamental object of critical scrutiny in Jonson's poem has been its "nativity," its very Englishness, which is cannily plucked from the constraining discipline of translation. *Imitatio* has been the great concern of the best criticism of Jonson's verse, and the slant power of this pervasive renaissance procedure is on brilliant display in this invitation poem.[4] "Inviting a Friend to Supper" is, after all, almost entirely a translation from Martial, a conflation of several such invitation

From *ELH* 53 (1986): 491–518. Reprinted by permission of the Johns Hopkins University Press.

poems. Recently, Thomas Greene has summarized the readings that address this poem specifically as an imitation, by showing how this, like many other poems by Jonson, figures imitative creation as a ceremony of entertainment, a hospitality, both dignified and festive, by which antiquity and Renaissance England engage each other in a mutual "receptivity." Greene suggests that, for Jonson, poetic tradition is, in effect, a receiving line.[5]

This particular pattern of figuration has its tonal uncertainties. I have written elsewhere of "the perilous ethics of festivity" in Jonson's dramatic writing. Not only *Bartholomew Fair* may be said to involve considerable broodings on the tense play between moderate individuality and the various forces (purgative, ensnaring, celebratory, anarchic) of social festivity: an earlier play, *Cynthia's Revels,* locates these tensions indoors, in a more settled environment, but without any relaxation of ethical tension. "Entertainment" is an equivocal value throughout Jonson's works: in the seminal *Masque of Blacknesse,* a dance at the mutable shore separating audience and spectacle, Britannia and the sea, self and social others may consummate the fiction of the masque, but it is said to be measured out to the tune of siren-song and its dangerous entanglements are designated "intertaynment."[6]

Of course, in "Inviting a Friend to Supper," Jonson speaks of an "entertaynment perfect," a private festivity that may seem to slip the trammels of those noisy and theatrical sociabilities of fair-grounds or banqueting hall:

> your worth will dignifie our feast,
> With those that come; whose grace may make that seeme
> Something, which, else, could hope for no esteeme.
> It is the faire acceptance, Sir, creates
> The entertaynment perfect: not the cates.
>
> (4–8)[7]

I wish to press, though gently, the fact that the indicative of this last couplet is without deictic force, that, firm as it is, the assertion made here is no more than a proposition. To sidestep the dicy question of what linguistic modality actually means, observe that what is affirmed is, precisely, contingency, the dependence of occasional value on the will of the grave guest: the poet's power, the power of the host, is limited to graceful deferral. And there are more fundamental uncertainties. Consider rhythm: the Folio texts of Jonson's verse are notoriously heavy in their punctuation, but lines like

> grace may make that seeme
> Something, which, else, could hope for no esteeme

so outstrip the norm that one feels compelled to acknowledge that here—in the precarious enjambment, negotiated under the sign of mere semblance, in the wary footfall of the next half-line, setting out from the nominal inadequacy of "Something"—here we have the very form (the very imperfect Form) of the negative compliment. "Something, which, else, could hope for no esteeme": the "something" of cultural value cannot quite be named, much less called into existence, can only be *entertained,* and "the entertaynment perfect" is utterly subjunctive.

Observations on the place of the subjunctive in this poem are hardly new. The meal proposed is sumptuous—

> An olive, capers, or some better sallade
> Ushring the mutton; with a short-leg'd hen,
> If we can get her, full of egs, and then,
> Limons, and wine for sauce: to these a coney
> Is not to be despair'd of, for our money.
> (10–14)

—but it is a curiously soluble sumptuousness. An old joke is being played here: nowhere is the incongruity of *res* and *verba* more nagging than when earthly delights are listed, yet nowhere does the word have more power. Jonson mocks advertising at its birth ("Ile tell you of more, and lye, so you will come: / Of partrich, pheasant, wood-cock" [17–18]), but only after more rueful humor has had its play. For not only nominal inadequacy or nominal deceit is being dramatized: urbane delicacies betray the hungers concealed by the graces of language. "An olive," the habitual litotes of polite invitation, "capers," the suggestion of piquancy—here we have the Anacreontic elegance of little things, and it would be boorish for the grave guest to remark on Anacreontic scale (*an* olive), for, after all, the lines open out toward "some better sallade / Ushring the mutton." (And yet, after the olive and capers that alternative salad threatens to wilt toward ontological vagueness, and the syntax withholds the mutton, slices it thinly). Hearty human generosity is perhaps always threatened by haunting human niggardliness, but these lines suggest that the language of verse is far more apt to withhold than to dispense. The turn from line 11 to line 12 makes a joke of this mean aptitude—"a short-leg'd hen, / If": one feels here that enjambment is the perfect prosodic correlative of conditional grammar, and that both are inevitable. The hen may not materialize; that which *is* not cannot be full (yet how enticing is the thought of plenitude); we are left with a koan of cuisine: can real wine and real lemons sauce an immaterial hen? Lassitudes of syntax are rife. "Limons, and wine for sauce": the "for" constructs what might be called a dative of delicious intentions. On and on: "a cony / Is not to be despair'd of."

It makes us hungry—one notices that a menu makes one hungrier than a cafeteria ever can—but the hunger goes beyond (or beneath) belly-hunger. Nominal detail is haunted by its syntactic contexts:

partrich, pheasant, wood-cock, of which some
May yet be there; and godwit, if we can:
Knat, raile, and ruffe too.
(18–20)

"May yet be there," "if we can": the locutions express longing distilled to abstraction. (By the time we get to "knat, raile, and ruffe," the syntax has so betrayed our hopes, so steadily thwarted hope, that what might in another context be taken as the purest of deictics—an assertion of available presence so full that the predicate may be ellipsed—actually seems to display how confidence in predication has, finally, failed altogether.) What is remarkable about this menu is that it converts belly-hunger into an appetite increasingly ontological. We are readied for the turn. With our appetites thus made metaphysical, the sustenance that Jonson now promises betrays the habitual bias of the humanist:

Knat, raile, and ruffe too. How so ere, my man
Shall reade a piece of VIRGIL, TACITUS,
LIVIE, or of some better booke to us,
Of which wee'll speake our minds, amidst our meate.
(20–23)

Here the conversion of belly-hunger into more consuming appetites receives a settled representation, for under the steadying influence of classical books, mind finds a place "amidst our meate." This is a consumption devoutly to be wished.

Here in the very center of the poem the sway of the subjunctive ends: we can see how much more solid the ground is by noting how the "olive, capers, or some better sallade / Ushring the mutton" is enriched and affirmed almost past parallelism by the "piece of VIRGIL, TACITUS, / LIVIE, or of some better booke . . . / Of which wee'll speake our minds."[8] But the implications of parallelism are not quite effaced and they insist on a question that may, at first, seem silly. We casually speak of the sustenance of books—does not this poem revivify, and so challenge, the figure? Put otherwise, what do the nourishments of body have to do with those of mind?

Such a question is quietly propounded, barely more than implied, in this the first half of the poem and perhaps it will be easier to answer after a more obtrusive problem is addressed. In the next line, Jonson promises the purity of the literary entertainment—"And Ile professe no verses to repeate" (24)—but the promise has already, in a sense, been breached. He *has* been repeating verses. One might as well cite:

vinum tu facies bonum bibendo
[The wine you will make good by drinking it]
(Martial, *Epigrams* 5.78.16)[9]

cetera nosse cupis?
mentiar, ut venias: pisces, conchylia, sumen,
et chortis saturas atque paludis aves
[Do you want to know the rest? I will deceive you to make you come: fish, mussels, sow's paps, and fat birds of the poultry-yard and of the marsh]

(Martial, *Epigrams* 11.52.12–14)

nostra dabunt alios hodie convivia ludos,
conditor Iliados cantabitur atque Maronis
altisoni dubiam facientia carmina palmam.
[My feast today will provide other performances than these. The bard of the *Iliad* will be sung and the lays of the lofty-toned Maro that contest the palm with his.]

(Juvenal, *Satires* 11.179–81)

plus ego polliceor: nil recitabo tibi
ipse tuos nobis relegas licet usque Gigantas,
rura vel aeterno proxima Vergilio
[More I promise you: I will recite nothing to you, even although you yourself read again your "Giants" straight through, or your "Pastorals" that rank next to immortal Virgil's]

(Martial, *Epigrams* 11.52.16–18)

I expect it to be objected that Jonson's promise "no verses to repeate" means something else, that it is a promise to recite no verses of his own. I must insist against the objection. The host's promised self-effacement should be taken in context, for it is part of a pervasive modesty that is made thematic at the poem's outset with the leveling of host and home:

TO night, grave sir, both my poore house, and I
Doe equally desire your companie.

(1–2)

The "subjunctivity" of this feast, the host's professed and implied inability to guarantee the luxury invoked, all of this situates generosity in a field of contingency. Individual will expands to express itself in festivity, and that expansiveness, inhibited at every turn becomes exquisitely articulate, made definitive by constraint. The modesty of Jonson's profession "no verses to repeate" is the will's answering mirror to the world, a self-restraint to match the subjunctive constraints of living. To remark this ethical position is to remark that Jonson's ethics are the perfect analogue to an imitative poetics, with its self-restraint of the expansiveness of individual poetic will. Jonson's profession here, to silence himself, does pun toward a promise not merely to repeat the verses of others. *Imitatio* makes possible a profoundly articulate poetic individuality, a voice made both quiet and personal by its knowing submission to the constraints of others' voices. If he professes not to repeat, it is because, repeating, he has made Martial's poems his own.

Jonson's profession is, specifically, the tongue-in-cheek profession of the poet. It is difficult to judge how familiar Jonson's reader may be expected to have been with the invitation poems that are the objects of imitation here; to me, the wit of Jonson's profession here seems to have a gentle privacy. Many of the best poems of the *Epigrammes* hover between a private and a public rhetoric (no doubt this is a strategic effect, part of Jonson's campaign to select, if he cannot create, the ideal reader). But certainly the wry attention to the ethics of imitation discernible here at the center of the poem loses its privacy in short order:

> Ile professe no verses to repeate:
> To this, if ought appeare, which I not know of,
> That will the pastrie, not my paper, show of.
> (24–26)

The lines need a bit of glossing, which editors of the *Epigrammes* consistently fail to provide. Fortunately, Roger Gognard came up with the ingenious and convincing explanation that Jonson is simply bolstering his promise by assuring the guest that the only way in which his, Jonson's, poetry could possibly manage to intrude itself upon the evening's entertainment is if the pastries bought for the occasion come wrapped in waste sheets from unsold copies of Jonson's poetry.[10] Apparently, the shortening in the baked goods made the ink on printed sheets fugitive, so that the pastries often took an imprint from their wrappers. The poet's modest suggestion that his work has not sold and is now being used to wrap custard tarts certainly accords with the themes of the first half of the poem—that is, the modesty has a context, as does the subtler humor of this evocation of an actual contact between tantalizing words and edible things. But a new pattern of concerns begins to take shape here, for which the printed pastry may function as an emblem. What we have here is false imitation.

There is much to say about these printed pastries. In this the first Age of Mechanical Reproduction, the automatism of publication has a haunting quality: even as the word loses its artisanal aura, as it sinks toward the commonplace, there is a historical moment, furiously reinforced by Reformation and Counter-Reformation celebrations and repressions of the disseminable word, when the new iterabilities of the word provided the central category around which the logocentrism of the West organized itself. (Spenser's Error is a sort of printing press; her most horrifying aspect is her fecundity.) Here the uncanny, if banal, offspring of the multiple, marketable literary text unexpectedly returns to its grandparent, reminding Jonson—as he would be regularly reminded—that the urban marketplace has its own energies (one would wish to say its own logic, though Jonson could seldom calm his gaze to see through its apparent chaos). Commit a poem to the bookseller and it comes back, reversed, automatically transformed into cipher, on shortcrust.

The mediation of the marketplace is important to the personality and "nativity" of Jonson's imitation. Martial delights in the miraculous appearance of the foreign at the domestic board (one thinks of Pope thrilling over Belinda's dressing-table):

> et nomen pira quae ferunt Syrorum,
> et quas docta Neapolis creavit,
> lento castaneae vapore tostae
>
> succurrent tibi nobiles olivae,
> Piceni modo quas tulere rami,
> et fervens cicer et tepens lupinus
>
> [pears that bear the name of Syrian, and chestnuts which learned Naples has grown, roasted in a slow heat. . . . Choice olives which Picenian branches have but lately borne will relieve you, and hot chick-peas and warm lupines.]
> (*Epigrams* 5.78.13–15, 19–21)

At least part of Martial's relish has to do with how the There gets Here. Jonson knows something of this pleasure:

> But that, which most doth take my *Muse,* and mee,
> Is a pure cup of rich *Canary*-wine,
> Which is the *Mermaids,* now, but shall be mine.
> (28–30)

Jonson succeeds in finding the exoticism in his Canary (and he will continue his efforts, chortling over the effort as he goes: "*Tabacco, Nectar,* or the *Thespian* spring, / Are all but LUTHERS beere, to this I sing" [33–34]). But the perspective on the foreign is obstructed by the Mermaid Tavern in the middle distance. Martial seems so to rely on the smoothly rational economy of the Empire that no such obstruction takes place. The market, of course, is central to that which throws Jonson's feast into the subjunctive: he will serve "a short-leg'd hen, / If we can get her," the "coney / Is not to be despair'd of, for our money," the wine is to be secured through the agency of the Mermaid.

Which is to say that the movement toward modernity in Jonson's imitation of Martial involves the recognition of middlemen. In Martial, the produce appears with the stamp of the foreign, to be sealed again within the domestic economy by elegant preparation:

> ponetur digitis tenendus ustis
> nigra coliculus virens patella,

> et pultem niveam premens botellus
> [There will be served—to be handled with scorched fingers
> —on a black-ware dish light green broccoli, and a sausage
> lying on white pease-pudding.]
>
> (*Epigrams* 5.78.6–7,9)

The economic drama of Jonson's feast is located precisely in the interstices of Martial's: between Martial's (often foreign) agriculture and his domestic cuisine, we find Jonson's marketplace. This marketplace is an unsettingly amorphous economic space, one that intrudes its vague rigors on Jonsonian festivity. Foodstuffs "may yet be there" in that unsettling space, and we will purchase them, "if we can."[11] This brings us back to the pastry. Baking is not part of Jonson's domestic cuisine: the pastry originates in the mysteriously contingent marketplace. Neither foreign nor domestic in origins, the pastry is brought home smudged with the imprint of uprooted privacy, marked by the wandering word.

The automatic reproduction of the word in the marketplace, the work of the printing press, is extended by a further automatism: the pastry brings the iterability of the literary text to the point of parody. Both page and pastry are constituted as comic versions of the literary imitation. (The comedy of the custard tart is broader, of course, than that of the printed page, just broad enough, it turns out, to render the austere comedy of print conceptually visible.)[12] The act of literary imitation, having begun its emergence as thematic within the poem at the central moment of Jonson's "profession," now obtrudes in oddly twisted modern forms: imitation is measured against market iterabilities, against automatic repetition. This comic torsion prepares a context for a final turn that earlier commentators have tended to regard as something of a tonal excrescence:

> Of this [i.e., the canary] we will sup free, but moderately,
> And we will have no *Pooly'*, or *Parrot* by;
> Nor shall our cups make any guiltie men:
> But at our parting, we will be, as when
> We innocently met. No simple word,
> That shall be utter'd at our mirthfull boord,
> Shall make us sad next morning: or affright
> The libertie, that wee'll enjoy to night.
>
> (35–42)

Here the iterability of the word has nothing to do with the automatisms of an amorphous marketplace, for the publicity from which private festivity here guards itself is the secretive violence of a repressive state.[13] Poley and Parrat were professional informers; not surprisingly we know rather little about their careers. Mark Eccles did the most authoritative detective work on the two men in 1937: though he was unable to determine whether Jonson was referring to Henry or William Parrat, he did find reference to a prisoner at Newgate who filed complaints of bribery against "one *Paratt.*"[14] Both Poley and Parrat seem to have specialized in accusations—true and false—of religious heterodoxy: indeed Robert Poley, one of Walsingham's most efficient agents, was one of the key figures in the betrayal of Anthony Babington. This specialization no doubt explains the slightly gratuitous detailing in Jonson's praise of the Mermaid's canary—that "*Tabacco, Nectar,* or the *Thespian* spring, / Are all but LUTHERS beere, to this I sing." "Luther" is hardly standard slang for "a German": he is mentioned to heat up the atmosphere. Though one means nothing by such a phrase as "LUTHERS beere," one is not at liberty to mean so little when such specialists as Poley and Parrat are at hand. It is just the sort of innocent glance at controversial materials so abundant in normal intercourse, but so hideously imperilled within repressive contexts. Any stray remark becomes an occasion to name names.

The *Epigrammes* is a book of names, a collection that exploits the fact that "the proper name . . . is bound by mysterious ties to the individuality of an *essence.*"[15] The adequacy of "Bedford," "Cecil," or "Pembroke" as self-sufficient panegyrics, the magical decorum of "Benjamin" or "Mary" as names for particular, and particularly beloved, children, the discovery of the truer name of "Sidney" in the person of Mary Wroth—these are the book's topoi of praise; if praise involves the discovery of the truth of given names, blame involves the furious giving of truer names—FineGrand, Sir Luckless Woo-All, Lip, Don Surly, and Sir Voluptuous Beast. As satirist, Jonson joins a tradition of prudence within the larger tradition of Juvenalian satire, claiming that "I have avoyded all particulars, as I have done names." But he breaks the rule of reserving given or family names for poems of praise (however moderate) in "Inviting a Friend to Supper": Poley and Parrat are named, singled out for an especially personalized blame. We know that Jonson took the threat of such men personally, for he said as much to Drummond:

> In the tyme of his close Imprisonment under Queen Elisabeth his judges could gett nothing of him to all their demands but I and No, they placed two damn'd Villains to catch of advantage him, with him, but he was advertised by his Keeper, of the Spies he hath an Epigrame.[16]

Eccles has convinced some students of the period, myself included, that the epigram referred to here is "Inviting a Friend Supper" and not the slighter, and completely unspecific "On Spies." To be sure, Parrat has a particular place in the historical record as a prison informant and Eccles supposes that it was Parrat himself who must have informed on Jonson: this would have been during Jonson's imprisonment at Marshalsea, for his part in the composition and performance of the ostensibly seditious *Isle of Dogs.* It is even more difficult to link Jonson directly with Poley, yet William Bakeless has pointed out that the only time between 1593 and 1599 when Poley was not in official government employ coincides exactly with the period of Jonson's Marshalsea imprisonment: Bakeless thus takes up Eccles's standard and argues that Poley made a second "damn'd Villain" to Parrat.[17] The argument is fairly persuasive. Certainly the men were not so notorious that their names had become slang for "informers": local reference, and not mere colloquialism, certainly seems the best explanation for their use as eponyms here. And even if there is not a direct personal connection between Jonson and Parrat or Jonson and Poley, the heat of the attack on the latter is not difficult to explain, given Poley's connection to the death of Marlowe, stabbed during a violent quarrel bursting out among spies, taking place after a tavern banquet. It is bitterly true that to exclude a Poley or a Parrat from a dinner party is the most fundamental defense of poesy.

On the other hand, one might argue that little should be made of the personal naming of these two spies, since the names may be taken as satiric ones, of a piece with the likes of "Bank, the Usurer." A Poll, a Parrot, these less-than-men give satisfaction to their keepers by their distorted repetition of the words of others, a repetition neither mechanical, nor human. It is not easy to determine the semantics of these names: are they truly personal names, eponyms, or satiric names?[18] Reference slips into a curious suspense, analogous to the subjunctive status of the feast, if somewhat more eerie. This is, I take it, a way of describing the nature of the aggression that animates Jonson's defense of poesy here: the "damnable iteration" of a Poley or a Parrat depletes them of personality, suspends their political being. That suspended being provides a perfect contrast for the private "libertie, that wee'll enjoy to night," a state of political being that grounds itself on the possibility of the simple utterance of simple words, a possibility that Jonson knew to be in constant peril.[19]

Two summary observations are in order. First, that this is a political poem, one that ends with a meditation, not on some merely abstract "civility," as many writers on Jonson would have it, but on a very particular sort of "libertie." Another way of putting this is to point out that for Jonson—ex-resident of debtors' prison, Catholic, convicted felon—an ethics of moderation was adaptive, part of the protection of endangered liberty. Moderation may not be such a considerable achievement, since it is very nearly one of the givens of this necessitous world, where the marketplace imposes its inevitable contingencies and domestic espionage threatens the simple festivity of private life. But—and here I come to my second observation—moderation in the practice of *imitatio* may very well be an achievement of distinction, given the aptitude of the world to iterations both uncannily automatic and slavishly politic. Recitation of verse, printed publication that in the marketplace acquires its own comic extension into the bake-shop, and the fatal parrotings of government spies provide a steadily sinking sequence of analogues for that essential of poetic strategy which shapes the poem. This may well be the center of this poem's distinction, its capacity to find a route of uncanny extension from the private concerns of the Renaissance artist to the public sphere, from the intricacies of literary self-construction to the exigencies of political life and economic livelihood.

Jonson may have found this route, may have discovered this sequence of analogues, as he contemplated one of his models in Martial. I suspect that his idealization of the "simple word," safe from modern iterabilities, involves a complex reflection on the terms of Martial's promise of the purity of conversation at his table, "sed finges nihil audiesve fictum" (you will speak no *fictum,* nor hear one [*Epigrams* 5.78.23]). Martial's phrase suggests a link between creative utterance and a whole range of social duplicities; for Jonson, the engagement in an imitative creativity has led to an address to imitative depredations. What does it mean to suppose Jonson aware of this link, of the lockstep from poet to poetaster to print to pastry to parrot? Among other things it forces us to see the full complexity of the assault on Poley and Parrat. By this nominal play, Jonson implies the slipperiness of their very being, their aptitude for the slide from agency to mere instrumentality. But these spies merely end a sequence that begins with the figure of the poet himself.[20]

The sequence raises insoluble critical problems, given the current state of scholarship on Jonson and his canon. B. N. De Luna has persuaded few people that Jonson participated extensively in the domestic espionage that followed—and perhaps also led to—the discovery of the Gunpowder Plot.[21] Perhaps Cecil's knowledge of the plot did not long antedate the moment of its official discovery; perhaps Jonson had nothing to do with any such foreknowledge. Perhaps his work as a liaison to the network of conspirators after the discovery of the plot was merely the public effort of an eminent Catholic who was also a political loyalist; perhaps it was not the secret activity of an agent of uncertain political sympathies, working to encourage the mutual betrayals already beginning to flourish within the embattled Catholic community. Perhaps Jonson was indeed not a spy in 1605, or did not consider himself one. But even so, what is one to make of Jonson's dinner in ordinaries, on or about the ninth of October, that is, within four weeks of the discovery, with several of the key conspirators, including none other than Robert Catesby? The document attesting to Jonson's presence at this supper may even be one of the government's put-up jobs, a facile construction to secure Jonson's service in the repressions that followed the fifth of November (though this, of course, would imply that Jonson did become a parrot in November).[22] Whether or not this supper did take place, the document represents a meal to which domestic espionage may be attached either as present danger (these men would have feared a Poley or a Parrat), present fact (there was such a figure present, and that figure was Jonson), or future consequence (because of his attendance, real or imputed, Jonson was eventually forced to convert into just such a figure). We cannot know how fully or how earnestly Jonson became implicated in Cecil's espionage, yet he was implicated. And yet—a final qualification—we cannot be certain how these implications bear on the apprehension of imperilled liberty in "Inviting a Friend to Supper," for the poem may have been written long before 1605. Still the poem gives us a Jonson who knows himself to be as corruptible, potentially as impersonal, as a Poley or a Parrat—although whether that sickening knowledge came from private meditations and was soon to be proven accurate or was already a lesson of history, a modern reader cannot say. Somehow or other the poem burns close to home, and it is a tottering home in a burgeoning state.

So the hiatus of the subjunctive in the middle of the poem must stand as a rather small achievement—inconclusive, really, for even Jonson's most grammatically assertive words could falsify as often as anyone's. One need not look beyond this poem for evidence, for his praise of the canary (another bird, more *subtly* ominous than the ones to follow) is sufficient to raise doubts.

> That, which most doth take my *Muse,* and mee,
> Is a pure cup of rich *Canary*-wine,
> Which is the *Mermaids,* now, but shall be mine
> Of which had HORACE, or ANACREON tasted,
> Their lives, as doe their lines, till now had lasted.
> (28–32)

This egregious hyperbole is, in more ways than one, a condition contrary-to-fact: promising immortality within this world of precarious being, the lines throw a shadow over the next and final promise of the poem, the assurance that no spies will be present, that nothing will threaten the simplicity of the word.

If the poem has subtly dramatized the potential failures of the sovereignty of self—the poet's collapse into bourgeois contingencies, his slipping control over the life of his own words, the threats to his exclusive right to self-representation in the political sphere, the tottering home—if all of this is plotted, it is also anticipated in the very opening clause of the poem:

> TO night, grave sir, both my poore house, and I
> Doe equally desire your companie.

It is a light enough touch, the urbane conflation of the straightforward ("I desire your company") and the conventional ("My poor house desires your company"). A form of zeugma much slighter than Pope's, but also more subtly implicative: I referred to its effect above as one of "modesty," yet it is more than that. It suggests how that most cherished Jonsonian entity, personhood, might find itself drained of its own distinction, objectified, if only rhetorically. ("If only": yet if personhood cannot sustain itself rhetorically, how may it be expected to thrive?)

Elsewhere, Jonson does not require a complete descent of the slippery slope from poet to parrot in order to dramatize the failed sovereignties of a modern self. His own comic Archimago, Volpone, as he moves from the private theater of the sickroom out into the public theater of St. Mark's Place, initiates the sequence that leads to his own downfall with a climactic self-dramatization as the mountebank, Scoto of Mantua. Alone on his small stage, Volpone would seem utterly self-possessed, however protean that self may be. Yet self-possession is undermined by his commitment to involvement in the community of others (a commitment that destroys him, for his agent, Mosca, turns out to be an instrument, but not an extension, of himself). The self-destruction in this public commitment finds its perfect emblem as he peddles his elixir: the litany of diseases responsive to his drug rises to its climax with the claim that it "cures *melancolia hypocondriaca,* being taken and applyed, according to my printed receipt" (2.2.108–10). Hardly a remarkable moment, yet the slightest turn to the mediation of print bears considerable weight for Jonson. He takes pains that the moment receive its exact theatrical inflection, stipulating gesture in one of his rare stage directions: "*Pointing to his bill and his glasse*"—

> For, this is the physitian, this the medicine; this counsells, this cures; this gives the direction, this workes the effect.
>
> (2.2.110–12)

Again, the iterable text usurps upon the personhood of its author. It is certainly true that the "printed receipt" is no more qualified a physician than is this "mountebank"; my point is that the focal figure for this investigation of the depletions of integral personhood is the substitution of print for person. Volpone revels in the self-representations that eventually subvert him. In "Inviting a Friend to Supper" the revelry itself dissolves as print passes on toward parrot. The analogy between poet and spy which this reading encourages enriches the perplexed questions that seem regularly to spring from the student who learns of the practice of *imitatio* and wonders, "What happened to creativity? Doesn't that turn the poet into a mouthpiece and no more?"

> "O rare Ben Jonson!" is an exclamation of delight that breaks seldom from the compressed lips of his critics. O learned Ben Jonson, they chorus; O hard-working Ben Jonson; O cantankerous, O unromantic, O fat Ben Jonson. . . .[23]

What follows has been cited with stultifying frequency; it is Jonson, from the *Discoveries,* on imitation:

> The third requisite in our *Poet,* or Maker, is *Imitation,* to bee able to convert the substance, or Riches of an other *Poet,* to his owne use. To make choise of one excellent man above the rest, and so to follow him, till he grow very *Hee:* or, so like him, as the Copie may be mistaken for the Principall. Not, as a Creature, that swallowes, what it takes in, crude, raw, or indigested; but, that

> feedes with an Appetite, and hath a Stomacke to concoct, divide, and turne all into nourishment.
>
> (*Discoveries,* 2466–75)

The metaphor is traditional, deriving ultimately from Horace. But its special relevance to "Inviting a Friend to Supper," to central themes in Jonson's poems and plays, and to Jonson's vocation (what might now be designated "his incarnation as a poet") needs to be acknowledged. Richard Peterson has cited the passage with particular shrewdness, as part of his eloquent discussion of the "Poet as Vessel"—an examination of Jonson's tendency to figure himself as container and as ship in order to suggest the conceptual plenitude from which his creativity flows.[24] Peterson shows how important the idea of fullness is to Jonson's notions both of Art and of the Artist. What I would wish to add is a remark on the peculiar fleshiness of this figure.

"O fat Ben Jonson," say the critics of Jonson, according to Professor Jackson. Of course, Jonson said it first, and often, and often wryly. He grouses that an unnamed beloved has no doubt seen, by means of "My Picture Left in Scotland," "my hundred of gray haires," has already

> Told seven and fortie years,
> Read so much wast, as she cannot imbrace
> My mountaine belly, and my rockie face.
>
> (*Underwoods,* 9.14–17)

But this is not quite a light and simple touch: the poem was written in 1619, the year just after the performance of one of Jonson's great masques, in which the central image is the Virgilian Mount of Atlas, another anthro-mountain of which it is said

> That men may read in thy misterious map
> all lines
> and signs
> of roial education, and the right.
>
> (*Pleasure Reconcild to Vertue,* 220–23)

We are to recognize the transfiguration here of Virgilian martial heroism into Stoic moral heroism. The massive-man is the emblem of that heroism within this public fiction—the explication of this emblem is only a stage in the masque: the transfigurations do not cease until the massive-man has been taught to dance—but "My Picture Left in Scotland" suggests that this emblem has a similar special import within the private mythology of this poet, that to make a mountain of the belly (the villain of *Pleasure Reconcild* is Comus) is to perform some privileged ethical labor.[25] For Jonson, what Hopkins called "selving" seems to involve a complicity of the mind and the digestive tract.

This is deftly implied in the exquisite lines near the opening of "His Excuse for Loving" in "A Celebration of Charis in Ten Lyric Pieces." His age and girth again threaten to obstruct his erotic appeal, yet he argues that

> it is not alwayes face,
> Clothes, or Fortune gives the grace,
> Or the feature, or the youth:
> But the Language, and the Truth,
> With the Ardour, and the Passion,
> Gives the Lover weight, and fashion.
> (*Underwoods,* 2.1, 7–12)

(Again, Jonsonian punctuation sustains more than a common share of the argument.) The cumulative effect of the repeated strong caesura is to display the light comedy of earnest self-promotion. But the sudden displacement of the caesura in line 12 from after the fourth to after the fifth syllable gives the line a somewhat more mechanical clunk than usual; the weight of "weight" is thus particularly sinking, with the further result that the contextual sense of the word—persuasive power, or what a rhetorician would call "ethical appeal"—loses its primacy, staggers. That is, the prosody forces the ethical metaphor to revert toward a lexical fundament, the weight of person to recover its origins in physical heft.[26]

Perhaps it is a small point to remark on the place of the bodily in Jonson's career. Its ramifications are various indeed: one could point to the place of gusto in the contemporary record of Jonson—the Tribe of Ben was more than an eating club, but not other than one. The debate with Jones over what constituted the true soul of the masque, painting or poetry, was equally a debate on the constitution of its true body, performance or publication, and Jonson's vigorous obsession with the printing of his works may well be taken as a labor on behalf of the material or bodily life of art, the generation of a literary corpus. Edward Tayler once remarked on the powerful voice of the "Celebration of Charis," the sense of the personal presences in the sequence. It seemed an odd remark, since those terms are usually reserved for the poetry of Donne in his fabled libertinage. But the Donne of "The Canonization" is personal because of the figured violation of his privacy, whereas the Jonson of "Charis" is personal because of a figured pleasure in public self-presentation, a desire that the poem be taken as the densely occasional speech of "a Bigg fatt man, that spake in Ryme."[27] We might speak of Jonson's as a corpulent, though not ungainly, poetic.

So it is hardly surprising that on certain crucial poetic occasions we find Jonson attending with special seriousness to matters of cuisine. The famous passage in *Neptune's Triumph for the Return of Albion,* based on a commonplace from Athenaeus and appropriated later in Jonson's career for inclusion in *The Staple of Newes,* in which a Cook and a Poet debate the relative merits of their two arts is more than a diverting fantasia on the idea of "taste." We can see a half-serious Jonson standing behind the Cook when he says that "a good *Poet* differs nothing at all from a *Master-Cooke.* Either Art is the wisedome of the Mind" (42–44). As a masque-maker, Jonson was particularly concerned that his devices should have the rhetorical power to move their audiences to virtuous and heroic action, and he surely envied the Cook's authority over human bodily impulses.[28] But the analogy between poetry and cookery may have been with Jonson for some time, perhaps since *Every Man Out of His Humour,* spiced with such minor characters as Clove and Orange, or *The Case is Altered,* seasoned with Onion and Juniper.[29] Still, the analogy always presents itself as parodic and the celebration of cuisine—by the Cook of *Neptune's Triumph* or by Comus's Bowl-bearer in *Pleasure Reconcild to Vertue*—is the stuff of antimasque. Even so, the characteristic choice of gourmandise as a special sign of vice betrays a curious aspect of Jonson's private mythology: for Comus, Sir Epicure Mammon, and Volpone, elaborately conceived gourmandise is a central act of self-indulgence, which only confirms the sense one gets of the ideal Jonsonian self as that which has dined appropriately.

I note the gentle recurrence of the idea of cuisine in Jonson's *corpus* (the term begins to boom a bit) in order to suggest that certain of the biographical origins of Jonson's creativity are peculiarly situated. I have already said a good deal about how contemporary political suspiciousness impinged on both Jonson's life and on Jonson's art; now I simply want to submit that Jonson has allowed his very body to leave an imprint on his creativity. Such an argument particularly recommends itself by the way it accords with what stands as one of the finest biographical, specifically pyscho-biographical, readings of Jonson, Edmund Wilson's impressive account of patterns of anal eroticism in his art—themes of hoarding, the aesthetic of nearly obsessive formal regularities, the exclusion of such common comic plots as might be associated with genital eroticism, the habitual replication of the poet's own melancholic furies in the behavior of those retentive misanthropes that crowd the society of Jonsonian drama.[30] Jonsonian gourmandise catches the physiology of hoarding at a profoundly ambivalent moment, a moment at which Rabelaisian gusto is on the verge of collapsing into an antisocial, indeed repulsive, miserliness of the body. Volpone fascinates us as he pursues his seduction by gastronomy precisely because of the way his Epicurean imaginings teeter between Rabelaisian gusto and Puritanical retentions. Lurid and alluring, this is not quite the salacious imagination of a Malbecco; at its gastronomic wildest, it is no worse than the imagination of a Trimalchio.

And perhaps it is a bit better. Given the limits of evidence, it would be difficult to produce a more precise psychological profile of Jonson than that Wilson provides. But it may be that one can flesh out Wilson's profile by describing the psychology of the creativity sustained—nourished—by Jonsonian gourmandise. The attempted Epicurean seduction in *Volpone* (3.7) will be especially pertinent here. The seduction is wonderfully elaborated: if it fails to better the later fantasies of Sir Epicure Mammon, which are clearly developed from this exercise in the rhetoric of extravagance, it surely rivals Volpone's performance as mountebank as the finest set piece in this particular play. Jonson has consulted his usual treasurer of enormity, Pliny, and then gone on to consult Lampridius's *Heliogabalus,* his favorite encyclopedia of luxury, for an ideal menu:

> The heads of parrats, tongues of nightingales,
> The braines of peacoks, and of estriches
> Shall be our food: and, could we get the phoenix,
> (Though nature lost her kind) shee were our dish.
> (3.7.202–5)

But the Epicurean fantasy is placed within the attractive, though curious, context of Jonson's most famous and most melodious imitations, the adaptations of Catullus's *Carmina* 5 and 7, "Vivamus, mea Lesbia, atque amemus," and "Quaeris, quot mihi bassationes." What makes this such a curious context is that, however attractive, the imitations (as well as the imagined feasts) are specified as the work of an almost willfully unstable self. Volpone seems to rejoice in his own self-desertions, though Celia is blamed for that instability:

> applaud thy beauties miracle;
> 'Tis thy great worke: that hath, not now alone,
> But sundry times, rays'd me, in severall shapes,
> And, but this morning, like a mountebanke,
> To see thee at thy windore. I, before
> I would have left my practice, for thy love,
> In varying figures, I would have contended
> With the blue PROTEUS, or the horned *Floud.*
> (3.7.146–53)

It is a commonplace of criticism that this instability of the self is for Jonson, the quintessence of vice. The commonplace can be stretched. In *Volpone,* censure of the unstable self creates an especially scrupulous context for the practice of imitation. Volpone's private vices parallel the political viciousness of Poley and Parrat in "Inviting a Friend To Supper"; both works bring the poetics of imitation into the sphere of ethics. Volpone implicates Jonson the actor, and (more stringently) Jonson the imitative poet. It is worth recalling that Jonson lifted Volpone's imitations of Catullus and reclaimed them as his own by including them in *The Forest,* a collection of those poems most characteristically, most quintessentially, his own. And one more observation might be made: in Jonson, when the self is flexed to the point of deformation, the presence of images of unwholesome dining is hardly fortuitous. Eating is as dangerous, as value-laden, as uncertain an activity as poetic imitation. The stable Jonsonian self must eat moderately.

It may be that for Jonson, as for many people, eating is a defense of the ego, an attempt to shore up a fugitive being within a bulwark of flesh.[31] The passage on imitation from the *Discoveries* is particularly interesting here, if only because it figures the relation of one poem to another as a nutritive relation between poets. The object of imitation proposed in Jonson's digestive metaphor is not a poem or poems, not a style, but a particular human being—we recall Volpone's confounding of physician and written prescription; here the pattern of substitution is reversed—and this involves a significant variation in the handling of this traditional metaphor.[32] The representation of eating here specifically implicates the *poetic* ego. But further, that representation implies a defense by means of the incorporation of others, the fugitive self replaced by "an other *Poet*," himself presumed to be wealthy—one ingests "the Riches of an other Poet"—which brings us back to the private thematics of Wilson's impoverished anal erotic, as well as to the terms of Volpone's rich diet:

> See, here, a rope of pearle; and each more orient
> Then that the brave *Ægyptian* queene carrous'd:
> Dissolve, and drinke 'hem
> (3.7.191–93)

and

> A gem, but worth a private patrimony,
> Is nothing: we will eate such at a meale.
> (3.7.200–201)

For the poet striving to preserve a stable self this defensive pursuit of wealth is itself costly—a common enough problem is budgeting defenses—for it risks the expenditure of all that is properly one's own to guarantee the more secure presence of the incorporated other.

The terms of Jonson's description of an ideal *imitatio* will sustain even further examination. At first, he only hints at the digestive metaphor, after which the poet is encouraged

> to make choise of one excellent man above the rest, and so to follow him, till he grow very *Hee:* or, so like him, as the Copie may be mistaken for the Principall.

Such a mistake would be a devastation, a devastation that the description itself risks and survives: the "him" of "so like him" is certain of reference and "the Copie" may be distinguished from "the Principall" at the end of this sentence; but in mid-sentence, at the moment of figured incorporation, which is "he" and which "*Hee*"? The blithe identifications of infantile feeding may be remembered with nostalgia, but for the mature poet-critic identification must give way to similitude—"so like him." The shift defends the differentiated self, traces the pain that inevitably stalks nostalgia. Only at this point does Jonson elaborate the digestive metaphor, insisting that the modern poet fully internalizes, decomposes, and transforms the ancient.[33] This is hardly surprising: the defensive aspect of the metaphor responds immediately to the threatened devastation of the self. To eat is to be less vulnerable; to eat the ancient poet, to incorporate, say, Martial, is to secure the poetic ego.

The hungry flesh. In his great book on Rabelais, Bakhtin argues that the hungry flesh is essentially festal, assertive, jubilant.[34] Yet for the Jonson who wrote *Bartholomew Fair* bodily hunger is precisely the net in which one is caught within a world of sharpers, a world in which jubilance itself appears as one commodity among many. The hungry flesh of Jonson's experience seems less like that Bakhtin discovers in Rabelais and more like that described in Sartre's definition of the modern body: "the body is the contingent form which is taken up by the necessity of my contingency."[35] This modern body is precisely that which seeks nourishment in "Inviting a Friend to Supper," a body apprised of its own contingency, aware of how fully exposed it is in a marketplace in which adequate foodstuffs at best "may yet be there." There is no heroism, no grandeur, and little power in this knowledgeable poem: the marketplace is unreliable and mysterious, it compromises our power of self-representation, it reminds us of the fragility of our integrity.

Near the beginning of this essay I raised the question of what might be the relation between the aroused appetite of this poem and its imitative activities, the question of what might be the relation between the nourishments of the body and the sustenance of books. It seems fair to assert here that the attempt to digest Martial is specifically a response to the poem's disabused awareness of the contingencies of the modern bodily self. But at the subjunctive feast to which the poem looks forward, Jonson expects to be silenced, his verses—poems that evidence a successful self-defense founded on the digestion of the cultural past—will be excluded. Virgil, Tacitus, and Livy will have ultimate authority, while the hungry moderns will satisfy themselves with commentary: "wee'll speake our minds, amidst our meate." This carefully delimited satisfaction, this calculus of appetite and digestion is moderated by necessity and not by will. Jonson's dignified humility before necessity is anything but existential, yet Sartre's expanded discussion of the body almost perfectly glosses the contingent creativity of this hungry poet:

> I exist my body: this is the first dimension of being.

("My mountaine belly, and my rockie face.")

> My body is utilized and known by the Other: this is the second dimension.

(The other: Poley, Parrat, Cecil, Martial; the reader, "grave sir.")

> But in so far as *I am for Others,* the Other is revealed to me as the subject for whom I am an object. Even there the question, as we have seen, is of my fundamental relation with the Other. I exist therefore for myself as known by the Other—in particular in my very facticity. I exist for my self as a body known by the Other. This is the third ontological dimension of my body. . . . With the appearance of the Other's look . . .

—as the poet submits himself to the gaze of others—like Scoto on his platform—writes, offers himself for comparison to Martial, goes into print—

> I experience the revelation of my being-as-object; that is, of my transcendence as transcended. . . . It is my being-there for others for which I am responsible. This *being-there* is precisely the body

—a body anticipating its inevitably imperfect satisfaction, inviting a friend to supper, letting itself figure against the ground of cultural history, exposing itself to view with somewhat less gusto than usual.[36] To have entertained this poem is to understand much that life implies when we find ourselves, as we are forever finding ourselves, feeling a bit peckish.

Washington University

Notes

1. Judith Kegan Gardiner makes excellent observations concerning the rhetorical schemes that make this calibration of ethical moderation possible: see her *Craftsmanship in Context: The Development of Jonson's Poetry,* Studies in English Literature, no. 110 (The Hague: Mouton, 1975), 24–31. Michael McCanles uses this poem to initiate his discussion of "Festival in Jonsonian Comedy," (*Renaissance Drama* 8 [1977]: 203–19), yet he is primarily concerned to describe not the Latinate festivity of the epigram, but a more popular form affiliated with the utopian folk culture that Bakhtin finds in Rabelais.

2. Wesley Trimpi, *Ben Jonson's Poetry: A Study of the Plain Style* (Stanford: Stanford Univ. Press, 1962), 185–90.

3. On the early English verse epistle, see Jay Arnold Levine, "The Status of the Verse Epistle before Pope," *Studies in Philology* 59 (1962): 658–84.

4. See Richard S. Peterson, *Imitation and Praise in the Poems of Ben Jonson* (New Haven: Yale Univ. Press, 1981), 31, for a glancing reference to this particular poem; for a general introduction to imitation in Jonson, see Peterson's first chapter, particularly 6–9.

5. "The temptation to turn the reception of the unnamed guest in Epigram 101 into a crude allegory of the reception of Martial's invitation poem should be resisted. But it would be a mirror perversity to ignore the duality of the poem's involvement with *conversation.* Just as it acts out proleptically an entertainment in which the speaker is active while remaining fixed at home, it engages Martial in an exchange that "confirms" the speaker's selfhood while extending his range of accents and his mastery of echoes" (Thomas M. Greene, *The Light in Troy: Imitation and Discovery in Renaissance Poetry,* Elizabethan Club Series, no. 7 [New Haven: Yale Univ. Press, 1982], 283). Greene's full discussion of the poem occupies 278–84.

6. *Responsive Readings: Versions of Echo in Pastoral, Epic, and the Jonsonian Masque,* Yale Studies in English, no. 192 (New Haven: Yale Univ. Press, 1984), 98–100; for festivity in general in Jonson's court drama, see chapters 3 and 4. And see also Jonathan Haynes's forthcoming study of Tudor and Stuart party-going and its relation to Jonsonian festivity.

7. I have cited Jonson from the eleven-volume edition of his works edited by C. H. Herford, P. Simpson, and E. Simpson (Oxford: Clarendon, 1925–52).

8. Nothing could have more of the welcome, tonic certainty of line 26: "Digestive cheese, and fruit there sure will bee."

9. Citations from classical authors are taken from editions in the *Loeb Classical Library.*

10. Roger A. Gognard, "Jonson's 'Inviting a Friend to Supper,' " *The Explicator* 37, no. 3 (1979): 3–4. Thomas Greene, who was kind enough to comment on this paper in an early draft, has objected that the lines might be construed otherwise—his para-phrase would run something like this: 'I shall make no other written representation of anticipated dishes; if I should manage to provide another dish, a dish that even I do not anticipate, it will be up to the pastry to represent ("show of") it.' I find this reading a bit problematic, first because the preceding four lines have been concerned, not with the menu, but with what will be read at table. Moreover, Professor Greene's reading produces some slight problems of construction, largely because of the phrases "that will the pastry show of." Presumably the phrase either implies that the unnamed dish will be encased in pastry, which can then "show of" it; or, insofar as "the pastry" might be taken as naming a pastry course, a stage in the meal that would provide an occasion for the appearance of an unnamed dish (this alternative would represent a slight breach of lexical procedures within the poem); or—for myself the most appealing alternative because to some extent in keeping with the weird metaphysics of this menu—the witty suggestion that the pastry will represent undescribed dishes by *being* the undescribed dish (thus a wryly laconic *occupatio* in which the word "pastry" in the poem is *not* to be taken as an explicit reference to real pastry, which cannot be referred to because it is not preconceived; at the dinner the real pastry will figure—"show of," some curious form of ontological metonymy—itself). These constructions seem vexed, if not impossible. I have a final objection to the reading: in the first portion of the poem the poet anticipates dishes and then, by various means, undercuts the promise of their actually being served; to promise dishes without anticipating them is to reverse a genuinely significant pattern within the poem. Gognard's reading does not do so: indeed, it points a moment of particular, but consistent, wit: Gognard's Jonson is coyly making one of his few promises—there will be pastry—but the promise is buried in the apodosis of a *conditional* statement. And, of course, the promised pastry may, in fact, be stained with ink.

11. "By the early seventeenth century, there was a general feeling that the city's appetite was developing more quickly than the country's ability to satisfy it," according to F. J. Fisher in "The Development of the London Food Market, 1540–1640," *Economic History Review* 5 (1935): 64. For further information on food supplies and prices during the period, see *The Agrarian History of England and Wales,* volume 4: 1540–1640, ed. Joan Thirsk (Cambridge: Cambridge Univ. Press, 1967).

12. One might speculate that this is one of the traditional functions of food in comedy. Food is comedy's perfect transitional object, representing the world's stubborn intransigence to the will of the comic hero (Keaton's canned goods), the deluding mutability with which the world responds—like a movie screen—to the projections of the hero's desires (Chaplin's chicken), the playful tyranny of the world over the hero's various hungers (the vaporous allure of cooling pies in cartoons: steamy redolence becomes beckoning finger, lifts the alleycat off its paws, wafts it to transgression and doom). Perhaps Claudette Colbert's and Clark Gable's raw carrot is not quite so intractable, but its function is to stall these lovers, a deferral through the field of the symbolic of the satisfaction of their appetites for each other, a sign that their romance is not yet cooked. Finally, a custard pie tells us how pasty-faced we are to begin with, how readily individuality des(s)erts us before the merest slings of fortune.

13. Compare the (only slightly less topical) model in Martial's Epigram 10.48:

> accedent sine felle ioci nec mane timenda
> libertas et nil quod tacuisse velis:
> de prasino conviva meus venetoque loquatur,
> nec faciunt quemquam pocula nostra reum.
>
> [To crown these shall be jests without gall, and a freedom not to be dreaded the next morning, and no word you would wish unsaid; let my guest converse of the Green and Blue; my cups do not make any man a defendant.]
>
> (21–24)

Horace's version of the topos (*Epistles* 1.5.24–25) is extremely abstract: the poet reassures his guest that "ne fides inter amicos / sit qui dicta foras eliminet" (that there will be none to carry abroad what is said among faithful friends).

14. "Jonson and the Spies," *Review of English Studies* 13 (1937): 385–97.

15. Ernst Cassirer, *Mythical Thought,* vol. 2 of *The Philosophy of Symbolic Forms,* trans. Ralph Manheim (New Haven: Yale Univ. Press, 1955), 40; cited in Edward Partridge's unrivaled study of naming and design in the *Epigrammes,* "Jonson's *Epigrammes:* The Named and the Nameless," in *Ben Jonson: Quadricentennial Essays,* Studies in the Literary Imagination 6, no. 1 (April 1973) : 195. Partridge's entire discussion of naming in the volume is pertinent to my discussion here, but see particularly 190–98.

16. Herford and Simpson, 1:139.

17. *The Tragicall Historie of Christopher Marlowe,* 2 vols. (Cambridge: Harvard Univ. Press, 1942), 1:179. It might be added here that the inquisition at the Marshalsea into the extent and nature of Jonson's guilt was conducted by a panel headed by Richard Topcliffe, whose primary responsibilities to Elizabeth's government involved the suppression of Catholics: one suspects that the "two damn'd Villains" may have attempted to impute Jonson guilty of Catholicism. (He seems not to have converted to Catholicism until his next imprisonment, at Newgate, for having killed Gabriel Spencer.)

18. Harris Friedberg has made particularly useful observations on the linguistics of denomination in the *Epigrammes;* see his "Ben Jonson's Poetry: Pastoral, Georgic, Epigram," *English Literary Renaissance* 4 (1974): 111–36, particularly 113–24. The kind of problematic semantics I am pointing to here also presents itself in the poems "To Sir Horace Vere" (where "Vere" becomes adjectival) and "On My First Daughter" (where the ethical response of "ruth" rises toward the status of a proper name, one which must properly be rejected).

19. By describing liberty as a state of political *being,* not as merely accidental, I mean to suggest that Jonson's "liberty," like the Latin *libertas,* is an ontological term within the horizon of politics, corresponding, in effect, to *personhood* within the horizon of ethics; certainly *liberty* was beginning to recover just this etymological meaning. Thus the conservative Jonson—with his defensive effort to describe a liberty that can in no way be confused with license, despite external pressures toward such confusion—anticipates important aspects of English revolutionary polemic.

20. This pattern of association is certainly not an isolated instance in the Jonson canon. From early in Jonson's career, in *Poetaster,* we can find an uncannily similar juxtaposition of poet and informer. This time the poet is The Poet, Virgil, who is reciting The Poem to Caesar in 5.2, when he is interrupted by the nearly hysterical Asinius Lupus, come to accuse Horace of libel (against Lupus himself, and perhaps against Caesar as well). It is a particularly curious moment, since Horace is the Jonson-figure during the bulk of the play, the satirist under attack by various envious detractors, all modeled on Jonson's opponents in the notorious War of the Theaters. Yet at the moment of Virgil's recitation, the strict association, Jonson-Horace, relaxes, for the recitation occasions for Jonson a moment of poetic virtuosity, the translation of

among the most famous passages of the *Aeneid;* that is, Jonson graphs the display of his own virtuosity as a translator on the character Virgil's display of his own virtuosity before Caesar, as if Jonson were saying, "There is a Virgil in me, but he is constrained by cultural circumstances to give place to my Horace-self." The intrusion of Lupus instances such constraint, makes the Horace-self take over, as Horace begins to defend the purity of motive behind an emblem that Lupus would like to claim as evidence of malicious intent. This is precisely the sort of interpretive "application" that had occasioned Jonson's imprisonment a few years earlier for *The Isle of Dogs,* and it is precisely the sort of sequence we find in "Inviting a Friend to Supper": Jonson figures himself at the height of his (specifically imitative) powers only to be forced to figure a self constrained by political suspicions to a reduced, defensive self, the juxtaposition itself, as in "Inviting a Friend to Supper," providing a sad occasion to dramatize the instability of the poet's self-representations.

21. For De Luna's argument see her *Jonson's Romish Plot: A Study of "Catiline" and its Historical Context* (Oxford: Clarendon Press, 1967), particularly chapter 4, "Jonson and the Gunpowder Plot," 115–43.

22. The document, from the Gunpowder Plot papers in the Public Record Office (S.P. 14/216, pt. II/no. 132), is cited in De Luna, 117.

23. I cite the opening of chapter 1 of Gabriele Bernhard Jackson's *Vision and Judgment in Ben Jonson's Drama* (New Haven: Yale Univ. Press, 1968), 5.

24. Peterson, 112–57.

25. Richard Peterson has given a fuller treatment of the literary backgrounds of the animated mountain in his "The Iconography of Jonson's *Pleasure Reconciled to Virtue,*" *The Journal of Medieval and Renaissance Studies* 5, no. 1 (Spring 1975): 123–53; see particularly 127–30.

Swinburne no doubt responds to this crucial self-representation in his own poem, "Ben Jonson," from the *Sonnets on English Dramatic Poets,* a sustained rendering of the poet as anthro-mountain. Though Jonson's Virgilian mountain has been Hellenized, it is still recognizable as Swinburne's subtext:

Broad-based, broad-fronted, bounteous, multiform,
    With many a valley impleached with ivy and vine,
    Wherein the springs of all the streams run wine,
And many a crag full-faced against the storm,
The mountain where thy Muse's feet made warm
    Those lawns that revelled with her dance divine
    Shines yet with fire as it was wont to shine
From tossing torches round the dance aswarm.

(*The Complete Works of Algernon Charles Swinburne: The Bonchurch Edition,* eds. Sir Edmund Gosse, C. B. and Thomas James Wise, 20 vols. [New York: Gabriel Wells, 1925–27], 5:173).

26. These are the terms, then, that Jonson dictated to seventeenth-century reception, whether in Richard Flecknoe's assessment—"*Shakespear* excelled in a natural Vein, *Fletcher* in Wit, and *Johnson* in Gravity and ponderousness of Style" (*A Short Discourse of the English Stage* [1664], G_6)—or in Thomas Fuller's more famous anecdotal record of the "wit-combates" between Shakespeare and Jonson, "which two I behold like a *Spanish great Gallion,* and an *English man of War;* master *Johnson* (like the former) was built far higher in Learning; *Solid,* but *Slow* in his performances. *Shake-speare,* with the *English man of War,* lesser in *bulk,* but lighter in *sailing* . . ." (*The History of the Worthies of England* [1662], 126).

27. From a poem by Francis Andrewes in the Newcastle MS. (Harley 4955, f. 166b), cited in Herford and Simpson, 11:388.

Perhaps this is the place to answer the question, "How fat?" In the Epistle to Lady Covell (*Underwoods,* 56), he is specific: "His weight is twenty stone within two pound; / And that's made up as doth the purse abound"—that is 252 lbs., or 280 when he could spend freely on supper. This is hyperbole, no doubt—and "twenty" scans better than any of the "-teens"—but it suggests that either body, or body-image, were remarkable.

28. Jonson's slightly bullying defense of his decision to publish an annotated text of *Hymenaei,* one of the early maneuvers in the quarrel with Jones, ends with a sustained figure of obvious relevance here:

> And howsoever some may squeamishly crie out, that all endevour of *learning,* and *sharpnesse* in these transitorie *devices* especially, where it steps beyond their little, or (let me not wrong 'hem) no braine at all, is superfluous; I am contented, these fastidious *stomachs* should leave my full tables, and enjoy at home, their cleane emptie trenchers, fittest for such ayrie tasts: where perhaps a few *Italian* herbs, pick'd up, and made into a *sallade,* may find sweeter acceptance, than all, the most nourishing, and sound meates of the world.
>
> (19–28)

29. The primitive notion of an occult connection between feeder and food, central to the digestive metaphor in Jonson's discussion of imitation, appears in parodic form in *Every Man Out,* where Carlo Buffone gives his philosophical praise of pork: "nothing resembling man more than a swine, it followes, nothing can be more nourishing" (5.5.69–70; the entire passage, lines 38–79, is pertinent). And one of the heuristic myths of psychoanalysis is that the process of introjection constitutes a sublimation of cannibalism; see S. H. Fuchs's account of the early psychoanalytic discussions of the process in "On Introjection," *International Journal of Psychoanalysis* (1937), 269–93, particularly 277.

On eating and imitation in *Every Man Out,* see Terrance Dunford, "Consumption of the World: Reading, Eating and Imitation in *Every Man Out of His Humour,*" *English Literary Renaissance* 14 (1984): 131–47. Dunford finds both the world and the textual past more easily available to consumption for Jonson than I do.

30. "Morose Ben Jonson," from *The Triple Thinkers,* revised ed. (New York: Scribner's, 1938), reprinted in *Ben Jonson: A Collection of Critical Essays,* ed. Jonas A. Barish (Englewood Cliffs, N.J.: Prentice-Hall, 1963), 60–74.

31. I am speaking here, of course, of what eating means to Jonson; I am hardly suggesting that a modern critic could account for his girth. An adequate etiological account would obviously require unavailable genetic information.

Hilde Bruch has observed that obesity (and *anorexia nervosa*) often constitute a bodily rhetoric by which a person defends a claim to self-possession, or at least to possession of the body; see *Eating Disorders: Obesity, Anorexia Nervosa, and the Person Within* (New York: Basic Books, 1973), particularly 102–4. It is noteworthy that before the praise of cooking in *Neptune's Triumph* and *The Staple of Newes* is specified to a direct comparison between cookery and poetry, the cook describes his as an art of defensive military tactics; see *Neptune's Triumph,* 90–98 or *Staple of Newes,* 4.2.21–29.

32. Both G. W. Pigman and Thomas Greene have interested themselves in the history of the digestive metaphor; see Pigman, "Versions of Imitation in the Renaissance," *Renaissance Quarterly* 33 (1980): 1–32 and Greene, 74, 275–76. Greene remarks on how Jonson forsakes the conventional imitative goal, resemblance, for identification; neither makes explicit Jonson's curiously emphatic shift from imitation of poems to imitation of poets.

33. Finally, Jonson's analysis of imitation may be taken as a remarkably rich inquiry into what Roy Schafer designates as *Aspects of Internalization* (New York: International Universities Press, 1968). Schafer discriminates between the internal dialogue fostered by introjection and the more advanced internal unity that he calls identification: primary-process ideas of incorporation can express a wish to achieve either of these internalizations. Thus, incorporative ideas can take on a primitive, cannibalistic form (aimed toward introjection) or a form suitable to more "civilized" nutrition (aimed toward identification). Jonson's scrupulous distinction

between the two modes of incorporation (he calls one "swallowing," the other " feeding") perfectly marks off the boundary between these two forms of internalization. Yet the rigorous distinction also expresses ambivalence to feeding, to imitation, and to internalization *per se.* These ambivalences appear in the *Discoveries* in the balancing between growing "very Hee" and "so like him," a profoundly revealing rhetorical adjustment that displays Jonson's own awareness of the defensively *motivated* character of his drive toward identification. (See Schafer, 7–23, 32–34, 70–74, and 121–22; see also Hans Kohut's similarly illuminating account of identification—which he calls "transmuting internalization"—in *The Analysis of the Self* [New York: International Universities Press, 1971], 166–67).

34. I refer here, of course, to Mikhail Bakhtin's *Rabelais and His World,* trans. Helene Iswolsky (Cambridge: MIT Press, 1968).

35. Jean-Paul Sartre, *Being and Nothingness: An Essay in Phenomenological Ontology,* special abridged edition, trans. Hazel E. Barnes (New York: Citadel, 1965), 304. A useful complement to Sartre's formulation may be found in the last few pages of Richard M. Zaner's "The Radical Reality of the Human Body," *Humanitas* 2 (1966): 73–87, in which he elegantly adumbrates an application of Freud's concept of the uncanny to the phenomenon of "my being-embodied by a body so 'already-familiar'" (85). This uncanny bodily *subjectivity* seems to be proper to the same body the objectivity of which Sartre describes. On the necessary complementarity of the body-as-subject and of the body-as-object, the most delicate modern argument is Merleau-Ponty's in *Le visible et l'invisible* (Paris: Gallimard, 1964); see particularly 181.

36. Sartre, 327.

From the 1616 Folio of Jonson's *Works*

FRANCIS BEAUMONT

If thou had'st itch'd after the wild applause
Of common people, and had'st made thy laws
In writing, such, as catch'd at present voice,
I should commend the thing, but not thy choice.
But thou hast squar'd thy rules, by what is good:
And art, three ages yet, from understood:
And (I dare say) in it, there lies much wit
Lost, till thy readers can grow up to it.
Which they can ne'er out-grow, to find it ill,
But must fall back again, or like it still.

Commendatory poem in the front matter of the 1616 Folio of Jonson's *Works*.

Ben Jonson and the Modality of Verse

JOHN HOLLANDER

Considering that they are the work of a literary genius, Ben Jonson's poems have had a curious critical fate. The epoch that most intimately responded to their virtues never singled them out for special praise, while our own age, so acutely conscious of history, acknowledges their importance and success and at the same time retains a fundamentally unsympathetic view toward them, seldom praising without apologizing. It is true that the importance of Jonson's non-dramatic works as a source for the whole current of poetic style during the course of the seventeenth century has only been adequately assessed during the past several decades. But even at the height of the Augustan style whose origins must be traced to Jonson's influence, the fame of his poems lagged behind that of his plays, and even further behind that of his personality.

There is perhaps some irony in this. In the audaciously entitled *Works* that the poet himself, in 1616, collected in the folio format until then reserved for editions of the great writers of antiquity, it was the lyric and epigrammatic portions that were popularly neglected in favor of the plays that at the time seemed to have even less right to publication under the presumptuous rubric of "dramatic literature." Jonson was, in every sense, a man of letters. He always devoted great attention and care to the cultivation of an organized *oeuvre* or corpus of literary creation. To be fair to him, one should include in a balanced selection of his "poems" examples of all the verse and prose, dramatic and non-dramatic, lyrical, satiric, critical, didactic, and occasional, that he left behind him. Poetry, Jonson knew, meant "making," and the senses of "things," "actions," or "deeds" are partially conveyed in his translation of *"opera."* On the other hand, what we would today call "poems" he would consider a misleading category, lumping together and blurring distinctions between the sub-species populating his literary world. A lack of sympathy with Jonson's attachment to just these distinctions between literary genres has led to the peculiar judgment and appreciation of his poetry charac-

From John Hollander, *Vision and Resonance: Two Senses of Poetic Form,* 2d ed. (New Haven: Yale University Press, 1985), 165–86. Reprinted by permission of the author.

terized by the critical attitudes of the present age. That peculiar judgment has crystallized about a rival for Jonson's laurels: for if his greatness as a dramatist has always had to contend with often inappropriate comparisons of his plays to Shakespeare's, it is only recently that his poems have seemed to lurk behind the obliquely cast shadow of those of John Donne.

It was the rediscovery of Jonson's contemporary, and Donne's critical canonization in the past forty years, that have helped to establish the very criteria by which, three hundred years after his death, a poem is considered to be a poem. In the narrowest view of these criteria, Jonson does seem a strange sort of poet, perhaps. He informs us (through the offices of the obliging William Drummond of Hawthornden in his *Conversations*) that he wrote his poems out in prose before versifying them. It is only the Romantic belief that poetry is somehow inspired and mysteriously spontaneous, or the post-symbolist insistence that a poem must *be* its own meaning, scheme, and purpose, rather than have separable skeleton, flesh, and organs, that can make us blush for Jonson at such a remark. Donne's poems, far from having been formalized out of prose statement, resist even our own efforts at prose paraphrase; and Donne is, or at any rate until very recently has been, a model English poet.

It must always be remembered that Jonson often writes in the metaphysical style, and that in one mode of writing, at least, the two poets are almost indistinguishable, as continued scholarly argument about the authorship of one of the elegies in *The Underwood* would suggest. But in general, we may oppose them to each other. Where Donne is grotesquely original, Jonson strikes us as being overly imitative. Jonson, moreover, seems at once to brandish his Classical learning like a weapon, and to depend upon it for guidance and support, as if he were momentarily both halt and blind. Donne, conversely, subtly inoculates his rhetorically violent arguments with doses of sacred and profane lore. Donne is an ironist with no stage for which to write, and his poems seem as a consequence to condense the complicated structures of dramatic irony into a dramaturgy of image and tone: in a sense, Donne's poems are all dramatic monologues. Jonson, on the other hand, is a moralist with no pulpit. He makes of his theater a kind of complicated moral machine for projecting human behavior onto a screen so constituted as to reveal the true nature of that behavior, a nature always kept hidden by the distorted perspectives of mundane interests and commitments. For Jonson all of literature has this same moral purpose, and the poet is a secular priest.

But there are even greater differences between the two. Jonson, a schematic and devoted prosodist, declared that "Donne, for not keeping of accent, deserved hanging"; it is in just this metrical roughness of Donne's, however, that so much modern interest lies. Jonson writes in what look to be many styles, but all of Donne's verses, sacred or secular, amatory or satirical, songs or letters, are very much the same sort of intellectual ceremony, synthesizing the occasional and the spontaneous. It is this spontaneity of the dramatic rather than the inspirational sort that we miss in Jonson. Donne's wit often constructs a public or even a universal occasion from the most intimate and private ones, and "makes one little roome, an every where." But Jonson's occasional poems are frankly public, and it is significant that he makes pioneer attempts to adapt to English the Pindaric ode, that most ceremonial of forms.

A rewarding contrast might be drawn between two typical "occasional" poems: Donne's pair of "Anniversary" poems, in which the death of a patron's little daughter becomes the occasion for a lament over the passing of an epoch in the West's intellectual history, and Jonson's uncompleted elegy on the wife of Sir Kenelm Digby. In "Eupheme," Jonson commits himself to eulogistic extravagances, but struggles against them:

> What's left a *Poet,* when his *Muse* is gone?
> Sure, I am dead, and know it not! I feele
> Nothing I doe; but like a heavie wheele,
> Am turned with an others powers. My Passion
> Whoorles me about and to blaspheme in fashion![1]

Aside from a punning reference to the lady's heroic name in "blaspheme," it was just the charge of blasphemy that Jonson leveled at Donne's first "Anniversary," perhaps having taken much of it far too literally. But in "Eupheme," Jonson's own literalness often leaves him breathlessly hyperbolic.

Although Jonson indeed esteemed "John Donne the first poet in the world in some things," he added later on that Donne "for not being understood, would perish." The irony here is that our day, which understands Donne so well as to have resurrected and animated his remains, should still misunderstand Jonson in some basic ways. The same influential judgment of T. S. Eliot that praised Donne as one who "knew the anguish of the marrow / The ague of the skeleton" could not approve of Jonson without insisting that "His poetry is of the surface." This, I feel, lies close to the heart of the question of Jonson's reputation as a poet today. Modern poetic taste distrusts surfaces because they seem too detachable, and demands the extrusion of the core of a poem, so to speak, onto its outside. For us, the meaning of a poem consists in its imagery and elaboration as much as in its "subject," and the separation of "sense" from expressive content in poetry is the arch-heresy of orthodox reading today. Yet Jonson insists on in theory, and demonstrates often enough in practice, a view of the nature of poetry depending on the notion of a "core" of prose sense or even moral purpose, surrounded by an exterior added by art, rather than secreted by the poem's soul within. Similarly, his widespread use of Classical sources as models, texts, and themes, as well as for direct translation, seems to modern sensibilities somehow *inauthentic.* Indeed, the Classic poetry upon which he most frequently draws—

Horace, Catullus, Juvenal, Martial, the corpus of Greek verse called the Anacreontea—itself tends to buckle under the same analysis of structure and texture that college students are today taught to apply to English poetry as a test of its very essence.

Beyond all these things, however, modern poetic theory requires of a poet a consistently recognizable language of his own, a characteristic voice sounding through any masks he may choose to wear, and overriding the accents of any style or manner he may elect to use. For a true poet, we feel today, all occasions, subjects, forms, and conventions must come under the absolute command of one governing style, and a major poet like W. H. Auden was often treated suspiciously by many otherwise sympathetic readers precisely because of his *use* of so many voices and techniques. But here again, Donne serves as textual authority, and here again, Jonson resists automatic commendation. With Donne, lyric, epigram, longer satire, and prayer are all, as I have already observed, the same kind of poem. With one or two dubious exceptions, none of the *Songs and Sonnets* are primarily lyrical, affecting us as being, first and foremost, song texts. Jonson's most celebrated lyrics, however, such as the two-heavily anthologized "Drinke to me, onely, with thine eyes," or the "Hymn to Diana" from *Cynthia's Revels,* have accumulated about them modern critical clichés concerning their "purely" lyrical character primarily because of their radical difference in manner from his odes, and even greater difference from his satires and epigrams. Jonson's lyrics seem "lighter" than his other poems; it is certainly true that, in contrast with Donne's, they are more properly "songs."

If we look through the body of Jonson's non-dramatic poetry, we come across his own schematic arrangement of various types of poem, both in the 1616 folio edition and in the larger posthumous publication of 1640. The epigrams form a collection of their own. Then follows *The Forrest,* a short selection of pieces of many sorts that he considered at the time to be his very best accomplishments. In the 1640 folio, Jonson prefaced his volume called *The Underwood* with the explanation that

> With the same leave as the Ancients call'd that kind of body *Sylva* or *Hule,* in which there were workers of divers nature, and matter congested; as the multitude call Timber-trees, promiscuously growing, a Wood, or Forrest: so am I bold to entitle these lesser Poems, of later growth, by this of Under-Wood, out of the Analogie they hold to the *Forrest,* . . .

It is not surprising, incidentally, to find him carrying through this "analogie" in the naming of his prose miscellany, *Timber: or Discoveries Made Upon Men and Matter.* . . . But with the exception of the separate compilation of epigrams, Jonson's categories are based upon the departments of a literary *oeuvre,* and arranged with respect to relative importance, rather than to distinctions between literary genres as such and as represented in the poems themselves.

The fact that Jonson took these modes or forms utterly for granted is quite significant for any clear understanding of what he meant by poetry, or for that matter, by literature in general. One of the most overpowering myths of Classical antiquity was that of the power of music at the hands of heroes like the poet-musician Orpheus. Of all the lore about ancient music that was transmitted through the Middle Ages down to Jonson's time, the notion of what I shall call modality most fascinated Renaissance thinkers and writers who sought to understand that fabled power. The modes or keys of ancient music, called Dorian, Lydian, Phrygian, etc., were all held to affect the hearer's feelings and actions, each in its prescribed way. (Thus the Dorian had a manly and martial character, the Lydian was held to be voluptuous and relaxing, the Phrygian, frenzied, and so forth. The modern musician may think in terms of a whole species of distinctions corresponding to that drawn by the Romantic imagination between a "happy" major key and a "sad" minor one.) Great importance was attached to these modes, to the kinds of poetic texts conventionally sung to their melodies, the occasions appropriate to the use of each, and their respective characters. Socrates, it will be remembered, carefully indicates which modes are to be permitted in Plato's Just City. In general, the idea of modality in the music of the ancient world becomes a kind of standard or model of the relation of musical or poetic form to content or purpose.

Now for a Neoclassicist like Jonson, the music-poetry of antiquity is the unfallen ancestor of all literature, and Orpheus' lyre a heraldic bearing. The idea of musical modality thus expands into a general literary principle, analogous to the Greeks' purely musical one, in an age whose literary program aimed at the achievements, if not at the actual forms, of Classical literature. And thus, for a writer like Jonson who believed in a vital tradition embracing the poetry of the ancient and modern worlds, never are styles, forms, and conventions to be thought of as spontaneous channels of expression, shaped by the unique identity of the poet, his experience, and his voice. Only a Romantic writer would insist on that triumph of feeling over form. Rather would the Neoclassicist employ forms and styles of modes of discourse having certain quasi-musical effects upon the reader, perhaps, but more clearly serving as a proper vehicle or designation of an occasion, a subject, or an attitude. Granted the notion that art is to be a mirror of life, the relationship between poetic form and poetic purpose, between the public or private occasion of a literary utterance and the mode or style proper to it, becomes a moral one.

In praising a sentence of Demosthenes, the Hellenistic Pseudo-Longinus accounts for its power not only by allusion to its *dianoia,* "thought," but because of its *harmonia,* "melody": "Its delivery depends wholly on the dactyls, which are the noblest of rhythms and make for grandeur—and that is why the most beautiful of all known meters, the heroic, is composed of dactyls."[2] Here is a beautifully framed example of what would become a dogma of Classicism: a form or mode is seen to possess an ethos or attribute of its own by nature, rather than because of an association with certain kinds and occasions of utterance. A modern formalist critic would say just the opposite about the dactyls, namely, that they acquired an aura of grandeur because of their conventional use in heroic, epical poetry. Jonson, like many good Renaissance scholars, knew something of the arguments in antiquity about whether powers of language and music were to be ascribed to nature, or to convention. But like all Renaissance poets who drew on antiquity for anything more than stylistic models, he grasped the force of the idea of the naturalness of stylistic effects, and lived with that idea as with a most useful fiction.

He retained always a vigorous and healthy attitude toward the relation between the modern and the antique. He castigated Spenser who, he felt, "in affecting the Ancients, writ no language," although we may suspect that other aspects of *The Faerie Queene* may have troubled him as well, and that by concentrating on the language, he was anticipating the strategy of twentieth-century Moderns like Eliot and Pound in rejecting Milton, Spenser, and much more poetry of the past that posed aesthetic and moral problems far deeper than stylistic ones.

Jonson took no part in the attempt to employ Classical quantitative meters in English. He seemed firmly committed to the English iambic pentameter line from the outset. Drummond of Hawthornden reminds us that Jonson distrusted longer lines, denouncing the translations of Homer and Virgil "in long alexandrines as but prose," and having no patience for the twelve-syllabled line of Drayton's *Poly-Olbion.* With his knowledge of the ancients, Jonson must have understood well that the accentual decasyllabic that descended (although his generation did not yet know this) from Chaucer would have to do a variety of jobs in English poetry. In Classical verse, the modalities, or generic associations, of various meters are sharply differentiated. Thus, Classical iambics (usually an iambic trimeter of six feet because iambs and anapests were always doubled up as two to a foot) was a conversational meter, used on the stage and hence for some of Catullus' invective, for example. The heroic hexameter was the line of epic and, in the tradition that Theocritus inaugurated and Virgil confirmed, of pastoral eclogue. The couplet was the meter of inscription, epigram, and, later, satire and epistle. A modulation from one to another could constitute a revision of a genre. Thus Ovid's joke, in the first two lines of the *Amores,* about how he had originally planned to write of high heroic doings, but Cupid, the naughty thing, came along and filched a foot from his second line (thus, it went without saying, transforming the hexameters into elegiac couplets of alternating hexameter and pentameter lines). A modern analogue of this might be an improvising pianist who muttered as he played about how he had meant to play a rousing march in C major, but Sorrow came along and sadly draped three blue flats on his melody.

Jonson realized early that the English-stressed decasyllabic would have to serve as iambics when unrhymed on the stage, as hexameters and as elegiacs both when indented;[3] similarly, he would translate iambics of the Catullan sort by a shorter English line, usually tetrameter. The iambic pentameter line, he knew, would have to do, on and off the stage, for high and low matters. His brilliant translation of Petronius' epigram about sadness after sex that begins "Doing a filthy pleasure is, and short" maintains that wonderful balance between the schematic written grammar and the spoken force that we associate with Milton (the Latin original goes "*Foeda est in coitu et brevis voluptas*")—the sequential build from one of the paired modifiers of "pleasure" to the second, last, and most telling being the inner "narrative" of the line and the moral it embodies. It is no wonder that Jonson had written a (now lost) "discourse of poesie both against Campion and Daniel, especially the last, where he [proved] couplets to be the bravest sort of verses, especially when they are broken like hexameters." Here was Dryden's, and Pope's, direct ancestor.

Jonson thus seems to follow directly upon Sidney in his understanding of the relation between form and genre, and of the necessity of building a new world of expression, wielding style in the purposes of truth and right, upon the ruins of the ancient one. "He cursed Petrarch," Drummond tells us, "for redacting verses to sonnets which he said were like the tyrant's bed," by which he meant that of Procrustes; but as we shall see a bit further on, his one sonnet is an anti-sonnet, not merely because of distaste for the format, but out of revulsion against the institutionalized Petrarchan convention. (This did not prevent him, in "Eupheme" or, brilliantly, in the masques, from wrenching the rituals out of their normal molds, and reapplying the rhetorical and mythological strategies of celebration.)

Jonson's interest in form, then, is by no means superficial. The brilliance and permanence of many of his achievements in a purely technical direction lie close to the foundations of what he considered to be the fundamental problems of the man of letters. For him, poetry was the same mirror of life that it was for his contemporaries. It exercised a moral function by *illuminating* on the stage the hiding place of folly and vice, by calling down in satire nasty self-interest for what it is, celebrating the knowledge and generosity of individuals in commendatory poems, etc. But for Jonson in particular, the glass of poetry presented in addition a view of what might be. He flourished in a spiritual climate too close to the miasmas of medieval despair over nature, and was of too fierce and loathing a temper himself, to partake of any optimism for the economic, social, and religious consequences of the sixteenth century. Neither is his Neoclassicism to be considered a historical nostalgia for golden days: the virtues he responded to in Augustan Rome concerned what he felt to be a model relationship of literature to life, while life was as petty and vile, he knew, as ever. But without necessarily apologizing for any old order, he made his task as a poet the representation of the ideals of what he felt to be the most important Establishments of his day: aristocracy, order, and a kind of humanist orthodoxy. Prior to all these, perhaps, lay a notion of courtesy, no hodgepodge of chivalric ideology and scraps from medieval writers, but a more universal idea of civilization involving knowledge and enlightenment allied with power and effectiveness. Literature was for Jonson the language of that courtesy. The understanders of that language were the various aristocracies of enlightened courts, literate theatrical audiences, university intellectuals in public service, and a learned reading public. When eventually the playgoers proved too fickle, the court unappreciative of his greatest efforts in the form of the masque, and readers in general too unsubstantial an entity, he must have turned, in his later years, for more than consolation to the group of surrogate sons calling itself the "Tribe of Ben," and including in its numbers most of the distinguished poets of the Caroline age. The coterie of such younger men of letters as Herrick, Carew, and James Howell, such public men as Sir Lucius Cary, Sir Kenelm Digby, the Earl of Newcastle, and others, turned exclusively about "St. Ben," its unwobbling pivot in a mad world. It is perhaps as much as anything else the doing of this "cult of personality" of Jonson's later years that Jonson's public figure seemed for so long to eclipse the light of his works.

But the idea of a civilized society as well as its microcosm in the literary cabala of the Tribe of Ben were both modern versions, for Jonson, of the idea of a literate community that emerges from even a cursory reading of Classical writers. The sense of Augustan Rome that we get from its poets, for example, suggests the paradoxical condition of a tight coterie upon which, nevertheless, no sun could ever set. Jonson knew that of all the aristocratic Establishments, the most carefully preserved, pruned, cultivated, and revered is The Past. His Neoclassicism was the one element in his poetic program that brought together questions of purpose, theory, and actual practice. It is no wonder that his basic notion of what poetic language is by nature, and of how and when it was to be used, was so strongly conditioned by his self-adopted kinship with Latin writers.

The many modes of Jonson's poetry, then, betoken no superficiality or inconsistency. Although there may be recognized everywhere in his range of accomplishment the combination of toughness of wit and vigorous delicacy of control that characterize Jonson's unique poetic elegance, to list his very best poems is to include an astonishing variety of successes. From the half-wry, post-pastoral lyric of the "Celebration of Charis" or "The Musicall Strife," for example, is a considerable stylistic distance to the dramatic climax of the magnificent "Elegie on the Lady Jane Pawlet":

> What Nature, Fortune, Institution, Fact
> Could summe to a perfection, was her Act!
> How did she leave the world? with what contempt?
> Just as she in it liv'd! and so exempt

From all affection! when they urg'd the Cure
Of her disease, how did her soule assure
Her suffrings, as the body had beene away!
And to the Torturers (her Doctors) say,
Stick on your Cupping-glasses, feare not, put
Your hottest Causticks to, burne, lance or cut:
'Tis but a body which you can torment,
And I, into the world, all Soule, was sent! . . .

Then there is the dual brilliance of the famous "Come my Celia, let us prove": in its original context in the superb seduction scene in *Volpone,* it is no mere Classically imitated *carpe diem* lyric, but rather an expression as well of the whole play's themes of acquisition and deceit. But as printed with a companion piece in *The Forrest,* it presents itself to us as a Catullan adaptation made with an almost gnomic concision. Different again is the extreme Mandarin elegance of "To Penshurst," whose authoritative couplets frame a poetry of statement rather than of gesture or indirection:

The earely cherry, with the later plum,
Fig, grape, and quince, each in his time doth come:
The blushing apricot, and woolly peach
Hang on thy walls, that every child may reach.
And though thy walls be of the countrey Stone,
They'are rear'd with no means ruine, no mans grone, . . .

Even the complimentary conceits woven into the splendid tribute not only to the ancestral home of the Sidney family, but to a whole way of life as well, look ahead to the near-Augustan tone of Andrew Marvell: the "ripe daughters," a few lines further on, have baskets that "beare / An embleme of themselves, in plum, or peare." The tone of the closing lines might be said to resound at the tonal center of Jonson's highest commendatory mode:

Now, *Penshurst,* they that will proportion thee
With other edifices, when they see
Those proud, ambitious heaps, and nothing else,
May say, their lords have built, but thy lord dwells.

Jonson is perfectly capable of using the resources of metaphysical poetry, however, as in the great Pindaric ode, "To the Immortall Memorie, and Friendship of that Noble Paire, Sir Lucius Cary, and Sir H. Morison." At the very opening image, based, it is true, upon an obscure incident mentioned in Pliny, the wretchedness of a world that cuts off virtuous lives is figured forth in a conceit that makes one think of the wilder excesses of an extreme poet like John Cleveland:

Brave Infant of *Saguntum,* cleare
Thy comming forth in that great yeare,
When the Prodigious *Hannibal* did crowne
His rage, with razing your immortall Towne.
Thou, looking then about,
E're thou wert halfe got out,
Wise child, did'st hastily returne,
And mad'st thy Mothers wombe thine urne.
How summ'd a circle didst thou leave man-kind
Of deepest lore, could we the Center find!

In the antistrophe immediately following, however, Jonson employs a more Classically expository language to clarify that "deepest lore":

Did wiser Nature draw thee back,
From out the horrour of that sack,
Where shame, faith, honour, and regard of right
Lay trampled on; the deeds of death, and night,
Urg'd, hurried forth, and horld
Upon th'affrighted world:
Sword, fire and famine, with fell fury met;
And all on utmost ruine set;
As, could they but lifes miseries fore-see,
No doubt all Infants would returne like thee?

And then, again, Jonson is capable in the same frequently underrated poem of violent grammatical tricks, such as when he expresses the shock of the breach of friendship occasioned by Morison's death through a likening of the two men to the constellation of the Gemini ("this bright *Asterisme*" he calls it), and then writing

To separate these twi-
Lights, the *Dioscuri* . . .

whereby the "twin lights" are separated, by the enjambment of the line, from the unified word "twilights" in which they were joined. Here the meter imitates the action of death by cutting the word apart even as death divided the two men. In the previous stanza, Jonson has also employed a striking enjambment, where Morison leaps "the present age, / Possest with holy rage," into eternity. The strophe ends: "And there he lives with memorie: and *Ben,*" and there one tends to come to a full stop. But the next strophe begins "*Jonson,* who sung this of him, e're he went / Himselfe to rest." This is no arbitrary shock, but is again a kind of pun-by-discovery. Just "*Ben*" may appear overfamiliar; with the addition of the enjambed line, the poet, as he would have been known by the living Cary, the late Morison, and the whole "Tribe of

Ben" becomes the public figure, the author of the *Works.* Thus is the poem labeled with the poet's dual name, expressing his private and public roles and duties.[4]

But Jonson has countless other modes of performance. Even in satire, he can be as personal as in the account of the burning of some of his writings in the "Execration upon Vulcan," or in his attacks upon Inigo Jones. He can adopt the traditional genre of mock-epic for the magnificently Rabelaisian "Voyage" (which was apparently too scatological for Swinburne, incidentally, whom one would have thought barely capable of shock). He can adopt the varying tones of "Ben" the critic, in epigrams addressed to his fellow writers like Donne, Selden, and Drayton, and of the public "Ben Jonson," in occasional pieces on broader subjects.

Aside from the public theater itself, the "loathed stage" which he could never quite leave, perhaps the one poetic mode which Jonson found most congenial was that of the court masque. This peculiar form, for Jonson almost a miniature world of humane letters, is lost to us as dramatic literature today for it is impossible to resurrect the theater in which it occurred. The most devoted archaeology and technology might reproduce some of the brilliant scenic and mechanical effects of Jonson's great collaborator and eventual rival, Inigo Jones, or allow us to hear the music of such composers as Alfonso Ferrabosco. But nothing could ever really duplicate the total milieu relating author, musician, performer, and audience. Masques were more than merely festival pageants full of singing and mythological figures and clever stage machinery. The Jacobean masque was an elaborate kind of dramatized court dance, in which some courtiers themselves participated, while others observed, with the monarch, from the vantage point known as "The State." The masque in Jonson's hands became, over a period of more than thirty years, a unique poetic instrument. With the sovereign, his court, and "The State" in a Hall on Twelfth Night, say, and the world enclosed, so to speak, in a more ideally compacted microcosm than the "wooden O" of the public theater, the poet could lead his nobility through a series of allegorical dances. The texts of the songs surrounding and accompanying them explained and moralized the very patterns, often, of the intricate series of dance figures, just as their melodies and rhythms provided the proper measures to govern them. In Jonson's masque *Pleasure Reconciled to Virtue,* for example, the masquers, costumed as pleasures and virtues, are led through a "laborinth of love" by Daedalus, the fabulous artificer of antiquity. As they "put themselves in forme" for the various dances, he sings

Come on, come on; and where you go,
   So interweave the curious knot,
As ev'n th'observer scarce may know
   Which lines are Pleasures, and which not.
First figure out the doubtfull way

At which, a while all youth should stay,
Where she and Vertue did contend
Which should have Hercules to frend.
Then as all actions of mankind
Are but a Laborinth, or maze:
So let your Daunces be entwin'd,
Yet not perplex men unto gaze.
But measur'd, and so numerous too,
As men they may read each act you doo.
And when they see the Graces meet,
Admire the wisdom of your feet.
For Dauncing is an exercise
Not onely shews the movers wit,
As he hath powre to rise to it.

Here is the perfect combination of "pleasure and profit," that Renaissance cliché about the purpose of art to which Jonson did not hesitate to give assent. But in this masque, moral subject, poetic figure and dramatic action are all unified. (Is the first stanza actually *metaphorical,* by the way, or rather a literal injunction to embodied abstractions about the structure and value of their imminent dance?) The animated moral emblem of the masque, moreover, might be said itself to approach most closely to Jonson's ideal of the proper role of poetry in the real world, involving the principals of The State not as spectators only, but as amused, amusing, and profitable participants, instructed both in and by allegorical roles by the poet himself. Such songs as these (and, of course, the masques include almost every type of dramatic and non-dramatic lyric as well) are supreme cases of the lyric doing the work of dramatic, speculative, and didactic poetry as well. But they can do so only because of the perfect, artificial literary milieu in which they are conceived. As the work of such scholars as Stephen Orgel has shown us, the masque remains in some senses the form of Jonson's most original poetic achievement.

Yet the range of his technical accomplishments is quite broad. Among its high points must be mentioned the establishment of the couplet in form and purpose as it was to continue through the century, and the extremely original and personal tone, texture, and form of the odes. For lyrics Jonson employs a variety of forms extending from the tetrameter couplet (analogous to the meters of the Anacreontea?) to the complicated stanza forms taken by pastoral madrigals. Certain forms he eschews utterly. His sole sonnet is almost a joke; "To the Noble Lady, the Lady Mary Wroth" at once casts aspersions on the form as a kind of Sunday painting, and manages to celebrate most delicately the Lady's own accomplishments in just that form.

I that have beene a lover, and could shew it,
Though not in these, in rithmes not wholly dumbe,
Since I exscribe your Sonnets, am become

A better lover, and much better Poet.
Nor is my Muse, or I asham'd to owe it,
   To those true numerous Graces; whereof some
   But charme the Senses, others over-come
Both braines and hearts; and mine now best doe know it. . . .

It is the same impulse operating here that accounts for the "Fit of Rime against Rime," in which he can choose no other instrument to launch his complaint about the necessary barbarisms incidental to the carving of literature out of the living, rather than the dead, language. Jonson uses all the attacks on the debased state of modern languages and their need for rhyming that were employed in the turn-of-the-century debates over prosody. At the end of the poem, he condemns the imaginary inventor of rhyming to a fate no worse than what must have been the endemic agony of a conscience-ridden Classicist who, unlike Thomas Campion, for example, refused to write quantitative poetry for polemical purposes alone, while hewing to the line of rhyme in all the rest of his work:

May his joynts tormented bee,
   Cramp'd forever;
Still may Syllabes jarre with time,
Still may reason warre with rime,
   Resting never. . . .

Jonson's mastery of the short poem led him to avoid, in all but satires, the kind of drawn-out, dialectical elaboration which Donne delighted in producing. Consider the perfection of the little poem on the hourglass, from *The Underwood:*

Doe but consider this small dust,
   Here running in the Glasse,
      By Atomes mov'd;
   Could you beleeve, that this
      The body ever was
         Of one that lov'd?
And in his Mistris' flame, playing like a flye,
   Turn'd to cinders by her eye?
   Yes; and in death, as life, unblest,
         To have exprest,
   Ev'n ashes of lovers find no rest.

This is like a collapsed version of a Donne song, starting with a formal reading of the emblem of the hourglass (what does it mean? here is the signification: etc.) and ending up where Donne might have after several stanzas and much brilliant digression. It is brilliantly, and tactfully, compressed, and calls to mind several lines from Herbert's "Church-Monuments"; a Latin original on which it is based is three elegiac couplets, but Jonson modulates with line length and half-rhyming (the opening "dust" never rhymes with "this" or "was," and comes to an uneasy rest of closure in the triple-rhymed, final "rest"). Similarly, "My Picture Left in Scotland," with its opening casual paradox "I now thinke, Love is rather deafe, then blind" closes in a bluster of material from the opening of Donne's "The Canonization":

> My hundred of gray haires,
> Told seven and fortie years,
> Read so much wast, as she cannot imbrace
> My mountaine belly, and my rockie face,
> And all these through her eyes, have stopt her eares.

Between the intimately private and the didactically public, there are many modes, and Jonson played in them all.

But even Jonson's most personal triumphs of technical skill and concern cannot put off post-Romantic objections to his imitativeness. Originality and novelty are recent virtues, and the Renaissance did not demand of "making" or "feigning" as poetry was frequently called in English, that it work out of whole cloth. But even against such a background, Jonson seems often to be doing patchwork. Translations, adaptations, and borrowings appear almost everywhere in his poetry. A particular poem may echo several different sources, while the same classic text may show up in several poems. His "translations" proper never aim at preserving a particular poem, however, but at carrying over a method, a style, a way of writing, thought, and life.

But Jonson's adaptations betoken no failure of imagination; rather they reveal a particular kind of mind. Edmund Wilson, in an extremely provocative essay in literary psychology, likened Jonson to James Joyce, and the similarities he draws between the two writers apply to the question of their use of literary reference and allusion as well. Both Joyce's and Jonson's learning is like a kind of hoarding. Lines, phrases, patterns, shapes (as, with Joyce, sounds, fractions of syllables, rhymes, puns) become the objects amassed in the store of knowledge—in his feelings for language, Jonson seems much like one of his own stage misers. Learning is for him not so much a play of light upon, or elevation of, the self, or a metamorphosis in the inner life, but rather an accumulation of treasure which cannot help but overflow.

Moreover, Jonson, like Joyce, aims at the creation of language itself. The latter sought in his later writing to make the One Great Statement that, once made, would render all other assertions tautological or trivial, and he tried to cast that Statement in a Universal Language, assembled from all the tongues of men and of angels. But Jonson makes no attempt to go beyond English. Rather, he attempts to mark off a literary dialect within it, manipulating larger instead of smaller linguistic elements. He selects building blocks from Classic writers in much the same way that Modern poets will come to choose forms or styles in this eclectic age. Today, times past and places distant are raided for metrical and rhetorical schemes, or even for the very notions of what a poem *is,* in an attempt to find an authority broader and more compelling than that given by the uses of the previous generation. Jonson's tags, phrases, and comparisons become the counters in no universal language, but rather in a particular civilized one. It is the language of poetry whose ultimate constituents are not so much words, but rather combinations of and ways of using them.

And finally it must be said that Jonson's very way of being derivative was in itself original. F. R. Leavis has pointed out that if Jonson's followers in the seventeenth century seem to derive more from his own Classical sources than from Jonson himself, it is because "the indebtedness to Jonson's models is of a kind that it took Jonson's genius in the first place to incur; if the later poets learnt from these models, they had learnt from Jonson how to do so."[5] This is undoubtedly true; but it should be added that Jonson's own pioneer concerns were for creating discourse in an ideal community, within which the literary dialect would be as speech. His Classical allusions and quotations are not covert tricks hiding cosmic jokes, as in Joyce, just as his poems, unlike those of Donne, Herbert, and Vaughan, for example, are not modeled on difficult texts for study, contemplation, and close reading, rather than upon songs, letters, dialogues. Their allusions aim at being recognizable accents, recognizable not only to a coterie of poets and gentlemen-scholars, but to a whole culture as well. If the notion of a civilization seems today to demand something larger, and the idea of humanistic literacy to be something smaller, perhaps, than it was for Jonson, his poetry nevertheless remains a monument of a literature that sought to engage life, but on its own terms. This is surely at once the oldest and the most urgently modern demand made upon the poetic virtue.

For the student of poetic form, Jonson's contribution to literary history is immense. In his grasp of the modality of verse, of the inevitable "choice of meter" which must be made, he advances the original contribution of Sidney. The latter's myriad attempts at all sorts of lyric forms were in the main, experimental: whether in the variety of meters in which he versified the Psalter, or the quantitative poems in the *Arcadia,* sheer compositional exuberance, and the exigencies of a particular moment seem to be at work. It is either a matter of trying on a form for its own sake, or casting about for a structural idea. But there is no sense of metrical genre about Sidney's shorter poems. With George Herbert, we have a radical extension of Sidney's practice in one direction, that of expressiveness. The overflowing variety of invention in *The Temple,* the scores and scores of unique through-composed and strophic patterns—all these seem directed not at a modal or generic variation, but at an internalized array of states. The form is frequently "read" tropically or figuratively by the language of the poem cast in it. Each form, as each poem for Wallace Stevens, is "the cry of its occasion."

Another Sidneyan experimentalist is Coleridge, using an array of meters but so enmeshed in the Romantic struggle to evolve new genres that although he is keenly aware of Classical and Neoclassical modality, he is torn between theorizing about it and practicing in a more expressive tradition as far as metrical "choice" is concerned. An extreme of non- or even anti-modal variation of style in the short poem is presented by Thomas Hardy, who makes us feel uncomfortable, often, at a decision about form which seems to have been taken in caprice, and then stuck to at all costs. Indeed, it is just out of such a sense of difficulty overcome that he is frequently able to generate formal, rhetorical, and structural force. But Hardy is almost the textbook case of want of modality; perhaps it is traceable to his having started a serious poetic career so late in life, and bursting into the blossom of verse so frenziedly because his poems, although written since his twenties, had been more a matter of the left hand until he gave up novels in the 1890's. It was not a matter for Hardy of finding a voice by searching for style and form, but of singing as many songs as possible.

Hardy's vast formal and structural repertoire exerted, as by his own frequent admission, a considerable formal influence on the young W. H. Auden, who was also absorbing Edward Thomas, Frost, Hopkins, early Germanic verse structures, and, later on, Rilke and Brecht. But after an early, self-consciously experimental approach to form, Auden developed a keen modal sense, and he became in the twentieth century the epitome of the master craftsman of verse.[6] Modern poets can take one of two directions, it seems, in moving toward a characteristic use of form, in seeking to "learn a style from a despair" of belated arrival in a world where forms are not given, where style is not canonical. One of these is that of American Modernism, following the Emersonian injunction to "mount to Paradise / By the stairway of surprise"—in short, to seize early enough upon a poetic tessitura of one's own, to frame a mode of singing, as it were, that would make any other formal style impossible. The effect is to dissolve genre: it is not that the poet wishes to make distinguishable, say, "a short, ironic meditation on landscape by Poet X," but rather only "a Poet X poem." The other tradition is best exemplified by Auden, and in this he was Ben Jonson's heir in our age. His grasp of the competing necessities of the public and private realms were mirrored not only in his poetic morals but in his stylistic practice; using a vast array of forms, styles, systems, differentiating between private messages, songs, sermons, inscriptions, pronouncements, and so forth, he made of his technical brilliance more than merely a matter of his own delight. In craft began, for him as well as for his predecessor Jonson, responsibilities.

Notes

1. All quotations are from the text, based on that of Herford and Simpson, of my own Laurel Poetry Series *Selected Poems* of Jonson.

2. Pseudo-Longinus, *On the Sublime,* XXXIX, tr. W. Hamilton Fyfe, Loeb edition, pp. 236–37.

3. See Chapter XII, pp. 268–69.

4. Jonson's one other truly startling enjambment is in ll. 20–21 of his translation of Horace's *Ars Poetica* (Folio edition). It is the part about the purple passages, when he talks of "A Scarlet peece, or two, stich'd in: when or / *Diana's Grove,* or Altar, with the bor- / Dring Circles of swift waters that intwine / The pleasant grounds . . ." It looks to be most ingenious, along with the possible pun on "stitch-*stiche.*"

5. F. R. Leavis, *Revaluation* (New York, 1947), p. 20.

6. Consider, for example, the use of a wide array of conventional forms in *The Sea and the Mirror* for almost emblematic purposes, as opposed to the casually irrelevant use of particular lyric forms throughout *The Dynasts.*

Scribimus indocti doctique epigrammata passim (1615–1616)

ANONYMOUS

Jonson, they say, 's turned Epigrammatist
So think not I, believe it they that list.
Peruse his book, thou shalt not find a dram
of wit, befitting a true Epigram.
Perhaps some scraps of playbooks thou mayest see,
Collected here & there confusedly,
Which piece his broken stuff, if thou but note,
Just like so many patches on a coat.
And yet his entreat Cato sta[n]ds before,
Even at the portal of his pamphlet's door,
As who should say, this book is fit for none,
But Cato's, learned men to look upon:
Or else, let Cato censure if he will,
My book deserves the best of judgement s[t]ill.
When every gull may see his book's untwitten,
And Epigrams as bad as ere were written.
Jonson this work thy other doth distain,
And makes the world imagine that thy vein
Is not true bred, but of some bastard race,
Then write no more, or write with better grace,
Turn thee to plays & therein write thy fill,
Leave Epigrams to artists of more skill.

In The Times Whistle, ed. R. C. (rpt. 1871, ed. J. M. Couper). D. H. Craig translates the title as "Skilled or unskilled, we scribble poetry, all alike," citing Horace, *Epistles,* 2.1.117; his source is the Library of Canterbury Cathedral (Literary Manuscript D10).

From *Miscellanies, or Essaies* (1673)

EDWARD HOWARD

But how much more should our small siz'd Wits and Critics take care of their presumptuous Descants and carpings at men's performances, when they are scarcely well vers'd in the common places of Grammar and Sense? . . . Of *Johnson* I dare affirm that he is yet unparallel'd by the world, and may be some succeeding Ages: He gave our English Tongue firmness, greatness, enlarged and improved it, without patching of *French* words to our speech, according to some of our modern Pens: insomuch that I question whether any of the Wit of the Latin Poets be more Terse and Eloquent in their Tongue, than this great and Learned Poet appears in ours.

Sexual Politics and Cultural Identity in *The Masque of Blackness*

KIM F. HALL

When she commissioned Ben Jonson to write her first court masque, Queen Anne specifically asked for a performance in which she and her ladies would appear disguised as "Blackamoors." The result, *The Masque of Blackness* (1605), inaugurated a new era in the English court which demonstrated a renewed fascination with racial and cultural differences and their entanglements with the evolving ideology of the state. The Jacobean court was a crucial site for England's development of its sense of national empire: the country earnestly stretched its imperial grasp and England's poets began identifying it as "Great Britain" when James became king of Scotland, England, and Wales. *The Masque of Blackness* and its later counterpart, *The Masque of Beauty* (1608), became the catalyzing agents for a discursive network of "blackness" which participated in this process of identity and empire formation by dramatically reconfiguring issues of racial/cultural identity and gender difference.

Many critics who study *The Masque of Blackness* hasten to note that the conceit of blackness in a court masque was by no means a new invention. Enid Welsford argues that Jonson was influenced by the Florentine tournament which commemorated the marriage of Francesco de' Medici and Bianca Cappello.[1] Stephen Orgel minimizes both the significance of the disguise and the possibility of Anne's influence on the performance in noting that "Queen Anne's bright idea for a 'masque of blackness' was by 1605 a very old one."[2] More recently, Anthony Barthelemy has suggested that the request for blackness in the masque was "nothing extraordinary," given the history of Black characters in court masques, although he does concede that the masque itself had a recognizable impact on its audience.[3] Although it is very true that blackness was long a part of court tradition in Europe, critical attempts to

From *The Performance of Power: Theatrical Discourse and Politics,* ed. Sue-Ellen Case and Janelle Reinelt (Iowa City: University of Iowa Press, 1991), 3–18. Reprinted by permission of the University of Iowa Press.

discount the issue of actual racial blackness in the interests of historical continuity or misogyny ignore the persistent presence of a discourse of blackness in James's court.

In focusing merely on the chronological, such criticism works to preclude investigation of the issues of imperialism, race, and gender difference raised by the masque. The reactions of the audience to the masque and growth of actual contact with Africans, Native Americans, and other racially different foreigners (which went much beyond anything seen previously in England) indicate that a more disruptive reading of both the text and the performance may be useful. The political import of Anne's request for a racial disguise is often effaced by this insistence on locating the masque solely within a dramatic tradition. Interest in the importance of this first collaboration of Ben Jonson and Inigo Jones ignores the very central political question of why such a landmark production involves bringing "Africa" (albeit a European version) to the English court. By examining these masques in conjunction with other dramatic modes of court presentation and within a more overtly political context of empire formation, this essay insists on the centrality of racial difference in the Jacobean court as well as in the masques themselves. I further suggest that the "aesthetic" values of the audience, the playwright, and subsequent critics of the masque are actually political concerns which address crucial anxieties over gender and racial difference.

Representations of Blacks, as well as actual Blacks, were an integral part of Scottish court entertainment during James VI's reign. At his wedding to Anne, princess of Denmark, James arranged an entertainment for his Oslo hosts: "By his orders four young Negroes danced naked in the snow in front of the royal carriage, but the cold was so intense that they died a little later of pneumonia."[4] This spectacle, the first entertainment by the royal couple, was followed by a wedding pageant featuring forty-two men dressed in white and silver and wearing gold chains and visors over blackened faces. Such engagement with "outsiders" followed from the very inception of James I's reign in England and contrasted sharply with Elizabethan insularity. The cult of Elizabeth fostered an identification of the queen's bodily integrity as a virgin with the integrity of the English nation.[5] However, James's ascension brought to the surface acute and pervasive threats to that identity. His joint rule of England and Scotland and his pet project of creating a "Great Britain" gave rise to a more complex figure of English nationalism. James was himself a foreign king bringing a broad Scots accent and his Scottish cronies to court. The policies of a king whose motto was *rex Pacificus* (the royal peacemaker) and whose foreign policy involved the forging of political alliances with foreigners, including traditional enemies like Spain, contrasted strongly with Elizabeth's motto, *semper eadem* (always one—and always English). The Jacobean royal engagement with blackness and foreign difference created strategies in representation for articulating and thereby solving the problem of difference in this court through the manipulation of blackness and of gender.

One example of the primacy of blackness and gender is found in the objection of an observer who, in writing "to discerne the humor of the time," describes *The Masque of Blackness:* "At night there was a sumptuous shew represented by the Queen and some dozen Ladies all paynted like Blackamores face and neck bare and for the rest strangely attired in Barbaresque mantells to the halfe legge."[6] While this "humor of the time" was very likely the much-noted conspicuous consumption of the Jacobean court, it is equally likely that the reference is to the Blackamoor disguise itself and the entire aura of strangeness and novelty that the masque strives to attain. Fascination with the culturally different and ongoing anxieties over gender coalesce in the unsettling vision of these English ladies posing as African nymphs.

The twin concerns of patriarchy and imperialism meet as Jonson's masque dramatizes the collision of the "dark lady" sonnet tradition with the actual blackness encountered in the quest for empire. This collision was not necessarily to the popular taste, as Sir Dudley Carleton's now famous criticism of the masque illustrates:

> Their Apparel was rich, but too light and Curtizen-like for such great ones. Instead of Vizards, their faces, and arms up to the Elbowes, were painted black, which was Disguise sufficient, for they were hard to be known; *but it became them nothing so well as their red and white, and you cannot imagine a more ugly Sight, than a troop of lean-cheek'd Moors.* [The Spanish ambassador danced with] the Queen, and forgot not to kiss her Hand, though there was Danger it would have left a Mark on his Lips. (emphasis added)[7]

Carleton's description hints at the compelling "difference" of this masque.[8] Rather than using the vizards courtiers usually wore to impersonate Black characters, Anne and her ladies painted themselves, making this the first recorded use of blackface pageantry in a court masque. This is a crucial change which Carleton notes again in a later letter: "Theyr black faces and hands which were painted and bare up to the elbowes, was a very lothsome sight, and I am sory that strangers should see our courts so strangely disguised."[9] The connection of their face-painting with their "Curtizen-like" apparel points to a time-honored association of blackness with lechery as well as supporting the greater concern that the masque projects the wrong, "strange," image to outsiders, themselves strangers.

Carleton's first letter is telling in its comparison of the theatrical paint disguising the maskers with more traditional cosmetics, "their red and white." In borrowing from the sonnet tradition's praise to evaluate this "racial" disguise, Carleton touches on a link among poetic discussions of blackness, racial difference, and beauty practices which recurs throughout Renaissance texts and reveals one way in which the discourse of racial blackness is continually gendered. Praising blackness by denigrating face-painting is fairly ubiquitous. For example, in *Love's Labour's Lost* Berowne claims that this "black" beauty, Rosalind, is pure and needs no "painted rhetoric" (V.i.253):

> Devils soonest tempt, resembling spirits of light
> O, if in black my lady's brows be deck'd
> It mourns that painting [and] usurping hair
> Should ravish doters with a false aspect:
> And therefore is she born to make black fair.
> Her favor turns the fashion of the days,
> For native blood is counted painting now;
> And therefore red, that would avoid dispraise,
> Paints itself black, to imitate her brow.[10]

Berowne's description of Rosalind encapsulates much of the paradox of praise of blackness. The use of cosmetics is so pervasive that it literally taints all "native" beauties with the suspicion that they are painting. However, Berowne's "praise" paints women into a box, as it were, by suggesting that these women are painting themselves black to avoid the imputation of cosmetic use. This circular reasoning makes all women dissemblers because we cannot tell which women are truly "white" and which are not.[11] Jonson evokes this paradox in *Blackness,* when Niger speaks of how his daughters compare themselves to "the painted beauties other empires sprung" (133). Similarly, Jonson corners the royal maskers who are "painted" both in their roles as African nymphs and in terms of the "native blood" suspected of "red and white" painting.[12] This uncertainty is only broken by a powerful male, usually a poet (or a poet-king), who confers whiteness and "pure" beauty. Berowne's use of the proverbial "devils soonest tempt," also dramatized in Webster's *The White Devil* and *The Devil's Law-Case,* draws upon this misogynistic tradition: devils appear disguised as white and beautiful women, thereby throwing all women's virtue into doubt.

At court, Jonson reenacts and complicates the manipulation of blackness and gender inherent in the Elizabethan sonnet sequence, a process itself complicated by the conditions of performance. Although a troop of "lean-cheek'd Moors," the maskers are still aristocratic ladies who are part of the "golden world" of the court; this poses the problem for Jonson of presenting a spectacle of cultural difference without slighting the royalty and beauty of the participants. The conceit of *Blackness* is that twelve African nymphs, the daughters of the river Niger, discover that they are not beautiful, but Black, and are promised in a dream that if they find a country "whose termination . . . sounds -tania" (53) they will be turned white. In Niger's opening plea to the court, he laments his daughters' sense of inferiority. Alluding to the popular myth that the sun caused blackness, Niger claims that his daughters are beautiful as well as Black:

Of these my daughters, my most loved birth:
Who, though they were the first formed dames of the earth,
And in whose sparkling and refulgent eyes
The glorious sun did still delight to rise;
Though he—the best judge and most formal cause
Of all dames' beauties—in their firm hues draws
Signs of his fervent'st love, and thereby shows
That in their black the perfec'st beauty grows,

All which are arguments to prove how far
Their beauties conquer in great beauty's war.[13]

However, Jonson opens *Blackness* with a hymn of praise to Niger's daughters, which, in reminding us that the African nymphs are to be seen as beautiful in everything except their color, directly contradicts Niger's praise of blackness.[14] Here Jonson draws upon the "Black, but comely" formulation of the Song of Songs; like Solomon's Bride, Niger's daughters become the meeting ground between East and West, as the opening song announces:

Sound, sound aloud
The welcome of the orient flood
Into the west
With all his beauteous race,

Who, though black in face,
Yet they are bright,
And full of life and light,
To prove that beauty best
Which not the color but the feature
Assures unto the creature. (50–51)

The masque specifically warns the audience not to imagine these women as actual Africans ("not the color, but the feature") by pointing out that these disguised nymphs still have the features of European women, a paradox which ironically occasions Carleton's disparaging, "you cannot imagine a more ugly Sight, than a troop of lean-cheek'd Moors."

The masque reveals that these nymphs' dissatisfaction with their color springs from their contact with Western poets. The English poetry which celebrates bright/white beauty also represents them as inferior:

Yet since the fabulous voices of some few
Poor brainsick men, styled poets here with you,
Have with such envy of their graces sung
The painted beauties other empires sprung,
Letting their loose and winged fictions fly
To infect all climates, yea our purity. (50–52)

Jonson here reveals the cultural imperialism rampant in European discussions of beauty. The assertion that poets, with "their loose and winged fictions," were the promoters of eurocentric notions of beauty suggests that early cultural mavens such as Jonson well understood the damaging imposition of white standards of beauty, which author Toni Morrison has called one of "the most destructive ideas in the history of human thought."[15]

Empire works with the same efficacy in delimiting an Other. It is no accident that this first court masque is both an elucidation of the nature of blackness and a celebration of empire. *Blackness* was performed shortly after the coining of the term "Great Britain." Although the term was not legally adopted until 1707, James I spent much of his energies trying to make the term official; consequently, it was the site of much discussion and debate over England's imperial growth and identity. *Blackness* is filled with references to the new status of England as the seat of a growing empire and the significance of its identity as Britannia:

> With that name Britannia, this blessed isle
> Hath won her ancient dignity and style,
> *A World divided from the world,* and tried
> The abstract of it in his general pride.
>
> Britannia, whose new name makes all his wealth a ring,
> Might be a diamond worthy to encase it. (55–56)

This pride in the revival of ancient Britain is continually yoked to the glorification of whiteness. In guiding his daughters to the promised land, Niger circles the globe, finding "Black Mauretania first, and secondly / Swarth Lusitania; next we did descry / Rich Aquitania" (54). Visiting these countries in an ascending (lightening) order of color, Niger at last happens upon England, which is throughout associated with whiteness. England is identifiable by its white cliffs: "This land that lifts into the temperate air / His snowy cliff is Albion the fair / So called of Neptune's son, who ruleth here" (54). This primary name of England—Albion (white land)—assumes great importance as its repetition throughout the masque stresses England's titular link with whiteness.

While *The Masque of Blackness* does deal with the fact of "blackness" itself, it cannot be made too obvious that such discussions of blackness are almost inevitably yoked to problems of gender difference. The cultural imperative of both masques is turning females white: none of the male "Blackamoors" seems to feel any such need. In general, little critical attention has been paid to the place of gender either in the masques or at court. Anne's role as Jonson's patron is not much discussed, perhaps because of the widespread opinion that Anne was an empty-headed spendthrift in endless pursuit of the unusual or the bizarre.[16] Although Jonson's claim that Anne specifically asked for "some Daunce, or shew, that might precede hers, and have the place of foyle, or false masque" (*Masque of Queenes,* 14) does not suggest that her creation of the antimasque is anything more than a continuing quest for novelty, it is also possible that her request reflects some awareness on the queen's part of her own female estrangement from James's court. Further, it plays up the transgressive nature of female "painting" or the use of cosmetics, long a basis for attacks on women. The patriarchal structures which underlie many discussions of female beauty often create unstable subject positions for women. As women come to be judged solely by their adherence to male standards of desirability and decorum, they are often put into the position of competing for patriarchal approval.

Blackness, a culturally authorized trope for distinguishing between women, is rooted in such competition between women. Blackness is often a mutable and relative quality; in early modern England, it is less a sign of complexion than of status. Women are only "Black" or fair in competition with, or in relation to, each other. In this special sense of inequality, all women were "Black" in King James's court. Female beauty was fairly powerless next to the "fair" men who enjoyed James's acutest attention. If, in the play world, James beneficently integrates these "dark" ladies into court, in the real world, James's attentions to his favorites denied women the status that accrues from being sought-after prizes in erotic competition. Stephen Orgel suggests that *Blackness* and *Beauty* may work together as an antimasque and masque.[17] Jonson tells us that the idea of the "foyle or false masque" was also Anne's and it may be that her masque allowed her the creation of a strange Other which worked to place her closer to the center of court, much in the way that *Blackness* prepares for and privileges *Beauty.*

The promise of *Blackness*—turning the nymphs white—is fulfilled two years later in *The Masque of Beauty.* The denigration of Anne's part in the creation of the masques may be sparked by the dynamic of the masques themselves. The blackness which originally marks her as different also marks her as inferior. For, in the execution of Anne's royal will, the masques concede power to the court males. Although Anne was the impetus for the performance of the masques, the actual power to do the impossible, proverbially described as "washing the Ethiope white," is credited to Britain's chief poet and sun, James, "Whose beams shine day and night and are of force / To blanch an Ethiope, and revive a corse" (56); the force behind the masque becomes the royal James, who watches a spectacle brought about by his kingly powers, "Which now expect to see, great Neptune's son, / And love the miracle which thyself hast done" (66). James's authority is called upon to break the deadlock of feminine beauty, to make the maskers, neither painted Black nor painted white, but simply "beautiful." The whitening of the nymphs is presented in terms of conquest as the language of blackness surrenders to a more powerful heliocentric language:

Yield, night, then, to the light,
As blackness hath to beauty,
Which is but the same duty
It is for beauty that the world was made,
And where she reigns Love's light admits no shade. (71)

Such a "surrender," even more than beautifying the nymphs, glorifies the king and his country: "And now by virtue of their light and grace, / The glorious isle wherein they rest takes place / Of all the earth for beauty" (65).[18]

The completion of *The Masque of Beauty* proclaims the triumph of Albion and the return of proper Platonic order to the world.[19]

Now use your seat—that seat which was before
Thought straying, uncertain, floating to each shore,
And to whose having, every clime laid claim;
Each land and nation urgèd as the aim
Of their ambition beauty's perfect throne,
Now made peculiar to this place alone,
And that by impulsion of your destinies,
And his attractive beams that light these skies . . . (74)

As the verse suggests, James's England was beset by subterranean anxieties of cultural impotence which are offset by the cultural imperative, mandated by the demands of patriarchy and colonialism, of establishing the primacy of white/beauty. In asserting the power of Albion and of James to convert cultural difference into European whiteness through the return of the now-white nymphs to court, Jonson dramatizes a "positive" model for the confrontation of cultures. This model explicitly reveals the ways in which imperial contact is shaped by an organization of cultural and racial values rooted in the control of gender mandated by patriarchy.

The Masque of Beauty presents an idealized world in which normally intransigent blackness is subdued by a European order predicated on white, male privilege and power. In actuality, female unruliness was not so easily contained: the performance itself featured many women who resisted patriarchal standards of female decorum. Along with Philip Sidney's "dark lady," Penelope Rich, who was the mistress of Edward Blount and the mother of four illegitimate children, the play cast Lady Arabella Stuart, who would later be sent to the Tower (again) for her secret marriage to Lord Seymour; Frances Howard, who later became notorious for poisoning her husband in the Overbury affair; and Lady Mary Wroth, who had two illegitimate children by her first cousin and was sent down from court after the publication of her prose romance (the first by a woman), *The Countess of Montgomerie's Urania* (1621). From the first entrance of James into England, the ladies at court are associated with lawless, transgressive behavior. In her diary, Lady Anne Clifford comments on the reputation of the queen's ladies, connecting their scandalous behavior with the performance of masques: "Now there was much talk of a masque which the Queen had at *Winchester* and how all the ladies about the Court had gotten such ill names that it was grown a scandalous place, and the Queen herself was much fallen from her former greatness and reputation she had in the world."[20] If the imaginative control of women in the masque did not transfer into the daily life of the court, the uniting of English and Scottish differences under the glorification of whiteness proved equally problematic.

The Masque of Blackness was not an isolated incident of "strangeness," but the best-known (and most visual) sign of a discourse of blackness emanating from the court. While the implication of blackness in the masque depends on the actual painting of these court beauties, Jonson provides many verbal "signs" of Otherness in his printed text. The sight of blackness is invariably accompanied by a vocabulary similar to what Edward Said terms the representative figures or tropes of Orientalist discourse.[21] As Jonson himself notes in claiming that he chose hieroglyphics to signify the nymph's names, "as well as for strangeness as relishing of antiquitie" (239–240), these signs carry the religious and cultural associations of and assumptions about blackness. Jonson's textual emendations and stage descriptions contribute to the illusion of cultural difference even as they display his erudition; for example, he describes the nymphs as having ornaments of "the most choice and orient pearl" (60) and hair "thick and curled upright in tresses, like pyramids" (50).

By such specificity we see that, as early as *The Masque of Blackness,* blackness had become part of the linguistic currency of James's rule. Not only did James keep Africans at court as part of his passion for oddities: the actual excesses of the court seem to have been perceived as "Oriental." Racial difference, particularly in descriptions of the perceived decadence of the court, was a privileged idiom for self-description and critique. Orientalism, another trope of difference with a broad arsenal of effects, opens up religion as a category of difference. Sir John Harrington's description of the entertainments for King Christian of Denmark in 1606 links James's court with the alleged idolatry and licentiousness of Islam: "The sports began each day in such manner and such sort, as well nigh persuaded me of Mahomet's paradise. We had women, and indeed wine, too, of such plenty, as would have astonished each sober beholder. Our feasts were magnificent and the two royal guests did most lovingly embrace each other at table."[22] From the Middle Ages on, Mohammed and "Mohammedism" had been a sign for sexual and moral depravity.[23] Harrington's description of the court as Mohammed's paradise would seem to be less a way of bringing the East closer to the West than of distancing the "private" indecorous behavior of these Western rulers from their royal function. Indeed, the entertainments Harrington describes sound much like the representations of James's public kingly persona. For example, a masque designed for the same occasion used the common motif of James as Solomon:

> One day, a great feast was held, and after dinner, the representation of Solomon, his temple and the coming of the Queen of Sheba was made, or (as I may better say) was meant to have been made, before their Majesties, by device of the Earl of Salisbury and others. . . . The lady who did play the Queen's part, did carry most precious gifts to both their Majesties; but forgetting the steps arising to the canopy, overset her caskets into his Danish Majesty's lap, and fell at his feet, though I rather think it was in his face. . . . His majestie then got up and would dance with the Queen of Sheba; but he fell down and humbled himself before her, and was carried to an inner chamber and laid on a bed of state; which was not a little defiled with the presents of the Queen, which had been bestowed on his garments, such as wine, cream, jelly, beverage, ales, spices and other good manners.[24]

Harrington's rhetoric, which sounds much like the official descriptions of court entertainments, only throws into relief the strangely burlesque nature of the occasion. The fascination with alien difference Scottish James brought to court becomes speakable as Orientalism in Harrington's discourse.

Such a description of court debauchery takes on an added resonance when one remembers the popular representation of James as an English Solomon. The lengths to which the proponents of this analogy went can best be shown by Bishop William's funeral oration on James: "Solomon was of a complexion white and ruddy. . . . Solomon was a great maintainer of shipping and Navigation . . . a most proper Attribute to King James. . . . Every man lived in Peace under his Vine and his Fig-tree in the days of Solomon. And so they did in the blessed days of King James. And yet, towards his end, King Solomon had secret Enemies, Razan, Hadad, and Jeroboam, and prepared for a war upon his going to his grave."[25] For Renaissance England, the biblical Solomon provided two models for relations between Western males and "Other" females. In one, the Song of Songs, we see the white male refashion and whiten the dark foreign female into an object of a transcendent wedded love; this "positive" aesthetic model reverberates through sonnet cycles and *Beauty* and *Blackness*. In the other, we have a Solomon too much given to pleasures of the flesh, which are associated with the allures of a foreign female.

Thus, in the entertainments for King Christian, we see how easily the control exercised in the one model slips into the degeneration and excess warned of by the second. The domination over (and eradication of) foreign difference seen in *The Masque of Beauty* is inverted into a carnivalesque spectacle which shows the threatening nether side of cultural interaction when the powerful Western ruler is seen to succumb to Eastern disorder and riot. The king's drunken departure echoes the problematic side of Solomon's womanizing, described as "defiling" the bed of state (albeit with food and drink). Harrington also reads the scene as a subversion of gender roles and cultural imperatives: the aptly named King Christian is described as "humbling himself" before Sheba.

Traditional notions of "Englishness" and concomitant problems of social disorder were being interrogated and threatened on all sides by the growing pains of imperialism. For, in addition to internal court tensions, James's subjects were going abroad in increasing numbers, implementing his plantation policies, exploring "undiscovered" lands, and seeking new economic opportunities. These displaced subjects were forced to grapple with the problem of maintaining their sense of an "English" self in a strange land. While it is difficult to estimate precisely how questions of birthright, religious toleration, economic viability, and gender organization affected the English sense of self and country, one measure may be the predominance of the trope of blackness in the drama of the period. As Sander Gilman has noted, such an evocation of an Other is not unusual in times of stress: "A rich web of signs and references for the idea of difference arises out of a society's communal sense of control over its world. No matter how this sense of control is articulated, whether as political power, social status, religious mission, or geographic or economic domination, it provides an appropriate vocabulary for the sense of difference."[26] With the loss of this "communal sense of control" at a moment of real historical change, Black figures—both "actual" and disguised—become the focal points for an extraordinarily dense system of signification, which, unpacked, reveals layered and interconnected anxieties over difference. In court entertainments, tropes of racial and cultural difference are used to present this seat of political authority as the center of a stable, ordered, and ultimately English world. However, such manipulations reveal that race is indeed "a dangerous trope,"[27] which highlighted the problematic differences of the Jacobean court even as it helped create the illusion of power.

Notes

1. Enid Welsford, *The Court Masque* (Cambridge: Cambridge University Press, 1927), 170.

2. *The Jonsonian Masque* (Cambridge, Mass.: Harvard University Press, 1965), 65.

3. Anthony Gerard Barthelemy, *Black Face, Maligned Race: The Representations of Blacks in English Drama from Shakespeare to Southerne* (Baton Rouge and London: Louisiana State University Press, 1987), 20.

4. Ethel Carleton Williams, *Anne of Denmark* (London: W. and J. Mackay, 1970), 21.

5. Roy Strong, *Gloriana: The Portraits of Queen Elizabeth I* (London: Thames and Hudson, 1987), 96–99.

6. Charles Harold Herford and Percy Simpson (eds.), *Ben Jonson* (Oxford: Clarendon Press, 1925), 449. All texts from this edition have been normalized.

7. Herford and Simpson, 448.

8. Although Carleton at times displays a Bottom-like need for verisimilitude in his criticisms of the masque (for example, when he describes "images of Sea-Horses with other terrible fishes," he complains that "the indecorum was, that there was all Fish and no water"), his commentary in other respects is not very different from that of other court observers.

9. Herford and Simpson, 449. For more on the costumes worn by "Black" characters, see Barthelemy, 18–21.

10. *The Riverside Shakespeare* (Boston: Houghton Mifflin, 1974), IV.iii.254–261. All references to Shakespeare's plays are to this edition, hereafter cited in the text.

11. For more on the traditional criticism of face-painting, see Annette Drew-Bear, "Face Painting in Renaissance Tragedy," *Renaissance Drama* 12: 71–76; and Lisa Jardine, *Still Harping on Daughters* (Totowa, N.J.: Barnes and Noble, 1983), 93–95.

12. Anne Cline Kelly ("The Challenge of the Impossible: Ben Jonson's *Masque of Blackness*," *College Language Association Journal* 2 [1977]: 341–355) glosses "painted" in this line as "superficial" or "inconstant." However, I think at this moment the masque literally refers to the paint of the participants.

13. Stephen Orgel (ed.), *Ben Jonson: The Complete Masques* (New Haven and London: Yale University Press, 1969), 47–60. All references to Jonson's masques are to this edition, hereafter cited in the text.

14. Barthelemy, 21.

15. Toni Morrison, *The Bluest Eye* (New York: Washington Square Press, 1970), 97. For more discussion on the lasting effects of the imposition of eurocentric beauty standards on Black cultures, see Toni Cade, *The Black Woman* (New York: New American Library, 1970), especially 80–89, 90–100; Audre Lorde, "Eye to Eye: Black Women; Hatred and Anger," in *Sister Outsider: Essays and Speeches by Audre Lorde* (Trumansburg, N.Y.: Crossing Press, 1986), 145–175; Jeanne Noble, "Bitches Brew," in *Beautiful, Also, Are the Souls of My Black Sisters: A History of Black Women in America* (Englewood Cliffs, N.J.: Prentice-Hall, 1978), 313–344; and Alice Walker, "If the Present Looks Like the Past, What Does the Future Look Like?" in *In Search of Our Mother's Gardens* (New York and London: Harcourt, Brace and World, 1983), 290–312.

16. When she is even mentioned, Anne is roundly condemned by James's biographers and other students of the Jacobean court. Antonia Fraser (*King James* [New York: Alfred A. Knopf, 1975], 53–55) comments on the way this phenomenon overlooks Anne's significance as a patron. William McElwee (*The Wisest Fool in Christendom: The Reign of King James I & VI* [London: Faber and Faber, 1958], 122) faults Anne's spending and her "placid stupidity." Stephen Orgel (*The Jonsonian Masque* [Cambridge, Mass.: Harvard University Press, 1965], 65), although somewhat less scathing, notes Jonson's "sensitivity to his audience" and proceeds to ignore or belittle Anne's place as patron, most obviously in his comment on Anne's "bright idea" for *Blackness.*

17. Orgel, 119.

18. Richard Peterson ("Icon and Mystery in Jonson's *Masque of Beautie*," *John Donne Journal* 5 [1986]: 169–199) sees this as "the almost imperialistic conquest of night by day," but insists that it does not overcome "the genuine strain of seductiveness in the masque" (190).

19. For a thorough discussion on the basis of the masque's symbolism in Renaissance Platonism, see D. J. Gordon's "The Imagery of Ben Jonson's *The Masque of Blackness* and *The Masque of Beautie*," *Journal of the Warburg and Courtauld Institutes* 6 (1942): 122–141, and his expansion of those ideas in *The Renaissance Imagination: Essays and Lectures by D. J. Gordon,* ed. Stephen Orgel (Berkeley and London: University of California Press, 1976).

20. *The Diary of Lady Anne Clifford,* ed. Vita Sackville-West (London: William Heinemann, 1923), 17.

21. Edward Said, *Orientalism* (New York: Random House, 1979), 71.

22. John Nichols, *Progresses of James I,* 4 vols. (New York: AMS Press, 1972), 2:72. Samuel C. Chew gives further examples of English allegations of carnality in "Mohamet's Paradise," in *The Crescent and the Rose: Islam and England during the Renaissance* (New York: Oxford University Press, 1937).

23. Said, 62.

24. Nichols, 72.

25. Quoted in Robert Ashton (ed.), *James I by His Contemporaries: An Account of His Career and Character as Seen by Some of His Contemporaries* (London: Hutchinson, 1969), 19–20.

26. Sander Gilman, *Difference and Pathology: Stereotypes of Sexuality, Race and Madness* (Ithaca and New York: Cornell University Press, 1985), 21.

27. Henry Louis Gates, Jr. (ed.), *"Race," Writing and Difference* (Chicago: University of Chicago Press, 1986), 5.

On *Hymenaei* (1616)

BEN JONSON

It is a noble and just advantage, that the things subjected to *understanding* have of those which are objected to *sense,* that the one sort are but momentary, and merely taking; the other impressing, and lasting: Else the glory of all these *solemnities* had perished like a blaze, and gone out, in the *beholders* eyes. So short-lived are the *bodies* of all things, in comparison of their *souls.* And, though *bodies* oft-times have the ill luck to be sensually preferred, they find afterwards, the good fortune (when *souls* live) to be utterly forgotten. This it is hath made the most royal *Princes,* and greatest *persons* (who are commonly the *personators* of these actions) not only studious of riches, and magnificence in the outward celebration, or show; (which rightly becomes them) but curious after the most high, and hearty *inventions,* to furnish the inward parts: (and those grounded upon *antiquity,* and solid *learnings*) which, though their *voice* be taught to sound to present occasions, their *sense,* or doth, or should always lay hold on more removed *mysteries.* And, howsoever some may squeamishly cry out, that all endeavor of *learning,* and *sharpness* in these transitory *devices* especially, where it steps beyond their little, or (let me not wrong 'hem) no brain at all is superfluous; I am contented, these fastidious *stomachs* should leave my full tables, and enjoy at home, their clean empty trenchers, fittest for such airy tastes: where perhaps a few *Italian* herbs, picked up, and made into a *salad,* may find sweeter acceptance, than all, the most nourishing, and sound meats of the world.

From the 1616 Folio of Jonson's *Works,* 911–12.

Index

◆

The Volume Editor

Robert N. Watson is professor of English at UCLA. He received his B.A. summa cum laude from Yale University in 1975 and his Ph.D. with Highest Honors from Stanford University in 1979. He was previously associate professor of English at Harvard University, chair of the department of English at UCLA, and the William R. Kenan Professor of English at Middlebury College. Along with various teaching awards, he has received Whiting, A.C.L.S., U.C. President's, and N.E.H. fellowships. He is the author of *Shakespeare and the Hazards of Ambition* (1984) and *Ben Jonson's Parodic Strategy: Literary Imperialism in the Comedies* (1987), both from Harvard University Press, and *The Rest Is Silence: Death as Annihilation in the English Renaissance* (1994) from the University of California Press, as well as numerous articles and reviews. His edition of Jonson's *Every Man In His Humour* is forthcoming in the New Mermaids series.

The General Editor

Zack Bowen is professor of English at the University of Miami. He holds degrees from the University of Pennsylvania (B.A.), Temple University (M.A.), and the State University of New York at Buffalo (Ph.D.). In addition to the Twayne and G. K. Hall series, he is editor of the University of Florida Press James Joyce Series and the *James Joyce Literary Supplement.* He is author of six books and editor of three others, all on modern British, Irish, and American literature. In addition, he has published more than one hundred monographs, essays, scholarly reviews, and recordings related to literature. He is past president of the James Joyce Society (1977–1986), former chair of the Modern Language Association Lowell Prize Committee, and current president of the International James Joyce Foundation.